Bangladesh Liberation @50 Years

'Bijoy' with Synergy

Bangladesh Liberation @50 Years

'Bijoy' with Synergy

India-Pakistan War 1971

Editors

VK Ahluwalia | AN Jha

KNOWLEDGE WORLD
KW Publishers Pvt Ltd
New Delhi

CENTRE FOR LAND WARFARE STUDIES
CLAWS
VICTORY THROUGH VISION
Centre for Land Warfare Studies
Delhi Cantt
New Delhi

The Centre for Land Warfare Studies (CLAWS), New Delhi, is an autonomous think tank dealing with contemporary issues of national security and conceptual aspects of land warfare, including conventional and sub-conventional conflicts and terrorism. CLAWS conducts research that is futuristic in outlook and policy-oriented in approach.

Centre for Land Warfare Studies
RPSO Complex, Parade Road, Delhi Cantt, New Delhi 110010
Tel: +91.11.25691308 **Fax:** +91.11.25692347
Email: landwarfare@gmail.com **Website:** www.claws.in
CLAWS Army No. 33098

ISBN 978-93-91490-90-4 Hardback
ISBN 978-93-91490-91-1 ebook

Published in India by Kalpana Shukla

KNOWLEDGE WORLD

KW Publishers Pvt Ltd
4676/21, First Floor, Ansari Road
Daryaganj, New Delhi 110002
Phone: +91 11 43528107
Marketing: kw@kwpub.in
Editorial: production@kwpub.in
Website: www.kwpub.in

Printed and Bound in India

Dedicated to

The Spirit of Friendship between India and Bangladesh

Contents

Operations by the Indian Air Force

राजनाथ सिंह
RAJNATH SINGH

सत्यमेव जयते

रक्षा मंत्री
भारत
DEFENCE MINISTER
INDIA

MESSAGE

It gives me immense pleasure to learn that the Centre for Land Warfare Studies (CLAWS) is publishing a book to commemorate the 1971 War for the liberation of Bangladesh on its Golden Jubilee. The book will be an invaluable addition to the existing literature on the subject.

1971 was a year of seismic change in the South Asian subcontinent as the borders were redrawn and a new nation was born. The brotherhood that the people of India and Bangladesh displayed during this period of turmoil, hope and jubilation continues to be an epitome of good neighbourly relations in the world. The Indian Armed Forces and the Mukti Bahini gave a stellar account of their camaraderie, steadfast pursuit of objectives with professional elan and an unflinching commitment to their national resolve. Every battle that they fought bears testimony to this spirit that animated the rank and file of the forces. The saga of bravery and sacrifice of these warriors, many recognised but also those unsung, needs to be retold for future generations to draw inspiration.

As the world and the subcontinent continue to face new and multi-dimensional challenges, we must draw from the rich history of our two countries and the Armed Forces to reinvigorate our youth with an unimpeachable spirit of courage and tenacity. To that end, I must compliment the CLAWS for this very timely and purposeful effort.

'Jai Hind'

(Rajnath Singh)

Date: 17th Sept, 2021
Place: New Delhi

Office : Room No. 104, Ministry of Defence, South Block, New Delhi-110011
Tel. : +91 11 23012286, +91 11 23019030, Fax : +91 11 23015403
E-mail : rmo@mod.nic.in

MESSAGE

The Liberation War of 1971 is an incredible milestone in the history of the Indian Armed Forces and the people's movement of erstwhile East Pakistan, that led to the birth of a new Nation - Bangladesh. As part of Military History, the battles, both in the Eastern and Western theatres of India, have been read with great interest by military leaders, defence analysts, political scientists, psychologists, and civilians. The bonds of camaraderie forged between the Indian Armed Forces and the Mukti Bahini on the battlefield have evolved into strong institutional relationships between the Armed Forces of both countries. The gallantry & valour of the soldiers and the bold leadership of the Commanders is today ingrained in the culture and ethos of the Indian Armed Forces.

The Indo-Pak War 1971 was unlike earlier wars with Pakistan, wherein India had fought to preserve its territorial integrity. This time however, the focus was to assist the people of erstwhile East Pakistan, as part of humanitarian assistance, against atrocities being committed against them. This War showcased the operational preparedness of the Indian Armed Forces, with major battles fought under challenging circumstances. Effective planning, systematic execution, strategic decision-making, decisive leadership and the unstinted support of the people of erstwhile East Pakistan - together helped us achieve resounding success. The War served as a testimony of our resolve to employ all elements of National Power to realise our National Objectives. We have drawn important lessons from this War over the years.

This initiative by CLAWS to publish a book commemorating 50 years of the Liberation War, that includes both operational aspects and anecdotal accounts by both Indian and Bangladeshi authors would certainly be of immense interest to the present generation and veterans alike. The response to the compilation of the book has been overwhelming. I would like to compliment and convey my appreciation to all those who have shared valuable and lesser-known facts to make it an interesting read.

The heroic acts from the War would remain a source of inspiration to the serving soldiers of both the Nations. I am sanguine that the friendship and interaction between the Armed Forces of both our countries would continue to grow from strength to strength in the years ahead.

'Jai Hind'

(MM Naravane)
General
Chief of the Army Staff

INDIA INTERNATIONAL CENTRE

N N Vohra
President

FOREWORD

In Pakistan's National Assembly elections held in December 1970 the Awami League, the main political party in East Pakistan led by Sheikh Mujibur Rehman, swept the polls. However, the Awami League was denied its right to form the government.

As the military dictators in Islamabad continued to defer convening the National Assembly, violent protests and rioting erupted all across East Pakistan which had, almost ever since its birth, suffered continuing atrocities and serious political, economic and social discrimination at the hands of the Pakistan government.

In end March 1971, the Martial Law Administrator of East Pakistan launched a ruthless military crackdown which unleashed arson, loot, rape and wanton killings. This genocidal onslaught led to the internal displacement of tens of thousands of people and hundreds of thousands fleeing their homes to seek refuge in the neighbouring Indian states. The continuing flood of refugees, which touched ten million by the end of November 1971, had generated grave political, economic and social problems for India. Among the large number of those seeking refuge in India the Pak ISI had inducted its agents and operatives who lost no time in inciting communal tensions and carrying out varied acts of sabotage and subversion, which engendered serious security problems for the country.

India made sustained diplomatic efforts to secure a fair and peaceful solution to enable the millions of refugees to return to their homes. However, her initiatives were summarily rejected by Pakistan which, instead, commenced a rapid military build-up along India's western borders.

Pakistan resorted to all manner of false news and propaganda to create an international impression that India was preparing to attack East Pakistan at any time and, under this cover, solicited external aid from various quarters. USA responded by offering open political support and extensive military assistance to Pakistan. It also encouraged UK to deploy its Navy in our region. Using the good offices of President Yahya Khan, USA Secretary of State Henry Kissinger made a secret visit to Beijing and China promptly joined the nexus to openly deter and constrain India at all costs. USA went one step further: it deployed its Seventh Fleet in the Bay of Bengal, to deliver a final warning to India.

40, Max Mueller Marg, New Delhi -110 003
Telephones : 2461-7936 & 2460-9401 Fax : 91-11-2463-4224
E-mail : president@iicdelhi.in, nnvohra@nic.in

Prime Minister Indira Gandhi's continued initiatives, through the entire summer, to avert the possibility of a war with Pakistan did not meet with success. She made a final attempt in October 1971, when she embarked on a six-nation tour to France, West Germany, Belgium, UK, Australia and the USA, to personally voice the altogether unbearable financial and other burdens, and serious security problems, created by the unceasing flow of millions of East Pakistan refugees into India. As expected, the response of the world leaders was neutral to negative. However, thanks to the Indo-Soviet Treaty of Peace, Cooperation and Friendship, which Prime Minister Indira Gandhi had timely concluded in August 1971, the USSR stood by India and stoutly supported its position in the UN and all other fora.

By November 1971 there were growing protestations across West Pakistan which demanded their government to "Crush India" and to "Hang the Traitor", Sheikh Mujibur Rehman. Backed by USA and China, and supported by Iran, Jordan and several other countries, Pakistan was emboldened to launch a pre-emptive air strike on 3 December 1971, with the objective of destroying all the front lying air bases and radar stations in north-west India, penetrating as far deep as Agra (500 km away from the Indo-Pak border). Simultaneously, the same evening, Pakistan launched heavy artillery attacks across the LoC in J&K. Later that day, in a mid-night broadcast to the nation, Prime Minister Indira Gandhi declared Pakistan's hostile air attack as a "war against India" and, losing no time, our armed-forces responded by launching planned air, sea and land attacks on chosen targets in Pakistan.

The war lasted only thirteen days. The Indian Armed Forces decisively defeated Pakistan on all fronts and took 93,000 prisoners. The Mukti Bahini and the people of East Pakistan played an important role in Pakistan's humiliating defeat which resulted in the dismemberment of its eastern wing and the birth of "Bangladesh", a new nation.

India's glorious victories in all land, air and naval battles were achieved on account of the perfect tri-service military planning which had been done in the preceding months and the outstanding operational jointness which was secured by the Army Chief, General Manekshaw, in concert with the Air Chief Marshal P.C. Lal and Admiral S.M. Nanda, the Chief of Navy. Furthermore, as a result of the meticulous preparations, strong and timely support was provided by the Border Security Force, the Central Intelligence Agencies and the civil and police administrations of all the four Indian states neighbouring East Pakistan – West Bengal, Assam, Meghalaya and Tripura. This outstanding cohesion of the Indian Armed Forces and all other agencies involved in the war effort materialised as a result of the very strong politico-military understanding which obtained in the entire preparatory period preceding the war, during the period of the conflict and in the post war phase. Fully, backed by her Cabinet, Prime Minister Indira Gandhi had maintained close understanding on all major issues with General Sam Manekshaw (later Field Marshall). Jagjivan Ram, Defence Minister, and K.B.

Lal, Principal Defence Secretary, played quiet but extremely valuable roles in the preparation for the war, once it was clear that there was no other way of dealing with the situation created by Pakistan.

Pakistan's defeat, the end of the genocide and tyrannical rule of military dictators in East Pakistan, the birth of Bangladesh and the return of millions of refugees to their homeland were events of unprecedented historical importance about which the present generation is perhaps not adequately acquainted. In this context, this volume is of great significance. Besides celebrating fifty years of the War of Liberation, it educates the reader about the essential facts of this war and about the numerous deeds of heroism, valour and exceptional bravery of all those who fought the battles, and the many who made the supreme sacrifice.

I compliment Lt Gen V K Ahluwalia, the distinguished Director of Centre for Land Warfare Studies (CLAWS), for securing valuable contributions from several surviving veterans of the 1971 War and from many others who have deep interest in and knowledge of the business of war. I am of the view that the reading of military histories provides an excellent opportunity for the upcoming generations to get acquainted with the many grave challenges which their country had faced in the decades past, how these were dealt with and, besides, to learn about the enormous sacrifices which were made by the brave officers and jawans of our Armed Forces for defending and preserving the unity and integrity of our country.

It would be enormously beneficial if this volume were to be translated into the major regional languages and made available to schools and colleges across the country. This would enhance awareness and imbue our youth with the requisite pride and fervour which is vital for fostering national cohesion.

17 September, 2021
New Delhi

N. N. Vohra

Preface

This book is special, as it marks 50 years of the Liberation War, and the birth of a new Nation- Bangladesh. The war was a result of the situation prevailing in East Pakistan (later Bangladesh) in 1971 and Pakistan's proactive actions based on its propagated strategy of 'Defence of the East lies in the West'. Several books have been written on the subject in the past. The aim of this book is not only to highlight the strategy and operational plans executed by India and Pakistan, as well as the role of the Mukti Bahini and the people of East Pakistan, but also to talk about personal experiences, and accounts of soldiers and people alike. The book recounts some of the lesser-known anecdotes of soldiers, Mukti Bahini, and their families, both during the preparatory stage and the final blow to the Pakistan Armed Forces and its Governance system in East Pakistan.

While the Awami League led by Sheikh Mujibur Rahman had emerged as the majority Party during the elections to the National Assembly of Pakistan in December 1970, but it was denied the right to form the government. Pakistani leaders and the military junta were unaware of the deep-rooted differences between East and West Pakistan, as well as intolerable ground conditions prevailing in East Pakistan. More importantly, they did not understand the pulse, the aspirations, and the power of the people. The book covers wide range of issues, such as the genesis, geo-politico-strategic landscape in 1970-71, the strategies of the two countries, including role of Mukti Bahini and the people of East Pakistan, and narration of war accounts by veterans, people of East Pakistan and their families.

The book is divided into seven parts. Part 1 titled 'Defence of the East Lies in the West: Dynamic Leadership at Play' briefly discusses the genesis, ground realities of the conditions in East Pakistan, geopolitical and strategic situation, and broad framework of strategy, of both India and Pakistan. It briefly brings out how Pakistan's strategy was outdated, and was not in sync with the prevailing ground actualities in East Pakistan. This part also focuses on the role of leadership in achieving an overwhelming victory and Liberation of a new nation. Part 2 is one of the most important parts, as it gives a detailed account of the Liberation War on the Eastern Theatre (East Pakistan), along with the role of the Mukti Bahini and the people of East Pakistan. Part 3 provides an interesting and telling account by the authors from Bangladesh, of the lesser-known facts of the prevailing situation, their commitment and patriotism, and their exemplary role in the Liberation War. Part 4 discusses the strategy of Pakistan and India and their aims in the western sector, and gives operational cum anecdotal account of the war. Part 5 highlights the vital role played by the IAF and the Indian Navy at every stage of the war, and how they contributed to the overall aims and objectives of the war. The accounts narrated by the war veterans deserves a special word of praise. Part 6 gives an absorbing account of the war as experienced by newly commissioned subalterns – the Greenhorns- within two weeks of their commissioning. The spirit of the Greenhorn has the most moving impact when one of them, on being severely injured and had lesser chances of survival in East Pakistan, conveyed, "Write to my Parents, I fought Well". Part 7 has been discussed by both Indian and Bangladesh authors, with a view to highlight a few major takeaways of the war, and to integrate South Asia as a region, and measures to further strengthen India-Bangladesh relationship.

The response for subscription of articles for the book was overwhelming. It has not been possible to publish all the narrations due to understandable reasons of the book's capacity. However, those 'left out of the battle' (meaning the book) accounts will be uploaded on the web site of CLAWS: www.claws.in. We sincerely thank all our authors for their valuable experiences and contribution to the book. We would like to thank the Hon'ble Defence Minister of India and the COAS for writing a message for the book. We would also like to thank Shri NN Vohra, IAS, Padma Vibhushan, former Defence Secretary, and former Governor Jammu and Kashmir, for giving a Foreword to the book. Our thanks are also due to General NC Vij and Air Marshal VK Bhatia for giving blurbs to the book. At the end, we would like to thank the Indian and Bangladesh people for their continuous support to the Armed Forces of both the countries.

In addition to the Armed Forces, the contribution of the Border Security Force (BSF) of India and other paramilitary forces were also immense. Controlling the huge influx of refugees while also maintaining the security of the border, was a mammoth task. The BSF, in synergy with the Army, was able to execute in an efficient manner.

The War of 1971 saw many battles that were fought simultaneously on both the fronts. Battles like the battle of Bogra, battle of Bakshiganj (1 Maratha Li Infantry), were all fought with equal grit and courage and were important milestones in the victory of India and Bangladesh.

We would also like to pay tribute to all the 'sons of soil' and the 'family members' who placed 'Nation First'. To name a few, Lance Naik Albert Ekka (14 GUARDS), PVC (P); 2nd Lt Arun Khetarpal (17 HORSE), PVC (P); Maj Hoshiar Singh (3 GRENADIERS), PVC; Fg Officer Nirmaljit Singh Sekhon (Gnat Detachment Pilot), PVC (P) as also the other gallantry award winners.

It would be of a great interest to all – civilians and military personnel alike. The book also looks beyond the Liberation @50 Years, to analyse the host of challenges confronting South Asia, and the need to integrate the region as a whole. Therefore, the book would be of immense value to the policy makers, defence analysts, academia and students of strategic studies.

Jai Hind !

Editors

Introduction

VK Ahluwalia and *AN Jha*

When the Awami League, led by Sheikh Mujibur Rahman, emerged as the majority party during the elections to the National Assembly of Pakistan in December 1970, the writing was clear on the wall. It had swept the elections against its nearest rival party, Pakistan People's Party (PPP). However, Awami League was denied the right to form the government. What was the writing that the Pakistani leaders could not read? They did not realise the deep-rooted differences between East and West Pakistan, and the intolerable conditions that prevailed in East Pakistan due to gross discrimination and neglect. The Awami League, the main political party in East Pakistan, on the other hand, knew the pulse and the aspirations of the people. It had pitched its manifesto for the election on the issue of autonomy for East Pakistan, and had a landslide victory by bagging 167 seats (including seven indirectly elected women seats) out of a total of 313 seats. Zulfikar Ali Bhutto's Pakistan People's Party (PPP), won 81 seats out of 138 in West Pakistan, becoming the majority party in West Pakistan, primarily with the support from Sindh and Punjab. It emerged that neither of the two largest parties won a single seat in the other wing. On the other hand, interestingly, Gen Yahya Khan had ordered National Assembly elections on the premise, based on the inputs given by the military intelligence, that 'no single party would win a majority in the parliament, and, with a hung parliament, real power would still reside with the military-bureaucracy oligarchy.[1] It came as a rude shock to the ruling elite of Pakistan. The governance system simply did not understand the pulse, aspirations and power of the people of East Pakistan.

Over the years, due to economic, political, social and regional neglect, there was a growing realisation among the people in the eastern wing, that East Pakistan had become a simple colony of West Pakistan. On the contrary, East Pakistan always shared the composite culture of undivided Bengal in history, language, literature, art and music.[2] Mere emotional appeals on religious affiliation could not bridge the widening gap between the two wings of Pakistan. While the civil services were composed mainly of Urdu and Punjabi-speaking West Pakistanis, the majority of officers in the armed forces belonged to Punjab and NWFP.[3]

With the indefinite postponement of the National Assembly session, announced on March 1, 1971, there were several violent protests and riots on March 2-3 across East Pakistan. Due to the prevailing uncertain environment in East Pakistan, there was a frequent changeover of Martial Law Administrator and Governor of East Pakistan. Pakistan Government was in a state of panic. The talks between the Pakistan Government and the parallel government headed by Sheikh Mujibur Rahman had failed. Resultantly, 'Operation Searchlight' was launched by Gen Tikka Khan on the night of March 25/26, 1971, which manifested in firing from all types of weapon systems. Military crackdown, accompanied by massacres, loot, arson and rape, resulted in mass exodus of people from East Pakistan to the Indian neighbouring states of West Bengal, Assam, Meghalaya and Tripura. By the end of November 1971, besides internal displacement, 'about ten million people had already moved into India.'[4] All efforts at political and diplomatic levels did not yield any results.

Seeing the conditions in East Pakistan, Mukti Bahini, formed out of defected paramilitary and regular troops, as well as patriotic youth, had already started organising itself as fighting units in East Pakistan to conduct guerrilla raids, ambushes and attacks on military installations and communication nodes. While Pakistan chose a defensive strategy in the East to delay the fall of Dhaka, it followed an offensive strategy in the west to capture sensitive territories to compensate for its losses in the east. As Pakistan Government's considered strategy was that the '*Defence of the East Lies in the West,*' it launched air attacks on 12 Indian airfields at 4.45 pm on December 3, 1971. Therefore, India officially declared a war against Pakistan. It was fought on both the fronts – Western and Eastern – by all the three services.

Although the book discusses the broad framework of strategy for both India and Pakistan, India's aim in the Eastern Theatre is covered briefly as it relates to the Liberation War. With a view to achieve decisive results, the army had considered four major thrust lines, one each under the three corps and a communication zone: 2 Corps and two divisions to the Western Sector of East Pakistan, 33 Corps with a division plus two brigades in North Western Sector; 4 Corps with three mountain divisions to the Eastern Sector, and 101 Communication Zone Area with two infantry brigades to the northern sector.

Having got reinforcements from West Pakistan, Pakistan Army's strategy was three tiered: first, to hold outposts along the border with India; second, hold strong points at important communication centres along the axes leading to Dhaka; and third hold Dhaka strongly. On the contrary, the Indian Army contained and bypassed the strong points, including paradropping and helilifting troops in the depth areas, to contact Dhaka at the earliest. The IAF and the Indian Navy played a vital role at all stages of the war towards the overall aim of the war.

The situation in East Pakistan was grim, with the Indian Armed Forces, the Mukti Bahini and the support of the people achieving success in all sectors. General Quereshi highlights the difficulties of being a commander in a situation where Pakistani troops were being targeted, as well as the role of human psychology in such a fearful and uncertain environment. He shares his unit command experience, wherein the 'commanding officer has to be firm under pressure, dependable in a crisis, and compassionate in his dealings.'[5]

Finally, the Pakistan Army surrendered on December 16, 1971. Although the Shimla Agreement was signed in July 1972 to return 93,000 prisoners and to usher in peace in the region, there has been no peace as the Line of Control (LoC). The border between India and Pakistan, remains active and Pakistan continues to sponsor terrorists to operate in India.

This book titled "Bangladesh Liberation@50Years: 'Bijoy' with Synergy: *India-Pakistan War 1971*" aims to take a look at the prevailing regional dynamics and beyond the Liberation War with great focus on connectivity, culture, commerce and security. The book has been compiled carefully with a view to highlight the operational cum personal experiences of the Armed Forces of both the countries, the local populace of the countries and the contribution of the family members of the personnel. This book would be great interest to all – civilians and military personnel alike as also to the policy makers, defence analysts, academia and students of strategic studies.

Notes

1. Akbar Zaidi, "Special report: The Breakup of Pakistan 1969-1971", *Dawn*. Available at https://www.dawn.com/news/1359141
2. Prasad, Thapliyal, *The India-Pakistan War of 1971: A History* (Natraj Publishers), p. 3.
3. Jasjit Singh, *Role of Indian Air Force in 1971 War* (FPBA Publisher, 2013), p. 22.
4. Prasad, Thapliyal, n. 3, p. xvi.
5. Hakeem Arshad Quereshi, *The 1971 Indo-Pak War, A Soldier's Narrative* (Oxford University Press), pp. 86-87. Quereshi commanded an infantry battalion (26 Frontier Force) in East Pakistan through the 1970 general election, the civil disobedience movement, the insurgency and the 1971 war.

List of Abbreviations

ACT	Air Control Team
ADS	Advance Dressing Station
AGPL	Actual Ground Position Line
ARC	Aviation Research Centre
ASW	Anti-submarine Warfare
AWACS	Airborne Warning and Control System
AWWA	Army Wives Welfare Association
BBIN	Bangladesh, Bhutan, India and Nepal
BIMSTEC	Bay of Bengal Initiative for Multi-sectoral Technical and Economic Cooperation
BOP	Border Out Post
BPG	Bangladesh Provisional Government
BRO	Border Roads Organisation
BRI	Belt and Road Initiative
B3W	Build Back Better World
CAR	Central Asian Republic
CAS	Close Air Support
CEPA	Comprehensive Economic Partnership Agreement
CFL	Cease-Fire Line
CHM	Company Havildar Major
CIJW	Counter Insurgency and Jungle Warfare
CPEC	China-Pakistan Economic Corridor
DZ	Dropping Zone
EBR	East Bengal Rifles
ELINT	Electronic Intelligence
EPR	East Pakistan Rifles
FAC	Forward Air Controller
FDL	Forward Defended Locality

FOCEF	Flag Officer Commanding Eastern Fleet (IN)
FOO	Forward Observation Officer
FUP	Forming Up Place
GBR	Gilgit-Baltistan Region
GLO	Ground Liaison Officer
HADR	Humanitarian Assistance and Disaster Reliefs
HICDP	High Impact Community Development Project
ICT	Information, Communication and Technology
INS	Indian Naval Ship
IOC	Indian Oil Cooperation
JCP	Joint Check Post
JRC	Joint River Commission
LoC/LC	Line of Control
LST	Landing Ship Tank
MES	Military Engineering Service
NATO	North Atlantic Treaty Organisation
NEFA	North East Frontier Agency
NER	North Eastern Region (India's)
ORBAT	Order of Battle
ORP	Operational Readiness Platform
PAF	Pakistan Airforce
PF	Path Finder
PLA	People's Liberation Army (of China)
PoW	Prisoners of War
PMO	Prime Minister's Office
RAP	Regimental Aid Post
R&AW	Research and Analysis Wing
RMO	Regimental Medical Officer
RT	Radio Telephony
SACEP	South Asia Comprehensive Economic Partnership
SAR	Search and Rescue
SEATO	Southeast Asia Treaty Organisation
SIGINT	Signal Intelligence
SOP	Standard Operating Procedure
TAC	Tactical Air Centre
UNDP	United Nations Development Programme

SECTION 1

Defence of the East Lies in the West

Dynamic Leadership at Play

1

Historical Perspective and Geo-Strategy: 'Defence of the East Lies in the West'

VK Ahluwalia and *Narjit Singh*

Pamphlet Calling on Pakistani Troops to Surrender

> *"Officers and Jawans of the Pakistan Army, Indian Forces have surrounded you. Your Air Force is destroyed. You have no hope of any help from them. Chittagong, Chalna and Mangla Ports are blocked. Nobody can reach you from the sea. Your fate is sealed. The Mukti Bahini and the people are all prepared to take revenge for the atrocities and cruelties you have committed ...[...]".*[1]
>
> *Major General Hakeem Arshad Qureshi recalls his time as a Lieutenant Colonel and Commanding Officer of the* 26 Frontier Force Battalion at Saidpur, East Pakistan, during the 1971 war.[2]
>
> *"We were part of over 90,000 (45,000 army) Prisoners of War including a large contingent of Police, Civilians, and complement of East Pakistan Civil Armed Forces who had surrendered to the Indian conquerors on 16 December 1971. Now, on 17 October1973, after having given up half the country and having preferred, surrender to martyrdom, we were being received like heroes with bands playing stirring patriotic tunes. It was embarrassing and depressing. How had it come about? 1971 had turned out to be a year of trial for Pakistan. [...] Apparently, the Indians had chalked out a complete plan of action right from the Agartala Conspiracy to the final capitulation of the Pakistan Army at the racecourse ground. [...].*

> *"[..]In fact, we appear to have disintegrated as a cohesive fighting force somewhere between the borders and our envisaged first, or in some cases second line of defence. Hence à quick defeat in detail. Factually, we lost the war without losing a battle. Even the enemy was surprised at the speed of our disintegration. [...]"*
> *"Was it possible to live as one nation with a people who had been 'tamed' through use of force?* Qureshi asked.

The word 'autonomy, which would subsequently result in secession,' was anathema to the ruling elite of Pakistan. With the ground situation worsening in East Pakistan, and following hectic parleys at various levels, President Yahya Khan met the senior most army generals in a conference at the Army HQs on February 22, 1971, and a decision was taken against entrusting political power to Mujib and his party.[3] Admiral Ahsan, Martial Law Administrator of East Pakistan, was one of the few officers who disagreed with President Yahya Khan's proposal at the conference.[4] General Tikka Khan reportedly told President Yahya Khan, "*Give me one week's time, I will bring back normalcy in East Pakistan.*"[5]

Following Yahya Khan's radio statement on March 1 about the indefinite postponement of the National Assembly session that was scheduled to be held on March 3, there were many mass protests and riots on March 2-3. Maj Gen Palit describes this act as, '*Breach of faith at the last moment was the supreme act of treachery.*'[6] As a result, the soldiers opened fire on the demonstrators. On March 7, Lt Gen Tikka Khan was moved to Dhaka to take over as the Martial Law Administrator and Governor of East Pakistan from Lt Gen Sahabzada Yakub Khan, who had taken over just a week ago. Frequent changes in the governance system in East Pakistan showed that the ruling elite was in a state of panic. Meanwhile, the size of the processions continued to grow, with popular slogans filling the streets of Dhaka with '*Joi Bangla*' (long live Bengal) and '*Sonar Bangla*' (Golden Bengal).[7] With a military crackdown in mind in East Pakistan, General Yahya Khan and his commanders had commenced military build-up since mid-February, both by sea and air. While all preparations for the military crackdown had been completed by March 24, 1971, Sheikh Mujibur Rahman had also established a parallel government in East Pakistan by then.[8]

The Gathering Storm

The year 1971 brought with it ominous forebodings of war on the Indian subcontinent. In 1970, the Awami League, an East Pakistan political party, won majority of seats in Pakistan's federal elections, marginalising Zulfikar Ali Bhutto's Pakistan People's Party of West Pakistan. This made Sheikh Mujibur Rehman, a Bengali Muslim and the leader of the Awami League, the top contender for the post of Prime Minister of Pakistan. Mujib had previously offered a six-point proposal for the autonomy of East Pakistan in 1966. Mr Bhutto viewed this as secession and rejected it outright. In his address in a public meeting at Dhaka on March 7, Sheikh Mujibur Rahman made four demands, reflecting popular Bengali sentiments: immediate lifting of martial law; immediate withdrawal of all military personnel to their barracks; immediate transfer of power to elected representatives of the people; and a proper inquiry into the loss of life during the conflict.[9]

Despite a clear majority in 1970, the Sheikh was denied the opportunity to establish a government. This sparked a civil disobedience movement in East Pakistan prompting Gen Yahya Khan, the President and Chief Martial Law Administrator, to order a military crackdown in the East on March 25, 1971. Sheikh Mujibur Rahman was arrested and skirted away to West Pakistan in the early hours of March 26, 1971, and on March 27, 1971, Major Ziaur Rahman, based in Chittagong, declared the sovereign Republic of Bangladesh's Independence on behalf of Sheikh Mujib. East Pakistan was engulfed in flames, and without any dithering, East Pakistani Officers in the Pakistan Army deserted and formed the 'Mukti Bahini' or the Liberation Army. Gen Tikka Khan, who was tasked with putting an end to the uprising, launched 'Operation Searchlight', in which thousands of protestors, university intellectuals and innocents were mercilessly butchered, resulting in a mass humanitarian crisis and exodus of refugees into the border states of Assam, West Bengal, and Tripura. In East Pakistan, the Pakistan Army was considered as an 'occupation army.'

The talks between the two warring factions had failed. When 'Operation Search light' was launched by Gen Tikka Khan on March 25, 1971, both Gen Yahya Khan and Mr Bhutto were still in Dhaka. The H- Hour for the military crackdown 'Operation Searchlight' was set at 1 am on March 26. Having secured all key communication stations and locations much before the

H- Hour, the military filled the air, especially in the streets of Dhaka, with fire from all types of weapons, including strafing and bombing of pockets of resistance, by sabre jets of Pakistan Air Force. Seeing all this, Mujibur Rahman, immediately sent out a message, knowing that the Pakistani Army would make every effort to trace him and arrest him, "*This is my last message. From today Bangladesh is independent. I call upon the people of Bangladesh, wherever you are and whatever you have to resist the army of occupation to the last [...].*"[10] According to some analysts, 80 percent of the population fled Dhaka within two days of the military crackdown, about 150,000 people were killed in the city, and the massacre continued with accompanying collateral damage, loot, arson and rape.[11]

All preparations for the military crackdown were completed by March 24 and final orders were conveyed by Lt Gen Tikka Khan to Maj Gen Khadim Hussain at 1100 hrs on March 25, "*Khadim, it is tonight.*"[12] On the night of March 25, West Pakistani troops perpetrated mass killings in Chittagong. On 26 March, Chittagong was reinforced with troops by C-130 transport planes flying in from Dhaka. That same night, naval guns also opened heavy artillery fire, and Pakistani troops attacked select targets. 'At 7:45 pm on 26 March 1971, Maj Ziaur Rahman, an officer of the 8th Battalion of the East Bengal Rifles (EBR) at Chittagong, announced the establishment of an independent Bangladesh.[...]'[13] By early April, several prominent leaders of East Pakistan had crossed over to India, and on April 10, 1971, they decided to set up the Provincial Government of Bangladesh to carry out the mandate given to them by the people. The formal installation took place on April 17, 1971. Considering the growing strength of Mukti Bahini, envisaged violence and secessionist movement, Pakistan transferred large reinforcements from West to East Pakistan, and subsequently the columns were moved to different parts of East Pakistan, as shown on Map 1. Pakistan went on to adopt 'the fortress form of defence' by occupying important communication centres around the towns.

Lt Gen AAK Niazi took over the Eastern Command from Lt Gen Tikka Khan on April 11, 1971. He issued an operational directive giving out five phases, to be effective by May 15, 1971; the entire focus was on action with speed, that is to man all important border posts, to secure the ports of Chittagong, Chalna and Khulna and the railway communication between

Map 1: Movement of Pak Columns

Source: *The India-Pakistan War of 1971*, SN Prasad & UP Thapliyal, 2014.

important communication centres to be made operational. According to Bhuiyan, *"The main targets of the genocide were the Bengali elements of EBR, EPR, Police, Paramilitary Ansars, Mujahids, and the Awami League office bearers and volunteers.."*[....].[14] The exodus continued to increase progressively, 'from a figure of 3,158,000 in May 1971, it increased to about ten million by end November the same year.'[15] There were several Bengali soldiers and officers serving with EBRs and PAF. While some of them were killed, the others, along with the trained manpower, formed the nucleus of the Mukti Bahini.

Siddiq Salik was a Public Relations Officer in the Pakistani Army in Dacca (Dhaka) during the crucial period that led to the disintegration of East Pakistan in 1971. In his book, Salik presented a view of soldiers and sailors serving in the army and navy during a crucial period of insurgency, as well as the politics that revolved around the Yahya administration, which eventually led to the nation's break-up.[16] Many analysts have written that while West Pakistani politicians like ZA Bhutto were responsible for the constitutional failure by not accepting the popular mandate, it was the military leadership that was solely accountable for the massacres that took place in East Pakistan. The fact that the leaders of USA and China, and West Pakistan's intellectuals and opinion makers remained silent spectators to the massacre in East Pakistan, meant that they were equally responsible for the second partition of the subcontinent.

Mukti Bahini

In the liberation of Bangladesh, Mukti Bahini or '*Muktijoddha*' – the Liberation Army (freedom fighters) – played a vital role at all stages. Although the concept existed much earlier, it gained momentum following the crackdown and repression carried out by the Pakistani Army beginning on March 25. Mukti Bahini grew progressively, with a sense of urgency, into an organisation of armed and trained men owing allegiance to the Provincial Government of Bangladesh. With an added vigour and commitment towards the formation of a new nation, the students, and young men from all segments of the society came forward to actively participate in the liberation war. Col MAG Osmani, an elected member of the National Assembly, who fought in the Indo-Pak War of 1965, was appointed the Commander-in-Chief of the Bangladesh Liberation Army.[17] He posited, '*The Mukti Bahini was manufactured overnight by the Pakistani Army.*' By the end of April, the number of volunteers had risen to about 2,50,000.[18] It did take some time to organise the Mukti Bahini into a well organised fighting force. However, they continued to attack and harass the Pakistani Forces and their vital installations, communication nodes, armed constabularies and networks at different places in East Pakistan. They conducted successful forays to inflict casualties on the Pakistan Army while operating from safe locations along the Indian border, and obtained valuable information about their deployments and movement plans. The guerrilla tactics of 'hit and run', and sabotage created an uncertain environment for the Pakistani Army, which was considered an occupation force. On the other hand, the Pakistani Forces destroyed the harbours and safe bases of Mukti Bahini across the borders into the Indian territory.[19]

Influx of Refugees

On January 30, 1971, an Indian Airlines flight between Srinagar and Delhi was hijacked. The two hijackers directed that it be flown to Lahore. While the crew and the passengers were returned through the land route, the aircraft was destroyed in situ at the Lahore airport. The two hijackers were welcomed as heroes by ZA Bhutto personally.[20] It was evident that it was a pre-planned move of the Pakistan Government. India retaliated by banning all Pakistani civil and military flights over Indian territory, which proved too costly to Pakistan in the events that ensued thereafter in East Pakistan.

Given the genocidal, repressive, volatile and unsafe conditions from March 1971 onwards, millions of refugees from East Pakistan – uniformed personnel, intellectuals, poor illiterate people, Hindus, Muslims, Buddhists, Christians – were given shelter in India. The then Central Government decided to provide relief on humanitarian grounds to about 10 million refugees. Several refugee camps were established along the border. The Prime Minister of India stated on May 18 and again on May 26, 1971, *"Lakhs of refugees pouring into the border states had created a major problem for the country. This would severely affect the country's economic, social, and political life [..] The refugee problem was threatening the peace and security of India."*[21]

Geo-politics: Alignment of the Powers

A great power play was underway in the strategically important Indian Ocean Region (IOR), as powerful nations sought to establish bases there. The Indian Ocean provided the sea lanes for international trade, flow of oil, raw materials, and had the potential to influence the economic activity of the dependent great powers. The geo-politics of the region was undergoing a change with the growing nexus between the US, China and Pakistan, and their influence in the IOR. The warming of relations between the US and China came to be known as 'Ping Pong diplomacy'. While the US remained firmly committed to Vietnam, its major objective was to prevent Soviet

Russia to gain influence in South Asia. Quite naturally, Soviet Russia, a superpower, felt threatened with the developments in the IOR. The net result was that a new power alignment developed in the region. The United States and China emerged in support of Pakistan, and the Soviet Union in support of India. It resulted in the Indo-Soviet Peace, Cooperation and Friendship treaty in August 1971, which served India's interests at this critical juncture. It included clauses requiring consultations during a conflict or in the event of a third-party threat to the country.

While discussing the role of the US and China, the essence of Akbar Zaidi's article suggests that while the scale and nature of massacre and atrocities conducted by the military in East Pakistan were beyond imagination, both the countries remained silent due to their vested interests The US considered three different aspects of the situation arising on the subcontinent: refugee problem, political instability in Pakistan and the probability of a war breaking out between the two countries. The US sent elements of its Seventh Fleet (Task Force 74 led by the aircraft carrier USS Enterprise) to the Indian Ocean and Bay of Bengal to demonstrate its support to Pakistan. It also encouraged UK to deploy a naval battle group (HMS Eagle) in the region. China had openly condemned India at the United Nations and had pledged its support to Pakistan against foreign aggression. Soviet Russia came in support of India by vetoing a US-sponsored draft resolution calling for immediate cessation of hostilities. Simultaneously, it despatched its cruisers and destroyers, and a nuclear submarine into the Indian Ocean.

Build-up of War Hysteria

The relations between the two wings of Pakistan were worsening by the day. The trigger to explode was waiting to happen – something the Pakistan's leadership failed to read. In July 1971, Pakistan's President Yahya Khan threatened that if India tried to seize any part of East Pakistan, he would declare war.[22] During the latter part of summer of 1971, Pakistani Army had raised *Razakars,* who were subsequently renamed as *Al Badr* (the soldiers of the first battle of Islam) and *Al Sham* (The Sun). They were Bengalis who were tasked to collect information about the Awami League's sympathisers, especially the intellectuals, and keep the Pakistani Army informed. But the general perception that prevailed among the East Pakistan's Army personnel was, *"You can kill a man, but cannot kill an idea."*[23]

Besides the large influx of refugees into India, Pakistan Army's intrusion into the Indian territory in pursuit of Mukti Bahini posed an additional threat to India's security.[24] With the situation deteriorating in East Pakistan and statements given by Pakistani leaders, it was becoming increasingly clear that probability of war was imminent. The Indian Armed Forces had taken several measures to improve its operational preparedness: raising and reorganising units and formations; compensating for deficiency of officers and other ranks; terminating courses and advancing the commissioning dates of officers at the training academies and recalling the reservists.

Pakistan's Strategy: 'Defence of the East Lies in the West'

Pakistan's strategy was that its forces in East Pakistan were to hold out until Pakistan defeated India in the West. Therefore, it is evident that an offensive by Pakistan was already planned. Dhaka Bowl – surrounded by three mighty rivers Jamuna, Padma and Meghna – was to be defended till the end with strong forces. It was a gross over estimation of one's own capabilities by Pakistan and a strategic blunder. The leadership was not in touch with the ground realities in East Pakistan, and failed to realise the power of the people.

Lt Gen KP Candeth, the Army commander Western Command during the 1971 War, mentions in his book that by mid-September, *"Pakistan's attitude had become increasingly truculent."* It was estimated that they (Pakistan Armed Forces) could concentrate and mount an attack within a week.[25] Going by an Army Commander's appreciation, it is evident that the situation was rather ambiguous and uncertain, as there was no offensive on the western front till December 3, 1971. It appears that the Indian Armed Forces and its leadership were driven by Clausewitz, who said, *"War is nothing but political intercourse with a mixture of other means."*

Having commanded a battalion during the most crucial period in East Pakistan, Arshad Qureshi makes a critical-cum-apt observation, *"Instead of accepting an unmanageable upheaval in the immediate future, we closed our eyes to reality and tried to conduct business as usual – probably hoping to bluff our way out of a tough corner."*[26]

Eastern Front

To understand the broad strategy, operational concepts and the progress of operations, one must have fundamental knowledge of the geographical features, terrain and friction, the prominent five river system (Jamuna-Brahmaputra, Padma-Ganges, Surma-Meghna, when Padma joins Meghna it is called Padma-Meghna, and the four prominent rivers in the Hill Sector of Chittagong – Feni, Karnaphuli, Sangu and Matamuhari), the inland water system and the waterways, transportation system including rail and road system. East Pakistan was a low-lying, riverine country with a large marshy jungle coastline. It is characterised by a deltaic plain at the confluence of the Ganges (Padma), Brahmaputra (Jamuna), and Meghna Rivers, as well as their tributaries. These rivers are highly vulnerable to floods. With a tropical monsoon climate, it experiences heavy seasonal rainfall, high temperatures, and high humidity. These peculiarities of terrain and climatic conditions were also important factors for timing the operations in the land of rivers.

For operations, East Pakistan was divided into four sectors (covered in detail in Parts 3 and 4).

- *North-western Sector*: Indian Army was to advance up to the main communication centre Bogra, and pin down the Pakistan Forces there.
- *Western Sector*: Army was to capture major communication centres at Jessore and Jhenida.
- *Eastern Sector*: Army was to occupy the Meghna Bulge between Chandpur and Ashuganj.
- *Northern Sector*: Army was to launch a thrust along Jamalpur-Tangail line to secure the area. Chittagong was to be dealt with by the Indian Navy. The military action envisaged joint operations by all three services to ensure a quick success.[27]

Gen (later Field Marshal) Sam Manekshaw, Lt Gen JS Aurora -Eastern Army Commander, Maj Gen JFR Jacob-Chief of Staff, Eastern Command, assisted by their staff, analysed the deployments and options available to Pakistan in their Eastern Theatre. Thereafter, they drew operational plans against East Pakistan. The Indian Army, with its 2 Corps, 33 Corps, 4 Corps, and 101 Area, along with the support of the IAF, the IN and the Mukti Bahini

Map 2: East Pakistan showing Deployment of Indian Formations

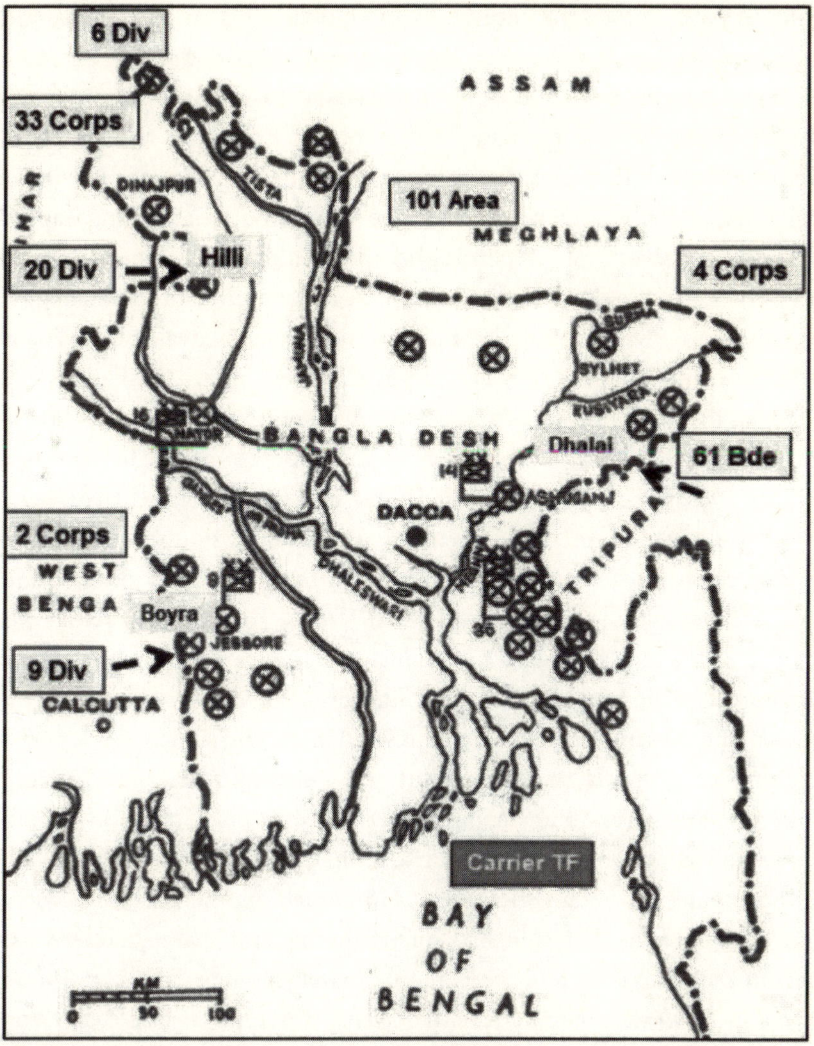

Source: http://www.indiandefencereview.com/spotlights/1971-war-a-tri-service-perspective/

and East Bengal forces, bypassed the strongly held fortresses and captured the initial objectives to reach Dhaka. Air Commodore Jasjit concluded that it was unparalleled synergy among the politico, military and diplomatic dimensions of national crisis management and decision making that enabled India to successfully undertakc military force application [...].[28]

Western Front

Unlike the other wars, the conflict in December 1971 was the consequence of an intensive conflict between the East and West wings of Pakistan. As Pakistan held the initiative, it was necessary to assess our own counter plans to neutralise any offensive action before executing the army's plan. This necessitated that the defensive posture be capable of withstanding shock first, and the Indian offensive be capable of threatening/capturing Pakistan's sensitive areas. According to information available, Pakistan had two Armoured divisions and two independent Armoured brigades, as against one armoured division and three armoured brigades available to western command, nine infantry divisions as against ten on the Indian side; one additional division was in Ladakh. Besides nine infantry divisions, Pakistan also had seven PoK brigades that could well be employed in Jammu and Kashmir. Of their nine Infantry divisions, it was appreciated that their 12, 23, 8, 15, 10 and 11 Infantry Divisions would hold ground in Jammu and Kashmir opposite Chhamb in the Sialkot and Shakargarh sectors, and in Punjab to protect the Lahore and Kasur front. Therefore, Pakistan would have the following in reserve for offensive action: 1 Corps consisting of 6 Armoured Division and 17 Infantry Division, 11 Corps with I Armoured Division and 33 Infantry Division and 7 Infantry Division.

The aspect which now stood out was that Pakistan could mount an offensive in any part of Punjab, Jammu and Kashmir or Chhamb with one of the reserve Corps, which could be further augmented by 7 Infantry Division. Yet, they could also retain the capacity to launch another offensive with the second Corps. Thus, Pakistan had many options and these increased as the waters in the rivers Ravi and Sutlej receded after the monsoon.

It will be pertinent to review the offensive options available to Pakistan, as was discussed in the Operations Room of Western Command. First was an offensive in Jammu and Kashmir, involving a Division together with about 10,000 infiltrators. 7 Infantry Division was a probability here, but as we approached end October and the snow blocked infiltration routes, the threat to the valley declined progressively. However, the infiltration threat into Poonch, Rajouri, Nowshera and Jammu remained. The other question was: would Pakistan transfer their reserve 7 Infantry Division so early and so far away from the decisive theatre of operations, which had always been Punjab? The second course was to use one of her reserve corps to isolate Jammu and Kashmir between Pathankot and Jammu. She could also combine this attack with another on Chhamb, Poonch and other parts of Jammu and Kashmir. Third, was an offensive from Nainakot to Gurdaspur with her 1 Corps to cut off and destroy our base in Pathankot. The fourth was an offensive through Dera Baba Nanak or Gill ferry to capture Amritsar or the Beas bridge. The fifth anticipated move could be against Amritsar or Ferozepore, or between the two, to capture Harike, but with a low possibility. Lastly, was an offensive in the south with her 11 Corps in the Fazilka region to cut off the Indian forces in Punjab.

The Western Front was divided into two sectors – Northern and Southern Sector.

To foil Pakistan's attempt to cut off connections between Pathankot and Jammu, as well as an offensive in the Hills Sector in Poonch-Rajouri sectors, India planned two thrust lines – one in Shakargarh Bulge, and the other from River Ravi at Thakurpur. Limited attacks were also planned in Shyok Valley, Kargil, Chicken's Neck and Dera Baba Nanak (DBN) bridge to improve own defensive posture. In comparison to the war aims of the 1965 War, which gave orders to the commanders to occupy minimum Pakistani territory and to destroy the offensive power of Pakistan, 'the war objectives of the 1971 War were more defensive and restrained'.[29] In the Southern Sector, an attack was planned in the Desert Sector (Barmer) along the rail lines towards Naya Chor, as also a thrust towards Rahimyar Khan (RYK) in the Jaisalmer Sector. Due to limited offensive by Pakistan in the Laungewala sector, 12 Infantry Division's plans to its objective at RYK could not materialise.

As the possibility of conflict seemed imminent, various formations such as 4, 6, and 9 Infantry Divisions, 23 Mountain Division and parts of 8 and 57 Mountain Divisions were deployed along the East Bengal border. Some of these formations were those which had earlier been earmarked for operations in the west. In a television interview in August 1971, Yahya Khan said, *"War with India is very near and in case of war, Pakistan would not be alone."*

On October 23, 1971, Prime Minister Indira Gandhi travelled to France, West Germany, Belgium, the United Kingdom, the United States of America and Australia in a last-minute attempt to avert war, highlighting the unsustainable load imposed on India by the refugees. At home, Lieutenant General K P Candeth, Army Commander was also concerned about the large troop movements to the eastern theatre, which he had been assured would be used for operations against West Pakistan. This had led to a void in guarding the western border, as Army Headquarters would not allow troops to fill the gaps lest it gave alarm signals to Pakistan. The view of the Army Commander was that the formidable concentration of troops in the east may be seen as a threat to their security and lead to a pre-emptive strike on the western border. In his view, it was more prudent to first secure the Western front before carrying out a massive concentration on the eastern border. Thus, until the third week of October, the western part was virtually open or so porous, that had Yahya Khan attacked, the Pakistan Army would have succeeded in achieving their objectives in Punjab and the narrow corridor to Jammu and Kashmir.[30] Pakistan's intelligence was highly active, as Pakistan Radio announced the accurate movements of our units every day.[31]

Pakistan had deployed its 1 Corps for the defence of the Shakargarh Bulge. 15 and 8 Infantry Divisions, 8(I) Armoured Brigade, and PMFs were deployed in a holding role. For its offensive, it had 6 Armoured Division and 17 Infantry division.[32] India's 1 Corps, with its 36 Infantry Division, 39 Infantry Division, 54 Infantry Division, were assigned both offensive and defensive roles in the Shakargarh Bulge. Although 1 Corps seized the initiative to launch the offensive, it was characterised by self-imposed caution. It was neither bold in planning nor in its execution. In Punjab, 11 Corps captured the DBN enclave and the Sehjra salient but failed to recapture the Indian enclave of Hussainiwala. In the north, Indian Army captured a few important heights in the Tangdhar, Lipa Valley, Shyok Valley and Kargil sectors.

The Indian Air Force

The Indian Air Force, too, had prioritised its agenda, with the primary objective of defending the home base against enemy air attacks, followed by a close support to the ground army's and navy's actions. Several counter-surface missions were flown, including interdiction and reconnaissance missions, counter air operations to gain control of the air and to destabilise Pakistan's air effort by attacks on their airfields and aircraft – both on the ground and in the air. Strategic priorities were put into place such as attacks on the Sui gas plant, Karachi oil storage tanks and refineries and also the Mangla hydroelectric power plant. In the east, the Air Force was able to achieve air supremacy mainly due to the higher force ratios, but this was not the case in the western theatre. The Indians had 34 fighter squadrons and 5 bomber squadrons making the force ratio against Pakistan in the west 2:1.[33]

On the other hand, in the eastern theatre, the Indians had a superiority of 11:1 over Pakistan due to the presence of just one Sabre Squadron comprising about 20 aircraft. The offensive Indian air strategy resulted in at least 11,548 sorties, out of which 44 percent were flown in the western front. Aircraft losses amounted to 43 in the west and 13 in the east. On the other hand, Pakistan flew 840 offensive missions in which they lost 27 aircraft in the west and 22 aircraft in the east. Maritime air operations were carried out at Masroor, targets next to Karachi harbour and their oil facilities in Karachi. These offensive missions were carried out by Hunters and wreaked havoc on Karachi's populace psychologically.[34] The first IAF dogfight was on November 22, when IAF Gnats shot down three PAF Sabres over Boyra in Indian territory, northeast of Calcutta. Yahya Khan was soon to announce that Pakistan would be at war with India in ten days. This became true when on December 3, Pakistan declared war on India by attacking airfields on the western borders attempting to imitate the Israeli strategy of the 1967 Arab-Israel War. However, due to poor planning and bad execution, these attacks had little effect on a well-prepared Indian Air Force and its assets. The Sukhois and the MiGs of India did an excellent during night strikes, confounding Pakistanis who 'thought' that the Indians were using the Soviet Airborne Warning and Control System (AWACS) – the pilots were going purely by compass, map and timing.

The Indian Navy

After nearly 25 years of Independence, the Indian Navy has now established its rightful place as an equal shareholder in national security alongside its sister services. Nothing exemplifies this coming of age than the daring strikes by Indian Navy missile boats on Pakistan Navy warships and shore-based installations at Karachi harbour on the nights of December 4 and 8. When the war broke out on December 3, naval commanders of INS Nipet, Veer and Nirghat were clearly instructed to fire their missiles at any enemy target within an arc of 100 nautical miles. INS Nirghat sank the PNS Khyber, and as they approached the Karachi coastline, INS Veer intervened and sank a minesweeper (PNS Muhafiz) on its way to pick up survivors from Khyber. Now just 25 nautical miles short of the Karachi oil refineries, INS Nipet fired a third missile at the refineries.

An interesting vignette on the Karachi harbour attack is narrated by Admiral Nadkarni while he was pursuing a course at the Naval War College in the US. His Pakistani naval counterpart was recalled at the commencement of the war, but on his return to continue the course after cessation of hostilities, he told Nadkarni that the attack on Karachi harbour was most 'unfair', as the Russians were manning the Indian attack ships. In fact, all the Indian crew of the missile boats had just returned from training in Russia and being fluent in the language would break into as Russians during the operation to confuse the Pakistanis. However, the sinking of PNS Ghazi outside Vizag harbour had shaken the Pakistan Daphne Class submarines. INS Khukri and INS Kirpan, two relatively new anti-submarine-warfare (ASW) frigates, were on aggressive patrolling on the night of December 9/10, when three torpedoes fired from PNS Hangor, a Daphne Class submarine, ripped into INS Khukri, drowning 18 officers and over 170 men down to a watery grave. Their brave captain, Mahindra Nath Mulla, who refused to abandon his command post on the bridge also went down with his sinking ship. This accident rekindled the fire among the Indian troops who were now even more determined to fight till they won as a tribute to their fallen 'brothers'.

The mood of the Indian Navy and their daring exploits have been aptly summed up by a naval midshipman in excerpts from his poem while aboard the INS TIR.

"[...] I remember the day when the navy went on a foray. My heart swelled with pride on being part of that historic ride. Delivering a crushing blow from which the enemy couldn't recover. Victory at sea was ours when we made him cower."[35]

The Indian Navy tasted blood during the 1971 war and struck deep into the heart of the Pakistan's maritime citadel. The maritime forces played a vital role in the Bay of Bengal, both by cutting off the logistics support and the escape routes of the Pakistan Forces from East Pakistan. Its hard-hitting attrition ratio in the Bay of Bengal contributed significantly to the victory and the liberation of East Pakistan.

> "At the end of the East Pakistan crisis...We (Pakistan Eastern Naval Command) had no intelligence and hence were both deaf and blind to the Indian Navy and Air Force pounding us day and night".[36]
>
> —Admiral Mohammad Sharif,
> Commander of Pakistan's Eastern Navy fleet

The mother of all battleships, 'INS Vikrant,' was despatched to East Pakistan on December 4, 1971 and launched air strikes along the coast, using Seahawks by day and Alizes by night. The carrier Task Force had, in fact, enforced total blockage within 48 hours, completely sealing any possibility of reinforcements from West Pakistan.

What then led to the commencement of war by Pakistan?

In November 1971, several hundred Pakistani politicians and leaders marched in Lahore and across Pakistan, demanding action by Pakistan to 'Crush India', and stickers with slogans like 'Hang the Traitor' presumably referring to Sheikh Mujibur Rahman, were also seen in West Pakistan. This news was covered extensively by the media. Pakistan was under tremendous pressure due to the hopeless reports being received from East Pakistan. Besides the support from the US and China, Pakistan was buoyed having received some military assistance from Iran and Jordan as well. The probability of war was being widely addressed at various forums.

On the evening of December 3, 1971 (at 5:40 pm on the Sunday), the Pakistani Air Force (PAF) launched 'Operation Chengiz Khan,' which consisted of pre-emptive strikes on several airfields and radar installations in North Western India. They struck at the airbases of Amritsar, Ambala, Agra, Awantipur, Bikaner, Halwara, Jodhpur, Jaisalmer, Pathankot, Bhuj, Srinagar and Uttarlai, and air defence radars at Amritsar and Faridkot. The strikes reached as far as Agra, which is about 500 km from the India-Pakistan border. It was accompanied by heavy artillery firing across the border in Jammu and Kashmir. These hostile attacks marked the commencement of the Indo-Pakistan War 1971. In an address to the nation shortly after midnight, Mrs Indira Gandhi announced that the air strikes were a declaration of war against India. In consonance with the Indian strategy, land, air and sea assaults were conducted in a planned manner.

Today, Pakistan refers to 1971 as the 'Fall of Dhaka' or 'dismemberment of Pakistan', whereas Bangladesh hails it as the year of the Liberation War. The 13-day war between India and Pakistan ended in India's resounding victory, the establishment of a magnificent nation – Bangladesh – and the surrender of 93,000 prisoners. The Indian Armed Forces' operations were fully supported by the Mukti Bahini and the people. In fact, the humiliating defeat resulted in greater animosity against India, which subsequently manifested through proxy war and state-sponsored terrorism in the late 1980s. It continues till date. On the other hand, despite rapid changes in the geopolitics of the region, India's relations with Bangladesh have continued to improve progressively to the mutual benefit of both countries. Some of the important takeaways of the War were: whole of nation approach, robust diplomacy, good leadership, employment of effective military strategies, timings of war, jointness among the armed forces, efficient logistical support, role of Mukti Bahini and support from the people of the country. The fact remains that the Pakistan was 'out manoeuvred' in their conventional and traditional thoughts and strategy 'Defence of the East Lies in the West', because they were not in sync with the prevailing ground realities of East Pakistan.

Notes

1. Hakeem Arshad Qureshi, *The 1971 Indo-Pak War: A Soldier's Narrative* (Pakistan: OUP) Only relevant excerpts have been produced.
2. Ibid.
3. Prasad, Thapliyal, *The India-Pakistan War of 1971: A History* (New Delhi: Natraj Publishers), p. 13.
4. Palit DK, *The Lightening Campaign, The Indo-Pakistan War, 1971* (New Delhi: Lancer Publisher), p. 29.
5. Prasad, Thapliyal, n. 3.
6. Palit DK, n. 4.
7. Hakeem Arshad Quereshi, n. 1.
8. Prasad, Thapliyal, n. 3, p. 14.
9. Moonis Ahmer, "History: Bhutto, Mujib and The Generals", *The Dawn*, March 4, 2018, at https://www.dawn.com/news/1392750/history-bhutto-mujib-and-the-generals
10. Prasad, Thapliyal, n. 3, p. 16.
11. Ibid., p. 17.
12. Ibid p. 15
13. Ibid., p. 23.
14. Bhuiyan, Md Abdul Wadood, *Emergence of Bangladesh and Role of Awami League*, p. 191.
15. Prasad, Thapliyal, n. 3, p. xvi.

16. Bahadur, Kalim, Book Reviews: Siddiq Salik. Witness to Surrender (New Delhi: Oxford University Press, 1977). First Indian edn 1979. Pp. x+map+235. Price Rs 55. *International Studies*, 19 (3): 544-546.
17. Prasad, Thapliyal, n. 3, p. 45.
18. Ibid., pp. 45-46, A regular armed force with 10 officers, including Col Osmani, Lt Col MA Rab, Gp Capt AK Khondekar.
19. Candeth KP, *The Western Front, The Indo-Pakistan War 1971* (Dehradun: The English Book Depot), pp. 6-7.
20. Ibid.
21. Ibid., p. 39,
22. Foreign Minister's statement in Rajya Sabha on 21 July 1971, BD I, p. 711.
23. Hakeem Arshad Qureshi, *The 1971 Indo-Pak War, A Soldier's Narrative* (Karachi: Oxford University Press), p. 35.
24. Prasad, Thapliyal, n. 3, p. 103.
25. Candeth KP, n. 19, p. 24.
26. Hakeem Arshad Qureshi, n. 23.
27. Prasad, Thapliyal, n.3, p. 105.
28. Jasjit Singh, *Role of Indian Air Force in 1971 War* (FPBA Publishers), p. 58.
29. Ibid., p. 86.
30. Candeth KP, n. 19.
31. Ibid., p. 23.
32. Prasad, Thapliyal, n. 3, pp. 158-59.
33. Jasjit Singh, n. 28.
34. Ibid.
35. Arjun Subramaniam, *India's Wars: A Military History, 1947-1971* (Noida: Harpercollins Publisher).
36. Ibid.

2

As India Decided, Pakistan Initiated the 1971 War

JS Cheema

Mr. DP Dhar, a member of the Indian Prime Minister's (PM) core group, made the remark, "*The fool has done exactly what one had expected,*" when Pakistan attacked the Indian airfields in the Western Sector on December 3, 1971.[1] It was a clarion call for India to enter the war zone and dispel Pakistan's misconceptions, that India will remain silent if attacked. By the end of April, the vast refugee influx comprising 20 per cent Bengali Hindus in March, increased to nearly 80 per cent. This raised apprehensions on their non-return, even on the conclusion of a political settlement. As this would have plunged India into a grave socio-economic crisis, the return of the refugees was to be viewed as a national political objective as part of the desired end-state, that is, 'the liberation of Bangladesh.' Dr. K Subrahmanyam, India's foremost strategic expert, described it as "a shift from the diplomacy of persuasion to the threat of force to avoid a compulsive drift into a war later on."[2]

The Government, till then, had resisted immense political and public clamour for immediate military intervention and recognition of Bangladesh's Provisional Government (PGB), established in exile on April 17, 1971. The Government thought it prudent to delay recognition, as most countries considered the developing situation as Pakistan's internal affair.[3] Despite the Prime Minister's initial enthusiasm, India wisely ruled out immediate military intervention, fearful of collective diplomatic isolation from the world community.

General Sam Manekshaw, then Chief of the Army Staff, briefed the Cabinet on April 25, highlighting China's threat along the northern borders, the impending monsoons, considerable time required for building logistics and advocated conducting military operations during the winter season for assured success. However, the briefing was 'misinterpreted' as a disagreement between the PM and the Chief, although both held similar views. The PM was also cautious as she apprehended being accused of double standards by recognising PGB and applying force in East Pakistan while maintaining that Jammu and Kashmir was an internal matter that brooked no interference.[4] Srinath Raghavan aptly commented that the Chief's decision suited the PM, who believed India should "tread her path with a great deal of circumspection, and not allow feelings to get the better of us." Rather than another Indo-Pakistan confrontation, India preferred to assist an indigenous Bangladesh liberation movement to loosen the Pakistan Army's grip and project its military intervention, when necessary, to support a 'Muslim' led East Pakistan liberation movement.

War Was Not The Only Option Explored

Diplomacy was the first line to avert war. India launched an extensive diplomatic campaign to restrain Pakistan from trying to ruthlessly oppress East Pakistan and seek a political solution to the East Pakistan refugee crisis – but it did not cut much ice. India failed to get the much needed support from the international community at this critical time.

However, considerable progress was made on this front on August 9, 1971, when the 'Treaty of Peace, Friendship and Cooperation' was signed between India and the USSR in New Delhi. The treaty assured India of the USSR's support at the United Nations, a continuous supply of arms and ammunition and foreclosing the same to Pakistan during the war. The treaty also reduced the possibility of China intervening on India's northern borders to support Pakistan militarily.

As the monsoon clouds were dispersing towards the end of August 1971, war clouds began to form. There is always a tipping point that unleashes the dogs of war! The war was waiting to happen 'like a small boulder coming loose on a sodden hillside followed by a few giant boulders, then more, and finally the roar of a landslide.' Blaming Awami League for the crisis, Pakistan ordered Sheikh Mujibur Rahman's trial for treason. It disqualified 79 of its 160 National Assembly members – charged 30 of them with treason, effectively ending any chance of a political solution. The refugee count published by Pakistan on August 5, 1971, that included only 2 million Muslim refugees.[5] It further reinforced India's apprehension that the remaining 8 million Hindu refugees would not return, thereby imposing a cost-prohibitive socio-economic burden on the country. According to Mr. PN Dhar, the then Secretary to the PM, the one-time cost of war was around Rs 500 crore, compared to the annual cost of hosting refugees at Rs 525 crore. The PGB, however, was disenchanted with India's slow progress to free their land.

India stepped up its qualitative and quantitative support to the liberation movement, and used operational measures like deploying regular commando troops with the Mukti Bahini. The frequency and intensity of border skirmishes between the two regular armies increased manifold. Recognising India's objectives to establish liberated zones around the borders and to install a puppet Bangladesh Government, the Pakistan Army withdrew from Dacca and started focussing on India. It also mobilised in the West to keep India engaged in its western sector and deter it from initiating war in the East. Undeterred, the Indian Army, from November 21, 1971, began securing key launchpads in East Pakistan for deeper operations when the need arose. For the first time, Pakistan used its Air Force in East Pakistan. India retaliated and neutralised three Pakistan F-86 aircraft. As it was becoming a challenge to justify East Pakistan's occupation, in the last week of November, India decided to launch an invasion in East Pakistan on December 4, 1971. East Pakistan's military-strategic needs of securing important communication centres near the borders were among the many reasons that allowed Mukti Bahini to operate with impunity. It prepared the stage for the success of the Indian Armed Forces' campaign in East Pakistan, a result they had not planned for.

India's involvement in East Pakistan with apparent intentions sparked anger and resentment amongst the Pakistan Army, who demanded military action against India. Mr. Zulfikar Ali Bhutto, in an impassioned speech at a meeting with Yahya Khan, remarked that unless he took a strong stance against Indian aggression, "he would be lynched" by the people.[6] Pakistan, therefore, launched pre-emptive airstrikes on Indian airfields, followed by a ground offensive in J&K on December 3, 1971, with a hope that international intervention would restrain India from getting involved in the war in the East. The 'roar of the landslide could be heard, and India had grabbed a fig leaf' for not initiating an all-out war and invoke the Indo-Soviet Friendship Treaty if required. However, US scholars Sisson and Rose observed that in real terms, the war began on November 21, 1971, when the Indian Army occupied East Pakistan territory.[7]

India's Obvious Victory

At the end of the war, nearly 93,000 Pakistan Armed Forces personnel, paramilitary and civil officials surrendered to India on December 16, 1971, and a new Nation Bangladesh was born. Historians are puzzled as to who won the war – the Indian Armed Forces assisted by the Bangla people or the Bangla people helped by the Indian Armed Forces? India extracted another 'fig leaf' by declaring a unilateral ceasefire on the Western Front. However, both the US and the USSR attributed it to their intense diplomatic pressure on India to prevent Pakistan's further division. But the Indian PM categorically rejected the claim and stated that "even a discussion (to further divide West Pakistan) had not taken place at any Cabinet meeting."[8]

Notes

1. Raghavan, Srinath, *1971 A Global History of the Creation of Bangladesh* (Ranikhet: Permanent Black, 2013), p. 234 quoting Dixit, JN, *Liberation and Beyond: Indo-Bangladesh Relations* (New Delhi: Konark Press, 1999), p. 89.
2. Subrahmanyam, K, Dr, *Bangladesh and India's Security* (Dehradun: Palit and Dutt Publishers, 1972), pp. 72 and 75.
3. Chopra, Pran, *India's Second Liberation* (Delhi: Vikas Publishing House Pvt Ltd, 1973), p. 79.
4. Raghavan, n. 1, p. 60.
5. Ibid., p. 209. Also see Agha Shahi to U Thant, September 2, 1971, s-0863- 0001-02, UNSG U Thant Fonds, UN Archives, New York.
6. Sisson, Richard and Rose Leo O, *War and Secession Pakistan, India, and the Creation of Bangladesh* (Berkeley: University of California Press, 1990), p. 230.
7. Ibid., p. 214.
8. Raghavan, n. 1, p. 262, quoting Jha to Haksar, February 7, 1972; Indira Gandhi's handwritten comments (emphasis in original), March 2, 1972, Subject File 243, PN Haksar Papers (III Instalment), Nehru Memorial Museum and Library (NMML).

3

Leadership@1971: An Amateur's View

Shreya Das Barman

The Prime Minister of India, Shri Narendra Modi visited Bangladesh from March 26 to 27, 2021 to participate in the Golden Jubilee celebrations of the Independence of Bangladesh, the Birth Centenary of the Father of the Nation *Bangabandhu* Sheikh Mujibur Rahman and 50 years of establishment of diplomatic relations between India and Bangladesh. It certainly made me curious to read more about Bangladesh and the 1971 War. As one reads the war accounts, one can sense the range of emotions experienced by the inhabitants of what is now Bangladesh. The fact that the 'very sound' of the Indian Air Force (IAF) fighter planes crossing the border into 'war-torn' East Pakistan (later Bangladesh) gave a 'ray of hope' to many who were detained by Pakistan junta and awaiting death. The sight of the 'Indian boots on ground' was like a 'light at the end of a dark tunnel' – after all what they witnessed for several months was only the 'ruthless killing' of innocent people. The 'sirens' of the Indian naval ships served as a death knell for Pakistan's atrocities and a 'soft tune' for the people.

The war of 1971, was not only a war of liberation; we witnessed the emergence of personalities who have become the 'epitome of leadership' – not only military, but also political. Although there were many prominent leaders, I would restrict my focus on only two distinguished political leaders: Sheikh Mujibur Rahman (Prime Minister of Bangladesh) and Mrs. Indira Gandhi (Prime Minister of India).

Sheikh Mujibur Rahman

Sheikh Mujibur Rahman or *'Bangabandhu'* (Bengal's Friend) as he was fondly called, was born in a humble family on March 17, 1920. Bangabandhu dedicated his life to the people of Bangladesh and envisioned an independent nation for his 'Bengali speaking brothers'.

Mujibur Rahman's actions inspired the people of Bangladesh to fight for the independence of their country. Not many would know that Rahman was the person who, upon realising the intensity of the situation, sent across a message to Mrs. Indira Gandhi (Prime Minister of India) seeking India's help in fighting the war against West Pakistan. Although he had spent half of his life in prison (not to forget that he was the first language prisoner), this did not deter him from thinking and working for the betterment of 'His Bengali Brothers'. The purity of his soul could be appreciated when reading about his little children who thought that "prison was the home of their father," yet he never regretted staying away from his family – for him the liberation of Bangladesh was all that mattered. Although Mujibur Rahman was arrested during the 1971 War, his sentiments of "*Amar Sonar Bangla, Ami Tomay Bhalobashi*" (Oh my golden Bengal, I love you dearly!) served as the main driving force behind the Mukti Bahini as well as the people of East Pakistan, military and civil alike, who fought for the liberation of the nation.

Mujibur Rahman's charismatic speech on March 7, 1971, provided East Pakistan with the much-needed impetus. Rahman's words were replete with references to strength, sacrifice and defending one's own country. Rahman instructed his 'brothers' to be prepared with whatever they had in order to fight the Pakistanis. It should be highlighted that before making such a speech, Rahman tried all possible means to solve the issue that the Bengali speaking people were facing, peacefully with Pakistan. He did not care about his own life, but he cared only for the Bengali people.

Rahman's love for his motherland grew even stronger after his release in 1972. He was an epitome of strength. He exemplified immense strength and charisma during his three-and-a-half-year tenure as the first Prime Minister of Liberated Bangladesh, during which he had to deal with critical problems like restoration of the communication system, restoring law and order, rehabilitating the *muktijoddhas* (freedom fighters) and feeding the people of Bangladesh. It was Mujibur Rahman's charisma, which earned Bangladesh a recognition in the international organisations such as the United Nations.

During his visit, Shri Narendra Modi described him as one of the greatest leaders of modern times, who will be remembered for his courage and indelible contribution to Bangladesh's emergence as a sovereign country. It was rather unfortunate that he was assassinated on his own land and among his own people. Nonetheless, Mujibur Rahman will always remain a great source of inspiration not only for Bangladesh, but also for us Indians. This year is rightfully called the *Mujib Borsho* in Bangladesh. It is rare to find a leader like Mujibur Rahman who 'lived with the people and died among the people'.

Indira Gandhi

India's win over Pakistan would have been stressful without a Prime Minister like Mrs. Indira Gandhi. Mrs. Gandhi's calm and composed demeanour as well as a well thought-out strategy helped India to strengthen its military might and construct necessary infrastructure before engaging in combat operations on ground zero. Although, Pakistan's atrocities started well early in March 1971, Indira Gandhi waited until December 1971 to allow her Military Commanders sufficient time and resources to prepare for the war. She gave a free hand to her military commanders to decide the modalities and conduct of the war – a characteristic of a true leader who had immense trust and confidence on her Military Chiefs. Mrs. Gandhi personally directed the responsible ministries to begin preparations on war footing – wherever slight delay was observed, Mrs. Gandhi ensured that the obligations are removed and smooth functioning commenced.

Mrs. Gandhi's efforts to draw the international community's attention (USA, Russia, China, etc.) towards the 'genocide' unleashed by Pakistan on East Pakistan, while also assisting the millions of refugees who crossed over to India, return to their homes, was indeed a sign of a true leader who pledged to help her country and also others in need.

Not only for the Military Commanders, Indira Gandhi was also a leader of the common people. This was evident when one reads her statement about India's involvement in the 1971 war. On the one hand, Mrs. Gandhi realised the intensity of the impending conflict; on the other hand, she assured her countrymen that India will win the war and also acknowledged that India would have to be prepared for a long period of 'hardship and sacrifice'. Indeed, she was *Durga* for her country. She rightly taught the Indians that, while we are peace loving people, however, if we wish to maintain peace, we must fight to guard our freedom, democracy and way of life. Mrs. Gandhi fought for the rights of the refugees, despite India's economic and social distress – it was not an easy task. She not only thought about India, but also worked for the liberation of Bangladesh.

A Friendship that would Never Die

Mujibur Rahman had met Jawaharlal Nehru in 1962 and shared his vision about a liberated Bangladesh – who knew that 9 years down the line, Mujibur Rahman would work with his daughter only to create a new history. Indira Gandhi, in the absence of Mujibur Rahman, provided full support to the Bangladesh guerilla fighters, so that they could gain a foothold along the Indo-Bangla border as also in the Bangladesh countryside. It is, indeed, ironical that both the Prime Ministers were assassinated on their home ground among their own people.

The War of 1971 witnessed some outstanding leaders whose contributions behind closed doors and in defining policies, actions and relationships were immense. Some of them who come to my mind are: Rameshwar Nath Kao (RAW Chief), Jagjivan Ram (Defence Minister of India), Bongobir MAG Osmani (C-in-C of the Bangladesh Liberation Army), Syed Nazrul Islam (Acting President of Bangladesh Government in exile), Tajuddin Ahmad (Prime Minister of Bangladesh Government in exile). These leaders demonstrated that leadership is more than displaying one's might – it is also about walking with the common people.

4

SAM: Our Chief during '71 Operations

Behram M Panthaki

In the last week of April 1971, General Manekshaw (later Field Marshal), the Chief of the Army Staff (COAS), was invited to participate in a cabinet meeting held in Parliament House. I, as his ADC, obviously accompanied him. While we drove back to the Army Headquarters, he said to me 'cryptically', "*Behroze (he always called me Behroze!), today you almost lost your job,*" and then added, "*so did I!*" – the order in which he said this reversed the importance of our roles!

The Game Begins

At the meeting, it transpired that the Prime Minister (Mrs. Indira Gandhi) and her cabinet persuaded the army to launch an immediate offensive in the east to 'stem the tide of refugees' and 'to provide moral support to the people of East Pakistan'. But the COAS had a different perspective and, true to his nature, he did not hold back from expressing the same – the army was facing a shortage of equipment which needed to be addressed first. The Armoured Division had only 11 operational tanks out of 189. Ammunition and petrol dumps had to be established in forward location and logistical support for the campaign had to be put in place. Railway lines and border roads required to be extended up to the war zone. It would take time to mobilise formations to their operational locations. Civilian aircraft and railway wagons would have to be requisitioned, thereby disrupting the normal services.

Additionally, the weather had to be conducive – during the monsoons, from June through September, the delta region of Bengal becomes swampy, restricting the movement of armour and the cloud cover limits the efficiency of the air force. Going to war meant preparedness on two fronts (west and east). He would rather wait to launch an offensive in the winter, when the Himalayan passes would be snowbound and block the Chinese from opening a third front in the north. Pressure was brought to bear on him, yet Sam stood his ground.

A very 'grim' Prime Minister (PM) dismissed her cabinet, but asked the Army Chief to stay back. Sensing her anger, he asked, "*Would you like me to send in my resignation? I could do that on grounds of health – mental or physical!*" "*Sit down, Sam. Is everything you told me true?*" "*Yes, it is my job to tell you the truth. It is also my job to fight and fight to win.*" With military acumen, he assured the PM that East Pakistan would capitulate within a month, but on the condition that he be allowed complete autonomy; the timing of launching the operation will be his choice; and he would report to one political master, that is the PM. She agreed to the terms of engagement, and with that, the preparations for war commenced in right earnest. Prior to the war, the Chief visited formations in forward areas to review operational plans and motivate the troops. He addressed the men in simple and clear words – "*A soldier's business is to fight and win battles, not to rape and loot. When you enter Pakistan, treat the women with respect like you would your own mothers and sisters. Anyone disobeying my orders will be court-martialed. I am commanding soldiers, not a pack of thugs!*" – However, Sam was much tougher with officers – "*Truth should not become a casualty of war. He expected honest reporting of gains and losses. He would accept an error of judgment, but any officer who deliberately gave misinformation about the ground situation would be sacked forthwith. Nor would he condone rape. If you feel the urge, put your hands in your pockets and think of Sam Manekshaw!*"

The Chief upheld the same level of honesty and truthfulness that he expected from his subordinates. During the war, he would brief the PM twice a day, or more often, with the exact situation on ground: gains, losses and reverses were faithfully reported.

The Indian Army made quick advances aided by the Mukti Bahini. Dacca airfield was strafed and rendered non-operational, therefore, air support from West Pakistan had been disabled. The Indian Navy blockaded the Bay of Bengal, preventing access by sea. Dacca had been surrounded by the 2 Para Battalion, which had been air dropped. Message intercepts between Lt Gen Niazi and GHQ indicated that his command was on the verge of collapse.

On December, as the fight drew to a close, Sam went on the airwaves calling on Pakistani troops to lay down their arms. Leaflets of his address were distributed in Urdu, Punjabi, Pashto and Bengali all over East Pakistan. On December 12, we received a message through the UNDP and the US Embassy that the Pakistan Army was ready to lay down their arms. In preparation, Sam drafted the 'Instrument of Surrender' that was cleared by Mr. PN Haksar (Principal Secretary, PMO) and Mr. KB Lall (Principal Defence Secretary of India).

On December 14, he dictated the document to Maj Gen (later Lt Gen) JFR Jacob, Chief of Staff, HQ Eastern Command, and requested that he create four originals and obtain Lt Gen Niazi's signature on each – one each for the records at Army Headquarters and Eastern Command, for Lt Gen Niazi and for the Army Chief. This War Trophy was displayed with pride in his office; hopefully, it is still there!

Mrs. Gandhi wanted Sam to take the surrender, but he refused to steal a march on Eastern Army Commander saying that he would have proudly done so if the entire Pakistan Army had surrendered. Prior to the surrender, a senior staff officer from HQ Eastern Command was required to go to Dacca to ensure all arrangements were in place. Sam deputed Maj Gen Jacob. When the Ministry of Defence got to know this, it expressed concern that a Jewish officer had been selected to make arrangements for the surrender of a Muslim Army. The government was apprehensive about how this would be viewed by Muslim nations that were friendly to India. Sam was outraged and asked why the government had been silent for 30 years when Jake (Jacob) had risked his life for the nation. The army was above religion, caste or creed and in any case, it was too late, for Jake was on his way. Sam hung up and immediately called Jake to inform him of what had occurred. Jake became sentimental and announced his intention to resign. This was the final straw for Sam and he said – "*Jake, don't give me a hard time after I went to bat for you. If you put in your papers, I promise I will accept them!*" – the matter was laid to rest!

A month after the war ended, Sam was summoned to PM's residence at 1 Safdarjung Road on a Sunday morning. Mrs. Gandhi handed him a dossier, compiled by R&AW, that documented transgressions of a handful of senior officers in East Pakistan. Sam advised the PM that public disclosure would be counterproductive and 'besmirch' the reputation of the entire army due to the lapses of a few. He assured her that each defaulter would be dealt with. One of the Generals in this list was an excellent field commander and was shortlisted to become Adjutant General. When the file reached the Chief's desk, Sam returned it with the comment, *"Over my dead body! The Adjutant General is the custodian of discipline in the Indian Army. If this officer becomes AG, this Chief will have sleepless nights!"* Career sealed; the officer retired. The axe fell, silently but surely. None of the officers on the list, in spite of their notable war records, rose to the next rank.

Following the surrender, India took 93,000 prisoners of war who were handled in accordance with Geneva Convention rules and granted unrestricted access to the camps to foreign journalists. On July 2, 1972, Prime Ministers Indira Gandhi (India) and Zulfikar Ali Bhutto (Pakistan) signed the Simla Accord. Sam met the PM on her return from Simla and told her that Bhutto had played on her softer instincts by convincing her to release and repatriate 93,000 Pakistani PoW and gave nothing in return! It was a lost opportunity – India could have converted the 'Ceasefire Line' into International Border and resolved the Kashmir Issue forever.

On November 28, 1972, we were scheduled to leave on an official visit to Tehran at the invitation of the Shah. Our luggage had reached Palam airport, when we received instructions from the PMO to abort the visit. Instead, the next morning we flew to Lahore for delineation talks to resolve the Thako Chak Enclave imbroglio – a contentious issue regarding territories captured by both sides which defied diplomatic solution. On the flight were two Pakistani Air Force PoW – Squadron Leader Amjad Ali Khan and Flight Lieutenant Wajid Ali Khan – who were being repatriated as a goodwill gesture.

General Tikka Khan, Chief of Pakistan Army, received us at the Lahore Airport, sporting his trademark dark glasses. We set off for the conference venue in Tikka's stretch limo. The tension in the car was palpable till Sam released the pressure valve, *"Tikka, why are you wearing dark glasses? You don't drink, you don't smoke, you have nothing to hide. It is I who should be wearing them!"*

The talks were held at HQ IV Corps followed by lunch hosted by the Governor of Punjab Province – Ghulam Mustafa Khar, a Bhutto confidante, at his official residence. After day-long deliberations, the delegation returned to Delhi in the evening without making any headway – the government did not consider it safe for us to stay overnight in Pakistan.

We travelled back to Lahore eight days later, on December 7, 1972, to begin negotiations. A few minutes into the flight Sam asked Maj Gen (later Lt Gen) Inderjit Gill for the map of Thako Chak. The Director of Military Operations turned to his staff officer who rummaged through his briefcase and broke into a cold sweat. There were maps of the entire western border with Pakistan except *Thako Chak!* An unfazed, Gen Gill told Sam, "*Sorry Chief, no luck, it's probably somewhere in my office.*" An equally unperturbed Sam replied, "*Never mind Inder, we'll use Tikka's map and will return with Thako Chak!*", prophetic words indeed, for that is precisely how the dice fell!

During this visit, lunch was arranged at the Corps Artillery Officers' Mess. Sam was viewing the trophies on display when he recognised one that belonged to his old battalion – 4/12 Frontier Force Regiment. He couldn't help but ask what it was doing at the gunners' mess. A Pakistani officer acknowledged that he was indeed right – it had been borrowed for this special occasion.

Mrs. Gandhi had initiated a case for promoting Sam to the rank of Field Marshal and appointing him Chief of Defence Staff (CDS) sometime in the later half of 1972. Politicians led by Defence Minister Jagjivan Ram opposed the proposal. Simultaneously, the Defence Ministry sent the proposal to Air and Naval Headquarters for their comments – the former opposed, the latter agreed. Scaling several hurdles, the PM finally had her way and Sam was promoted to the rank of Field Marshal on January 1, 1973, with a formal investiture ceremony held at Rashtrapati Bhavan on January 3. On January 15, after bidding farewell to his officers and men at the Army Day Parade, Field Marshal Sam Manekshaw drove to Army HQ, handed over the reins to Gen GG Bewoor and drove to the Military Engineering Service (MES) Inspection Bungalow, bringing an era to a close.

Every Successful Man has a Woman Behind

Like a good army wife, Silloo Manekshaw, who was also President of the Army Wives Welfare Association (AWWA) by virtue of being the Chief's wife, kept her distance from official matters. While she may have come across as casual, but behind this veneer of indifference was a sustained commitment to the plight of wounded and to war widows. The Commandant, Base Hospital, had been instructed to inform her whenever a fresh batch of battle casualties arrived. Regardless of the time of day or night she would be at the hospital to receive them.

Every morning, she would make her rounds with Mrs. Mona Batra, Secretary, AWWA, and wife of Lt Gen MN 'Bim' Batra, and other dedicated army wives, enquiring about the wounded, tracking their progress, and helping in the delivery of messages and letters to families to keep them informed and updated.

Pakistani PoWs received equal attention. For the first few days, a young Pakistani Officer at the hospital, refused to acknowledge Silloo's presence. Each time she passed by his bed, he would turn his face to the wall and pretend to be asleep. One day, curiosity got the better of him and he asked the nursing orderly who the *"lady in slacks was, who came by diligently each day and enquired after each patient."* When he learnt that she was the wife of the Army Chief he was filled with remorse. The next day he awaited her arrival and apologised for his behaviour, saying he could never have imagined in his wildest dreams that a Chief's wife would go to this length. Silloo reassured him and shared a cigarette with him. He confided in her regarding his hopes and aspirations to win the war and grieved at the shame of surrender. Thereafter, each day he waited impatiently for her visit.

Simultaneously, AWWA's fundraising activities were Silloo's top priority. She travelled across the country meeting CEOs of large corporations, people of the film industry and representatives of donor agencies.. She was able to raise Rs. 2.5 crore (Rs. 25 crore in present value) in cash and Rs 5 crore (Rs. 50 crore in present value) in kind which led Sam to say – *"My wife and I go around with a begging bowl so that my wounded soldiers and my war widows will never have to!"*

Image 1: Mrs Siloo Manekshaw, Wife of India's then Chief of Army Staff General [later Field Marshal] Sam Manekshaw, visiting soldiers injured in the 1971 War for the liberation of Bangladesh

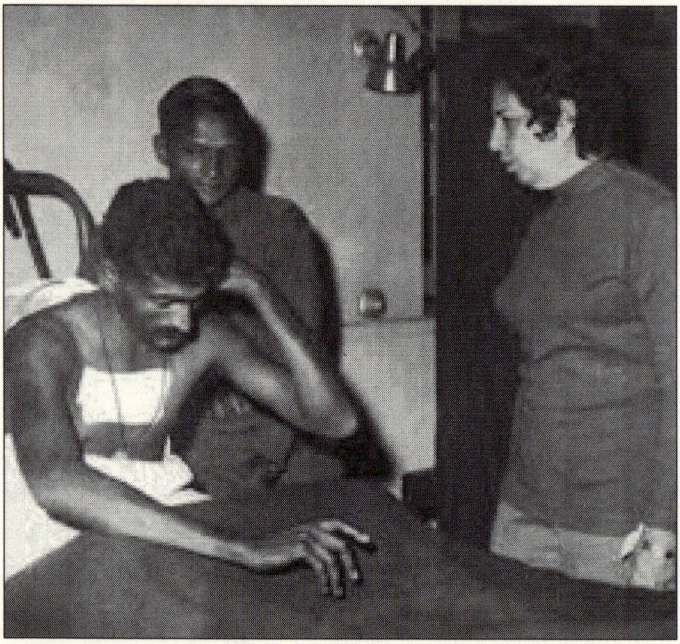

Source: www.spansen.com

Image 2: Indira Gandhi had a special fondness for Manekshaw. She ensured he was awarded Padma Vibhushan and made a Field Marshal

Source: tribuneindia.com

Image 3: In 1947, British officer Yahya Khan offered his colleague 1,000 rupees for his spiffy red motorcycle. His colleague, Sam Manekshaw, agreed. But before Khan could pay, he was off to what was going to become Pakistan. The British split its Indian colony, and things on the subcontinent have been pretty tense ever since. To top it all off, Yahya Khan didn't pay for the motorbike. But he would, even if it took almost 25 years.

Source: http://www.indiandefensenews.in/2019/11/yahya-never-paid-me-1000-rupees-for-my.html

SECTION 2

Eastern Sector

Acts of Valour

5

The War I Experienced: Armour and Air Battle

Ajit Apte

Greenhorn in Battle

During the 1971 war on Eastern Front, I was a subaltern with my first unit, 14 Field Regiment Artillery and was part of 9 Infantry Division under the newly raised 2 Corps in the Jessore-Khulna Sector, which was tasked to advance and capture Jessore and Khulna. I served as the Artillery Gun Position Officer (GPO) of my Quebec Battery, of the Field Regiment in Direct Support of 1 JAK Rifles Infantry Battalion.

Order of Battle

The build-up of forces had commenced in and around Calcutta, Barrackpore and Kanchrapara, and infantry began marching forward on the border with well-defined affiliations and allotment of artillery support. The process of shaping the battlefield started from November 11, 1971. For all operations by the brigades of the division, artillery was concentrated and provided fire power in all the battles, irrespective of our affiliations.

Garibpur the Armour Battle and the Air Battle of Boyra

The famous Tank Battle at Garibpur was fought on the morning of November 21, 1971. 14 PUNJAB was in Garibpur and fought gallantly. Our 14 Field Regiment had fired for the Battle, and my 99 Field Battery had been assigned at Priority Call to engage targets for Charlie Squadron of 45 Cavalry. Pakistan's 107 Infantry Brigade launched a counter attack with their 3rd Independent Armoured Squadron after dawn, and it was a fierce engagement.

I had redeployed my battery on the flanks of 6 Field Regiment, which was providing direct support to 42 Infantry Brigade for Garibpur battle. I witnessed the tank vs tank battle then, and my guns were already mounted on anti-tank platforms for direct shooting. I had ordered a 'Tank Alert Armour Piercing Charge 3', and all guns were loaded and ready to engage. We saw the enemy tanks doing a diagonal crosser in front of my guns at about 600 metres, when I was tempted to give the order to fire. My seasoned troop leader, a veteran of the 1965 war, Naib Subedar Raghunath Singh, squeezed my hand and said, "*Sahib don't give orders to fire, because it seems the enemy tanks have not seen us, and if we fire now, we will attract them to charge on our battery.*" Raghunath spoke sense and I listened to him. We waited for the next opportune moment and the enemy tanks moved across. Nothing happened thereafter.

When I returned to my regiment location after the battle, I heard the news on my transistor, and comfirmed what the BBC had reported. I had actually seen it happen – about nine enemy tanks were destroyed and the enemy armour Squadron had limped out with only three tanks intact. The Pakistani Tanks that had been destroyed were recovered and moved inside the Boyra Bulge. Our Defence Minister addressed the troops, congratulating them for their valour.

Air Battle of Boyra

The Battle of Garibpur and the Boyra Air Battle were actually intertwined. The Pakistan Air Force had been making frequent runs on November 21, in the Garibpur area, but was uncontested. In the absence of an Indian response, the Pakistani Sabres thought they could have a free run and thus were very active since 8 am on November 22. They conducted multiple treetop level runs intermittently over our corps zone, with special focus on our guns, tank concentrations and on the engineers bridging areas. Perhaps our Air Force was not deployed, as war had not been declared officially then.

The IAF Challenges the PAF in the Air Battle of Boyra

(Eyewitness Account from Ground Zero)

It was a bright Monday on November 22, 1971, when at about 2.40 pm (1440 hours) "Stand To" was ordered. All guns were manned and Light Machine Guns (LMG) were deployed on the Anti-Aircraft (Ack Ack) role. We were under an enemy air strike once again. We had been under continuous enemy air raids since the previous day, while providing artillery support for the famous Battle of Garibpur inside East Pakistan. The enemy guns had shelled our positions earlier, but fortunately there was no major damage. Our aggressive posturing had perhaps provoked the Pakistani Air Force (PAF) 14 Squadron to be unleashed on our Divisional Sector to engage our dispositions deployed.

Our earlier requests for Fighter aircraft cover over our Divisional Sector on the 21st of November were rejected by the Indian Air Force (IAF), perhaps because officially War had not yet been declared.

Earlier in the day I had seen the Sabres doing High Dive attacks on our position. One of the Sabres had flown just above Tree Top level, between my battery and the adjacent battery of Lt Gabriel Pereira, the other GPO. At 2.45 pm or so, I saw these Sabres climbing up to about 2,000 feet and then coming down to about 500 feet for the weapon release, similar to the German Stuka bombers during the Second World War.

Our LMGs on Ack Ack role and our Air Defence (AD) guns were ineffective, but we could see their white puffs trying to deter the enemy aircrafts. I very clearly saw a mission of three Sabre fighters from the East of my gun area swooping over us at low level. Just then, within a few seconds I noticed four aircraft heading from the West of my gun area, pulling out of formation to the west of my gun area, from a mission that was initially heading towards us but then swiftly swinging towards the enemy aircraft.

The Sabres were totally oblivious of these four Gnats heading towards them and instead continued with their Dive Attacks. It was clear to us now that our IAF had joined the Air Battle. We emerged from our bunkers and trenches looking skywards to see the action.

Our Forward Air Controller (FAC), Flt Lt Sharad Savur (Later Air Marshal, AOC-in-C), with our 350 Infantry Brigade was already located with 4 SIKH, which was ahead of my regiment. Our Infantry Brigade's other battalions deployed ahead were the 1st JAK Rifles and 26 MADRAS.

My regiment was tasked with providing Direct Support to 350 Infantry Brigade. Earlier that day on November 22, at about 1000h, there were two missions by the PAF Sabres. Our Gnats had then scrambled, but they did not reach the target area on time. They did not make contact and returned dejected. Wg Cdr Sikand was the Commanding Officer 22 Squadron IAF, who had led the two earlier sorties. He then moved out and handed over the lead to Flt Lt Roy Andrew Massey, with Flg Offr Sunith Francis Soares as his Deputy. Flt Lt Ganapathy and Flg Offr Don Lazarus retained their number 3 & 4 Positions. The Fighter Controller then was Flg Offr Bagchi. The Fighter Controller and the Operational Readiness Platform (ORP) Pilots were all in place.

All was quiet on the Eastern Front. Sunith Francis Soares and Don Lazarus were playing Scrabble and relaxing. It was now 1440h when suddenly the Klaxon started blaring, 'Intrusion and Pick Up'.

The Intrusion

The Radar had picked up the intrusion of the three enemy Sabres at 1440 h, and within a minute the ORP (Aerocorp) at Dum Dum Airport Calcutta, scrambled four Gnats, who were airborne without wasting any time, hurtling through the skies at low level, with full throttles against the Stop.

Dog Fight

Our Gnats reached the International Border (IB), and then Bagchi told Massey (On the Air Defence Interceptor Radio Channel), "*Enemy 2.O Clock 4 Nautical Miles*".

Massey replied, *"Contact. I see them pull up". "Murder Murder Murder Murder,"* was heard on Radio transmission and our IAF swung into action swiftly.

Ganapathy and Don, who were on the right flank, were unable to detect the hostile aircraft. Soares detected an enemy aircraft from a distance of 3 kilometres, poised and ready to dive. He called out, 'Contact' and Massey spotted the enemy aircraft, then pulled over the flank pair, to manouevre behind that aircraft. Soares then gave the running commentary on the flight path very effectively. Meanwhile, that Sabre tried to evade, but Massey's Gnat got within firing range and he fired a small cannon burst. It missed the target, but he followed quickly, with another cannon burst, which slammed the right wing, as we saw it near the fuselage. The enemy pilot soon ejected. The Sabres had now commenced another dive from 1800 feet altitude, diving down to about 500 feet in an attack, running over our positions. Massey, Soares, Lazarus and Ganapathy, just latched on to the Sabres (Like a hungry tiger would do to its prey) as the Sabres now tried to pull out of the attack. While Flg Offr Soares was in combat, he had heard Flt Lt Ganapathy report seeing a Sabre and manoeuvred behind him to fire on the enemy aircraft. He did, however, missed the target. Just then, the third Sabre cropped in behind Don and Ganapathy at a distance of 200 yards. Flg Offr Don Lazarus swerved now, manoeuvred into position alongside the enemy aircraft and fired. Don's reflexes and manoeuvring skills were exceptional, which enabled him to slam the cannons bang on target. It caused that enemy aircraft to explode, with the debris hitting Don's aircraft on the nose and Drop Tank. The enemy pilot then ejected. He was Flt Lt Pervez Mehdi. We on the ground, saw him coming down and were ready to welcome him. Ganapathy fired later accurately and hit the third enemy aircraft on its right wing setting it aflame, but that enemy aircraft perhaps escaped back to base.

Meanwhile, Flt Lt Ganapathy and Flg Offr Don Lazarus spotted an enemy aircraft each, and they split up to now shoot down one aircraft each. From the ground, we observed two Gnats in a pair were shooting at one enemy aircraft, while another pair of Gnats separated themselves and then shot one enemy aircraft each. Finally, two enemy aircraft were shot down and the two parachutes drifted to the ground. It was an unforgettable sight.

The third enemy aircraft with trailing smoke had evaded and most likely returned to their base. It was perhaps Wg Cdr Chaudhury, their leader from 14 Squadron PAF. The Dogfight was over in a jiffy. Our Gnats did the Victory Roll over us and Home they went. Within minutes the All-India Radio and the newspapers announced this news and the Nation's first three Gallantry Awards of Vir Chakra's went to Flt Lts Massey, Ganapathy and Flg Offr Don Lazarus, and Vayu Medal to Flg Offr Bagchi.

What the nation was reading or listening to was remote. We had witnessed it unfold in front of us, and had been part of that high-voltage drama. The two Pakistani pilots ejected and their parachutes landed, one over 4 SIKH that was Flt Lt Pervez Mehdi, where Capt H S Panag, (later Lt Gen and Army Commander) was the Adjutant of the battalion, who had initially apprehended the pilot and saved him from being massacred by the troops. Flg Offr Khalil Ahmed the other Pilot had landed on 1st JAK Rifles, where Capt Sharma, our Regimental Observation Post (OP) Officer saw him being captured by the battalion. Both these pilots were then sent to our 14 Field Regiment, which was about 1500 metres behind, on a flank. I was summoned together with Lt Gabriel Pereira, the other GPO, because I was closest to the Regimental Command Post (RCP). The Second in Command

(2IC) Maj Basudev Krishna and Capt Jay Sapatnekar, Adjutant, told us to attend to the two Prisoner of War (PoW) Pilots once they reached our station.

Flt Lt Pervez Mehdi, the senior of the two, was slightly injured, but luckily Panag had saved him from further injuries and he received First Aid in that battalion. We treated both the pilots with due dignity. They were even given tea and cigarettes.

Khalil Ahmed admitted that they were surprised by the Gnats and outgunned and outmanoeuvred by them. They were not hit by ground fire, as some believed. They informed us that the dispositions of our guns, tanks, and other details were given by the Mukti Bahini. I saw Pervez Mehdi's Shooting Map on his flying suit. I observed on it that we were identified as an enemy, in red, on his list of targets to be bombed. Our guns, tanks and engineer bridges were his main targets. Pervez said that they couldn't pin point the targets for shooting, because accurate spotting was difficult due to our good camouflage and concealment. They were also scared of our fire from the Air Defence Guns.

Both Pervez Mehdi and Khalil Ahmed pleaded with us, not to surrender them to the Mukti Bahini. Pereira and I then had the opportunity to blindfold the two enemy Pilots. Then, with a proper armed escort, we sent them in our regimental vehicle to the infantry brigade.

I had blindfolded a future Air Chief of the Pakistan Air Force, which I was unaware of at the time.

Image 1: Pervaiz Mehdi Qureshi

Source: https://twitter.com/RuthlessIndia/status/1229623954458935297/photo/1

PoWs Flight to Delhi

The two enemy pilots were well treated in accordance with the Geneva Conventions. I learned much later that two of my NDA classmates, Pilot Officers Pradeep Kapur and TV Abraham along with Flg Offr GS Bhullar as the Capt of the Dakota (DC-3) Carnicobar-Rangoon-Barrackpore Calcutta Courier, had taken the two PoW Pilots for interrogation with a proper escort to Delhi. They were accompanied by IAF officers. Pradeep Kapur said, that while Pervez Mehdi had kept quiet throughout the flight, Khalil Ahmed was talkative and easygoing.

The PoWs were given packed dinner on the flight from Great Eastern Hotel in Calcutta. Khalil Ahmed enjoyed the dinner, but Pervez Mehdi refused to eat at all. On reaching Delhi, the PoWs were dealt in accordance with the regulations.

6

The Battle for Sylhet

Ian Cardozo

Battles are won or lost in the minds of men, before they have been won or lost on the ground.

—Brigadier Desmond Hayde, MVC

It was December 6, 1971, and the 4th Battalion of the 5th Gorkha Rifles (FF) had just returned to Firm Base following the battles of Atgram and Gazipur. Although the battalion was victorious in both battles, it had sustained heavy casualties. Three officers and 19 other ranks laid down their lives, while four officers and 84 other ranks were wounded. It had originally entered the war with 18 officers and now only 11 Officers were left, and the war had only just started. The Commanding Officer – Lt Col Arun Bhimrao Harolikar, had asked for a few days to reorganise the Battalion, and was busy cross-posting personnel to make up the deficiencies in the Rifle Companies – he had asked for four days to reorganise the Battalion to prepare it for the next battle. This had been approved by Brigadier 'Bunty' Quinn, Commander of the 59 Mountain Brigade.

In the morning of December 6, Lt Gen Sagat Singh, GOC 4 Corps, received an intelligence report that the Pakistani Infantry Brigade, that was holding Sylhet, had moved for the defence of Dhaka. He quickly determined that Sylhet had to be captured and occupied, before it could be reinforced. Sylhet's capture would enable him to continue his mission of reaching the Meghna River and then becoming the first to reach Dhaka. He consequently decided to capture Sylhet in a heliborne operation, as this was the only way he would be able to reach and occupy it before it was reinforced or re-occupied by the Pakistanis. He wanted the Gorkhas to take on this task and passed on the directions to Major General KV Krishna Rao, GOC 8 Mountain Division, who in turn communicated the orders to 'Bunty' Quinn.

The Brigade Commander informed General Rao that the Battalion had been given a break after its two hard-fought battles. General Rao conveyed this to General Sagat, but the Corps Commander turned this down and said that "*there was no time for delay*". When another battalion was recommended for the same purpose, he likewise declined, saying: *"Nothing doing! I know the Gorkhas, they are best suited for this task. Tell them to move at once."*

The Sylhet Imbroglio

Sylhet was a part of Lieutenant General AAK Niazi's strong belt of defences, designed to defend East Pakistan. General Niazi was the General Officer Commanding-in-Chief of all forces in East Pakistan, and was known as 'Tiger Niazi'. His strategy was known as 'The Fortress Concept of Defence,' that is, strong defences based on important towns and communication centres built along river lines and strengthened with deep minefields. Sylhet was one such strong point, others included Jessore, Jhenida, Bogra, Rangpur, Jamalpur, Mymensingh, Bhairab Bazar, Comilla and Chittagong.

Being aware of the Pakistani defence strategy, Lt Col Harolikar said that it would be 'uncharacteristic' of the High Command of East Pakistan to remove Sylhet as a link from this strong belt of defences, and it was unlikely that Sylhet would be undefended. He was informed, however, that this information was received from the Corps Commander and it was doubtful that the Commander would be fed with wrong information.

> *"In the Army, one can protest up to a point. After that, orders are orders and that is that!!"*

Therefore, the task was to capture Sylhet.

The Operation Begins

The Battalion reached Kalaura the same evening as it was not very far away. Next morning, December 7, 1971, the Battalion received confirmatory orders through a signal message that it should be prepared to capture Sylhet in a heliborne operation the same day. It laid down the objectives, which included the Radio Station, a Road Cross Junction and a bridge – an ambitious task, even for a brigade! It seemed extraordinary to give it to a battalion, that too at half its strength. The Battalion was 'blooded but it had also been bloodied!'

As per plan, the helicopter for the Commanding Officer's reconnaissance arrived at 0930 hours. The Commanding Officer – Group Captain Chandan Singh of the Indian Air Force and Brigadier Bunty Quinn left for an aerial reconnaissance of the ground, we would have to initially capture. They hovered over the area and selected an open space at a place called Mirapara, southeast of Sylhet.

There was no reaction to the helicopter recce from the enemy. This seemed to confirm the Corps Commander's opinion that Sylhet was not held by a large force and that the brigade responsible for Sylhet had withdrawn.

On the Commanding Officer's return, the Battalion prepared quickly for the heliborne operation – the young officers were thrilled that our Battalion had been given the honour of launching the Indian Army's 'first heliborne operation'.

Lt Col Harolikar called his 'O' Group once again and briefed them on the operation. He added that, while the formation headquarters had assured him that the Battalion would be reinforced within 48 hours, it would be prudent to be prepared for the worst. He suggested that instead of taking food and water, a spare set of clothes and blankets, additional ammunition and grenades would be better. The officers and JCOs readily agreed to his suggestion.

The Battalion had lost its Second-in-Command during the battle of Gazipur, and the Commanding Officer was worried as to who would he be able to handover the Battalion, in case he was wounded in action. Although the officers who remained, had acquitted themselves well in the earlier battles, they were very young. A new second-in-command was on his way from the Staff College. That was me, and I had not yet arrived.

Priority had to be given to the companies' fly-ins to Sylhet. 'Major Mane Malik, Commander of 'C' Company, volunteered to fly in first, and thereafter the CO nominated the sequence of the remaining Companies.

The total strength of the Battalion had now been reduced to just 384 due to the casualties faced in the two previous battles, and also because of some of the 'leave parties' from Nepal that had yet not joined up.

Eight Mi-4 helicopters landed at Kalaura at 1415 hours on December 7, 1971, and the helicopters took off in waves of four at exactly 1430 hours. More than four would have cluttered the air space over the landing ground.

Major Malik and part of 'C' Company met with heavy fire as a part of the first two waves that landed. Each helicopter could take ten armed men, i.e. a Section. So, the first two waves managed to take 'C' Company. The next two waves were able to land the Commanding Officer, the Battalion Headquarter and part of 'B' Company. The total strength landed that evening was just 254.

The men had hit the ground running, fanned out and took up a perimeter defence. Attacks were launched by the Pakistani defenders with cries of *"Allah-o-Akbar,"* which were responded to by 'C' Company with counter attacks, and the war cry of *"Ayo Gorkhali"* filled the air. The situation is best described by the helicopter pilots through the writings of PVS Jagan Mohan and Samir Chopra in their book *Eagles over Bangladesh*:

> *"The SHBO at Sylhet began at 2.30 pm, with the first MI-4s taking off from Kalaura carrying the troops of 4/5 GR. The troops of 4/5 GR had no specialised training in heliborne operations. Indeed, this was the first time that they had ever moved by helicopter. Heliborne operations were still a novelty for the Indian Army and certainly no unit had acquired any expertise or training with helicopters. [...]*
>
> *Contrary to Indian expectations, the Pakistanis had not withdrawn troops from Sylhet, nor had they any intention of doing so. Sagat Singh had expected that the Gorkhas would face minimum resistance, but they were now caught in an awkward situation with a strong enemy just outside their landing area and their lines of supply restricted to aerial ones.*
>
> *[...] The Gorkhas fought back vigorously and soon established a perimeter, the Pakistani Army was unable to breach. [...]*
>
> *[...] By the time the day's operations were called off, in the evening, the helicopters had lifted 254 personnel to the landing zone in two waves over a total of twenty-two sorties."*

I landed at Dharmanagar Railway Station on December 6, and had driven non-stop to reach Kalaura just in time to catch the last wave of helicopters flying to Sylhet.

I met the Commanding Officer for the first time when he arrived to take over 4/5 Gorkhas from another Battalion of the Regiment. He was very relieved to see me, as at last he had a second-in-command after the battle of Gazipur!

I assisted him now and assumed part of his responsibilities, allowing him to concentrate on the battle.

The final wave of Mi-4s had landed an ACT (Air Control Team) and two mountain guns with ammunition. The helicopters departed for other tasks. We were now on our own. However, the ACT would subsequently prove to be a life-saver!

By mid-day December 9, 48 hours had passed and there was no indication whatsoever that the link-up would occur.

While we were aware that a sizeable force was opposing us at Sylhet, we were unaware that the 202 Pakistan Infantry Brigade had not moved out, and that 313 Pakistan Infantry Brigade had reinforced Sylhet. So, we were facing two infantry brigades and the Sylhet Garrison – an unequal ratio of 1:20. Our total strength was 384.

That evening, though, a 'stroke of luck' occurred. The British Broadcasting Corporation (BBC), which is known for its factual reporting, announced that a Brigade of Gorkhas had landed at Sylhet in a heliborne operation. It is unclear whether the reporter had got his facts wrong or got mixed up with the terms 'Battalion' and 'Brigade'.

The Commanding Officer and I decided to use this piece of 'misinformation' to convince the Pakistanis that we were a Brigade. Alpha and Delta Companies were pushed forward and laterally to simulate the deployment of a brigade. There were risks involved, i.e. if the enemy was 'worth his salt' he could take on the Rifle Companies one by one and dismantle our defensive layout. Also, due to the increased spread of the Rifle Companies, mutual support posed problems. We resolved this by placing machine gun nests in between the gaps and conducted aggressive patrolling of the no-man's land. Pakistanis lacked the bravery to engage us in a close quarters battle for whatever reason; the use of the khukri in the earlier two battles appeared to have frightened them. The remainder of the Units who faced us at Atgram and Gazipur were now part of the Sylhet

Garrison and they seemed to have passed the word around *"Do not mess with the Gorkhas. If you do, you are likely to lose your head!"*

By this time, the Pakistani force at Sylhet decided finallyto launch a major assault on our defences. Fortunately, one of our OPs were able to see them. The ACT called for our fighter aircraft from Kumbhigram to break up the attack. The fighter aircraft – MiGs and Hunters – were over us in minutes. They not only broke up their attack, but also attacked their gun positions. Thereafter, they used their artillery only at night and in the early hours of the morning against us.

By December 12, the condition of the dead and wounded had deteriorated considerably. Numerous casualties had accumulated and were strewn about. No medication was available to treat the wounded. We were unable to provide them with safe drinking water. We requested evacuation of the dead and wounded and were fortunate to receive a positive response from the IAF. Goose Necks[1] were lit at night to guide the helicopters to the landing ground, and two Mi-4s came at night to transport the dead and wounded. This was a great morale booster, as it was uncomfortable to have so many of the dead and wounded lying around and not being able to help the wounded in any way. We later learned that the Pakistanis thought that the helicopters had brought reinforcements at night.

The Commanding Officer and I discussed the matter as to what could we have done if we were in their place. We concluded that we would have attacked. We decided that we required a united front to defend against such an onslaught, which could come from any direction. We might as well give them a bloody nose if we're going to die. And so, Alpha and Delta Companies were brought back to their initial locations. We felt more compact and stronger when the companies had occupied their original positions.

We awaited the anticipated attack the following day and night. The Pakistanis increased the tempo and quantum of their artillery fire, but the expected attack did not come. The Commanding Officer and I went around the defences to check how the men were doing. Although we were low on ammunition, the men were unfazed. During lulls in the firing, they were sharpening their khukris. When asked, they said: *"As a weapon of last resort there could be nothing better than the khukri as a weapon for close combat."*

On December 14, General Sam Manekshaw issued the first of his three ultimatums to the Pakistani Army in East Pakistan to surrender.

On December 15, in the late afternoon, Major Mane Malik, Company Commander 'C' Company, reported over the radio, that two Pakistani soldiers (we learnt later that they were junior officers), were approaching his company-defended region with white flags. They reported on arrival, that they wished to deliver a message to the Brigade Commander. We straight away realised that our bluff, that we were a brigade had worked! At the same time, we also felt that if the Pakistanis realised that we were so few, the situation could turn dangerous. Most important, there was no Brigade Commander present!

A verbal message was sent back that the Brigade Commander had received no orders as yet to accept their surrender and they should come the next day at the same time and place, by which time the modalities of the surrender would have been worked out. The officers went back.

Meanwhile, we communicated with the Brigade Commander and notified him of the incident in coded language. The next day, Brigadier Quinn arrived in a helicopter and moved forward to meet the Garrison Commander of Sylhet.

After the customary salutations, the Pakistani Garrison Commander asked Brigadier Quinn about who had arrived in Sylhet via helicopter. Brigadier Quinn said that he had come in the helicopter.

"*Were you not here then?*" asked the Pakistani Brigade Commander.

"*No,*" said Brigadier Quinn.

"*Then what was here?*" the Pakistani Brigadier asked.

"*Half a Battalion,*" said Brigadier Quinn.

The Pakistani Officers and men who had come to surrender were stunned and could not believe what they were hearing.

However, it was also our turn to be surprised! Three Brigadiers, 2 Colonels, 173 Officers, 290 JCOs and approximately 8000 Pakistani soldiers surrendered to us. Our strength at that time was just 352.

General JFR Jacob gave credit to the 4th Battalion the 5th Gorkha Rifles (FF) for tying up the greater part of a Pakistani Infantry Division at Sylhet, allowing IV Corps to conduct its operations against Dhaka without interruption. This has been discussed in detail in General Jacob's book *Surrender at Dacc: Birth of a Nation.*[2]

Map 1: The War Zones

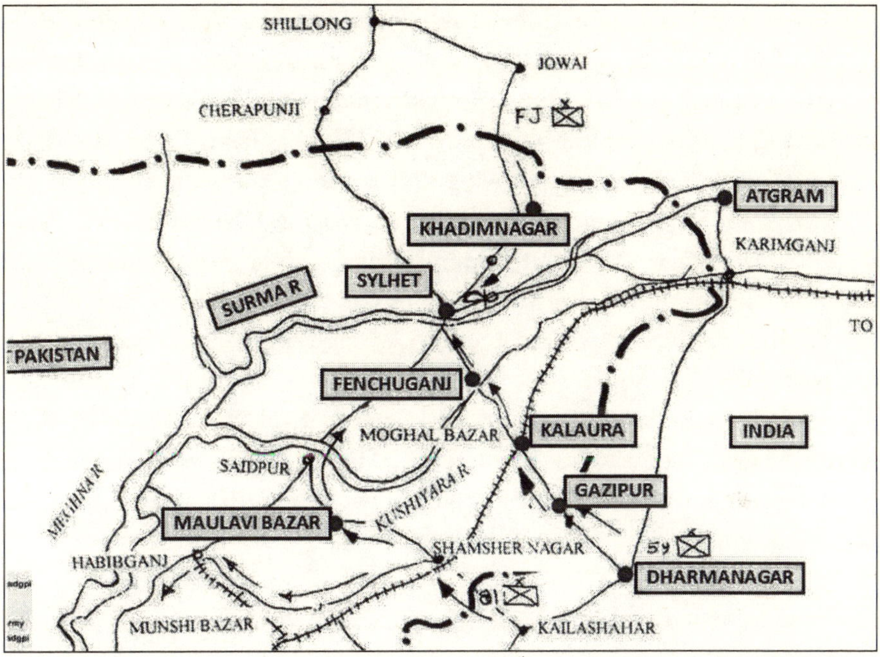

Source: Author's Own.

Reflections

Several principles of war were demonstrated during the Sylhet fight. They were as follows:

- ***Cooperation.*** Cooperation between the Army and the Air Force was critical to the operation's success. We discovered the critical role of air power in joint operations.
- ***Offensive Action.*** Offensive action in the planning and conduct of operations by senior leaders as well as the Commanding Officers and Junior leaders. The enemy must always be put under pressure relentlessly.
- ***Surprise.*** Unorthodox thinking and use of surprise to knock the enemy off balance is of primary importance. The use of weapon platform, such as a helicopter, caught the adversary off guard.
- ***Selection and Maintenance of Aim.*** The Corps Commander made up his mind to capture Sylhet in India's first heliborne operation and never deviated from the aim, irrespective of what happened thereafter. He was

fortunate to work alongside colleagues such as Group Captain Chandan Singh and Lieutenant Colonel AB Harolikar who were equally single-minded in the execution of that aim.

- ***Maintenance of Momentum.*** Notwithstanding the huge enemy force at Sylhet, the Commanding Officer of the Gorkhas kept the enemy on the backfoot by aggressive patrolling and constant engagement, giving the enemy the impression that his little force was much larger.
- ***Administration.*** Although administration was a major problem, the Commanding Officer of the Gorkhas decided to give a higher priority to ammunition rather than food, water, clothing and blankets and that paid off.
- ***Maintenance of Morale***. Great leadership was displayed at all levels, which ensured the morale of the men remained high. Officers led from the front, and faith and trust that the Air Force would never let us down kept the morale high.

In addition to the Principles of War, the success of the Operation came due to robust leadership, quick decision making, risk taken, the spirit of resilience and flexibility. The battalion was able to project that they were a 'Brigade', exhibiting exceptional flexibility and innovativeness.

Postscript

Although fifty years have passed since this battle took place, the Gorkhas of the 4th Battalion the 5th Gorkha Rifles (Frontier Force) feel that it is never too late to say 'Thank You' to the BBC for their inadvertent error that helped them turn the tables on an enemy that was twenty times their size.

Notes

1. Goose Neck – Kettle like contraption containing kerosene. It has a long spout that emits a flame when lit. This light assists helicopters to land at night.
2. Lieutenant General JFR Jacob, *Surrender at Dacca – Birth of a Nation* (New Delhi: Manohar, 2006), pp. 116-18.

7

A Rescue to Remember: First Family

Ashok Kumar Tara

As a young Major, I was involved in the Liberation War from the very beginning, that is from March 1971. As per orders, I had provided shelter, medicines and clothes to the refugees who came to India. I was also involved in training the young blood (both boys and girls) in weapons and field craft, so that they could go across the border and contribute to the East Pakistan man force in the struggle against the Pakistani Forces on a 'killing spree.'

On December 3, 1971, 14 GUARDS fought the famous 'Battle of Gangasagar,' which is 4 km south of Agartala (Tripura). I was awarded Vir Chakra. However, the dramatic surrender of Pakistan Forces to the armies of India and Bangladesh brought along with it additional responsibilities and protocols.

On the eve of December 16, 14 GUARDS was vested with the task of securing the Dhaka Airport. The unit was fully prepared to execute their allotted job by the early hours of December 17. Around 0900 hours the same day, while reassessing the arrangements with Major Shanti Khanna, I was hastily summoned by my commanding officer (CO) Lt Col VN Channa (later Brig, Retired). I thought of it as just a usual briefing session until I came to know the real reason that Muktijoddha told him – the family of Sheikh Mujibur Rahman was being held under house arrest (including now present Prime Minister Sheikh Hasina) by a contingent of enemy troops and that the possibility of them getting assassinated by the Pakistani Army was very high. Still nobody realised the sensitivity of the situation, as they thought that the

Pakistani Army had already surrendered on December 16. With the Mukti Jodha – Mr Hazi Golam Morshed as my guide and two Guardsmen to support the rescue endeavour, we arrived at the scene in Dhanmandi where the First Family was being held captive.

When about a hundred yards from the house, I was apprised by the locals about the 'trigger-happy' enemy soldiers guarding the premises with automatic weapons. They requested me to re-evaluate my approach, directing my attention towards a bullet-ridden car and a corpse in a pool of blood. While weighing the odds, it became apparent that attacking head-on was not a good option with limited resources and a well-entrenched enemy with effective weapons behind sandbagged bunkers, that were clearly visible from my position. Waiting for reinforcements would result in an endless stream of questions from my superiors regarding the situation, and reinforcements would take time to arrive. Additionally, any sudden attack on the premises would put the lives of the entire family in danger. Therefore, at that very moment instinctively, I decided to tackle the situation psychologically and get the enemy soldiers to surrender. Later it was called 'The Battle of Guts & Wits'. However, the chances for success were bleak and I had to 'play the game very tactfully'. I began by handing over my weapon to one of my Jawans and instructing them to take whatever advantageous positions they considered appropriate. Unarmed, I slowly approached the confinement. Upon reaching the bullet-ridden car – I hailed my Pakistani counterparts – "*Koi Hai*?" (*anybody there*) but failed to get any response.

Cautiously, I kept treading forward. About 10 yards from the main entrance of the house, a Pakistani soldier on the roof shouted in Punjabi to halt my approach or expect retaliatory fire.

Being fluent in the spoken dialect, I understood the gravity of the threat. I responded by apprising them that I was an Officer of the Indian Army in uniform and standing unarmed, warning them to lay down their arms as the Pakistani Army had already surrendered and that the war was over; however, they seemed unconvinced. They continued to threaten me, even using abusive language and fired at the onlookers, but to their disappointment, I stood calm without any reaction.

To my good fortune, at that very moment, an Indian Army Helicopter flew overhead. I grabbed the opportunity and, pointing towards the helicopter, re-conveyed the fact that the capital city was now in control of the Indian

Army. This trick played well, and the enemy asked for some time to speak to their commanders, to which I re-asserted that all the officers of the Pakistan Army were now Prisoners of War, and the communication grid was cut off. Simultaneously, I steadily paced towards the enemy positioned at the front gate of the house.

Suddenly, a woman waved frantically and shouted, "Do not believe, they are trigger happy and they would do any brute act". This reconfirmed my apprehensions about the Pak Army's intentions. Not wishing to give the adversary time to ponder options, I persuaded them to concede.

Finally, I was standing at the main entrance of the house while a young Pakistani soldier at the Gate was pointing the cold steel of the bayonet of his rifle under my right ribcage. His trembling hand and his jittery finger on the trigger of his rifle was a reminder of the delicate position I was in. It was quite obvious that he had never been in such close vicinity of his adversary.

Notwithstanding, gathering all my wits together, I continued to persuade the Pakistani soldiers to surrender while slowly pushing away the barrel from my body.

With the conviction that the enemy was almost swayed with my narrative, it was time for me to play the final card in the 'emotional salvo.' On the one hand, I engaged myself in inflicting constant reminders of their families back home who were waiting to meet them, and on the other, I reminded them about the death at the hands of the *Muktijoddhas* and the Indian Army, as a consequence of non-compliance. I reassured them that if they surrendered, as an Indian Army Officer, I would take them to their HQs in Pakistan and also allow them to meet their families. This tactic finally made them aware of the dire situation they were in, and eventually they yielded. Later, I was told by media person that the commander of Pakistani Army before sitting in the vehicle to move, remarked, "*I was a 'Bekhof'* (Fearless) *man.*"

I rushed in immediately and pushed the doors open to secure the family and eliminate any possibility of a foul play.

Mrs Sheikh Mujibur Rahman embraced me and said, "*God has sent you to save us ... you are like my son.*" The other members present were – Prime Minister Sheikh Hasina, her younger sister Rehana and younger brother Sheikh Russel. Around the same time, Mr Mominul Haq, cousin of Sheikh Mujibur Rahman, handed over the National Flag of Bangladesh and requested me to hoist their flag on top of their house. I immediately went up and hoisted the Bangladesh National Flag.

Sheikh Mujibur Rahman was in Pakistan under the custody of Pakistan Government at that time. He was released and reached Dacca on January 10, 1972, and invited me on January 12, 1972, to his residence. He conveyed his gratitude to me for saving his family and told me that I was like one of his family members. I finally left Dacca on January 23, 1972, for my home in Delhi and later rejoined my Unit in Mizoram.

Almost 41 years after the battle, on October 20, 2012, the Bangladesh Government conferred me with the award – 'Friends of Liberation War Honour.' Later, on October 21, Hon'ble Prime Minister Sheikh Hasina invited my wife Abha and me to her residence. There, I met her younger sister Rehana and her son with his family. She was very gracious and humble towards both of us.

The rescue act gave me a family in Bangladesh – a bond that I would cherish for the rest of my life. I am fortunate to have met Sheikh Mujibur Rahman and receive his blessings.

On April 8, 2017, I was invited to attend the 'Sommanona Ceremony,' where both the Prime Ministers of India and Bangladesh expressed their gratitude for my efforts in rescuing the 'First Family of Bangladesh.'

8

The Battle of Garibpur

Vijay Gidh

The Battle of Garibpur was fought from November 20 to 22, 1971, and was the first major battle during the India-Pakistan War of 1971, in which a single infantry battalion – 14 PUNJAB (Nabha Akal), ably supported by a squadron of armour and intimate artillery support, successfully fought a Pakistani brigade. This fight had a tremendous impact on the Pakistan Army's operations and morale.

Task

14 PUNJAB (Nabha Akal) was initially tasked to occupy the Battalion-defended area at Fatehpur under the command of Lieutenant Colonel (later Brigadier) RK Singh, which was located 6 km inside East Pakistan. The task was later revised 'to secure area Garibpur by first light on November 21, 1971. The Battalion was tasked to advance well inside to secure the enemy territory in order to interdict road Chaugacha – Jessore and trap the withdrawing enemy troops from Chaugacha, or prevent enemy reinforcements joining from Jessore. The unit was allotted 'C' Squadron of 45 Cavalry, one platoon of 102 Engineers Regiment under command, with 87 Battery of 6 Field Regiment in direct support, and the remaining 6 Field Regiment and 78 Medium Regiment in support.

Garibpur: Why was it Important?

The hamlet of Garibpur was located in the Boyra salient, about 9 km inside East Pakistan, and stood astride the highway from India to Jessore via Chaugacha, which was an important crossroad for both the nations. If a full military option had to be exercised, 9 Infantry Division had the initial task to capture the prestigious cantonment and vital communication centre of Jessore; one of its axis of advance was the Chaugacha – Jessore highway. Its control would create a road map for the Indian Forces to eventually defeat Pakistani troops in December 1971.

Assessment of the Enemy

A battalion of Pakistani 107 Infantry Brigade was located at Chaugacha, while the remainder of the Brigade and 9 Infantry Division was stationed in Jessore. Since, the Garibpur position would outflank the Pakistani battalion at Chaugacha, a strong enemy reaction was almost certain. By last light on November 20, 1971, 14 PUNJAB along with 'C' Squadron 45 Cavalry equipped with fourteen PT-76 tanks crossed the international border formed by the Kabadak River near Boyra and reached the Garibpur position.

Deployment and Preparation of Defences

Captain (later Brigadier) MPS Bajwa was the Adjutant of the battalion during the battle. The companies were allocated their area of deployment. Major NS Narang, 'C' Squadron Commander, 45 Cavalry, was ordered to deploy his tanks in conjunction with two recoilless (RCL) guns to cover the enemy armour advance from the direction of road Jessore – Chaugacha and the east between Garibpur – South Jagannathpur.

While the Delta Company under Captain (later Colonel) Balbir Singh, occupied a company-defended locality in South Jagannathpur to cover the tank approach with elements of armour, the Charlie Company, under Major (later Lieutenant Colonel) NJS Bains, occupied a company-defended locality further North at Track Junction near Pitambarpur, where the two tracks converged from Chaugacha. Alpha and Bravo Companies, under Majors (later Colonels) Vishwanathan and KM Machiah respectively, occupied the gap between Charlie and Delta Companies.

It was past midnight when Major DS Narang had deployed his tanks. The tank troops were commanded by Captain (later Lieutenant Colonel) Tejinder Singh Sidhu, located near a locality defended by Alpha Company; the other troops were commanded by Captain (later Brigadier) BS Mehta, which was deployed towards South-Eastern side, near Delta Company's farthest end; and the third troop was commanded by a JCO.

Map 1: Garibpur Area

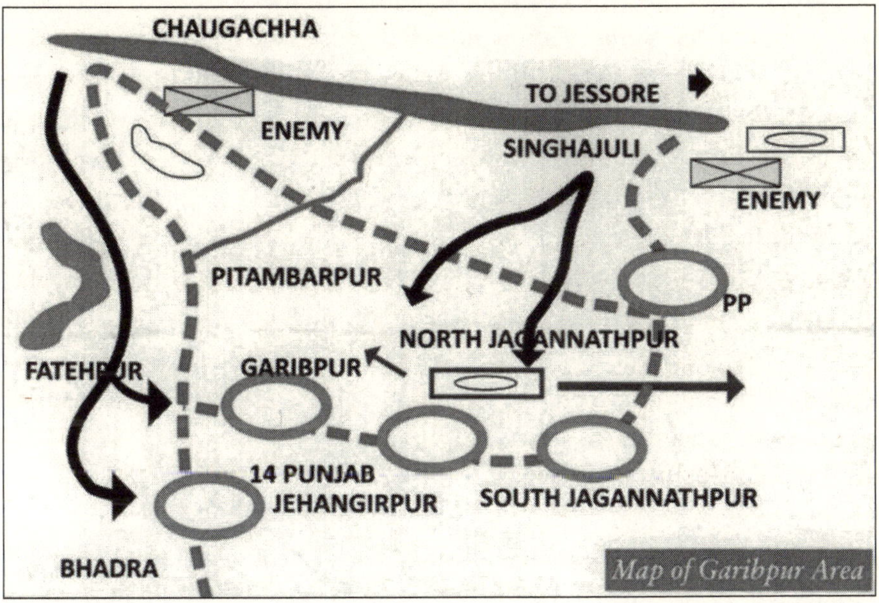

Source: 14 Punjab (Nabha Akal)

Bold Action of Protective Patrol

A patrol from 6 Field Regiment was deployed North towards Singhajhuli – Jagannnathpur, under the command of Captain (later Colonel) GS Gill – the MMG officer, and the artillery observer Captain PP Chaturvedi, to cover the enemy movement on road axis Jessore – Chaugacha. In the cold and foggy early hours of November 21, Captain Gill heard the 'unmistakable' sounds of enemy tanks moving south from the Chaugacha – Jessore road. The fog and poor visibility allowed the patrol to remain close to the enemy columns and keep an eye on them accurately. Captain Chaturvedi was able to take some very accurate artillery shoots on 'closely massed' Pakistani columns. The patrol was nearly encircled due to limited visibility and the noise of tanks and own artillery fire, but fought bravely and broke away. Captain Chaturvedi was wounded and was carried bravely by Captain Gill and others till they finally made their way back to the Company – both were awarded the Vir Chakra (VrC).

Although the radio silence had been lifted but Charlie Company under Major Bains was still out of communication. It was later found that Lance Naik Ajaib Singh, his radio operator, had carried a faulty AN PRC-25 (Radio Set)!

Brigadier Hayat Khan, Commander 107 Infantry Brigade (Pakistan), later stated in his interrogation report that he had definite information that one Sikh company of Indian Army, i.e. our Charlie Company had taken up position near Pitambarpur road junction. He was not aware of the remaining battalion (14 PUNJAB) having fetched up and deployed in the area of Garibpur with a squadron of armour and other supporting elements. So, he ordered his brigade and a squadron of 3 Independent Armoured Squadron to encircle the Indian Army's lone company (Charlie Company) from the southern and south western direction, preventing them from escaping towards the Indian territory. The aim was to capture them at first light, and show to the UNO team that Indian troops were fighting inside Bangladesh, though war had still not been declared.

Enemy Attack

At about 3.30 am on November 21, our patrol deployed near Singhajhuli passed on a message regarding roaring sounds of tanks from the direction of Jessore. At 5 am, Captain Gill reported on radio link that, he could see enemy armour and infantry lining up for assault in the Forming Up Place (FUP). Following the information, all companies were warned to be prepared for the impending enemy attack. Enemy artillery guns opened fire and started pounding our defences. As dawn broke, the enemy launched a brigade-size attack supported by a squadron of armour equipped with M-24 Chaffee tanks. Around 6 am on November 21, 1971, enemy activity was observed opposite Charlie company from Chaugacha built-up area side. The enemy's attempts to encircle the Company lead to a fierce encounter.

Captain Bajwa remembers how Major Bains had requested for defensive fire, DF (SOS), as the enemy had closed in and was preparing for the final assault. The artillery fire was promptly given by the battery commander – Major Kailash Nath – who ensured an accurate barrage of fire to break the enemy attack.

The enemy tanks had come in the open and most of the tanks rushed to the south, towards Captain Balbir Singh's Delta Company, with the intention of encircling Charlie Company from the south west. They were unaware about the deployment of the entire Battalion, which was supported by tanks.

By this time the 'C' Squadron, 45 Cavalry had swung into action and Major DS Narang had readjusted the position of all the three troops. Unfortunately, while doing so standing in an open cupola, he was hit by the enemy fire and we lost this brave officer. Major Narang was later awarded MVC, posthumously, and Captain BS Mehta being the second-in-command, took over the charge. In the meantime, Delta Company led by Captain Balbir Singh in the South had fought fiercely and was successful in repulsing the repeated enemy attacks. Later during the day, while searching for the dead bodies of enemy troops, an enemy soldier had hid in the paddy field. When he tried to escape, Captain Balbir chased him for 40–50 metres and apprehended him.

The Air Battle

Around 9.25 am on November 22, 1971, three enemy F-86 Sabres strafed the battalion defences, knocking out one PT-76 tank and injuring some troops on the ground. Around 2 pm three Pakistani aircraft roared in freely, when Major Kailash Nath, the Battery Commander, got a 'deceptive' smoke shot fired into the enemy position at Singhajhuli. This deception paid off well, as all the enemy aircraft diverted their attack on their own troops at Singhajhuli.

At about 2.45 pm the same day, three more Pakistani aircraft roared in and were having a free run, when suddenly four Indian Gnat aircraft from No 22 Squadron from Kalaikunda, appeared in the sky. In the first aerial combat between the two sides since the 1965 War, all three enemy aircraft were shot down in the ensuing dog-fight. Two of the Pakistani pilots – Flying Officers Khalil Ahmed and Parvez Mehdi Qureshi – ejected safely but were captured by the Indian troops and treated as Prisoners of War (PoW). As a result of the PAF's decision to cease sending fighter-bombers to support their own soldiers following the intercept of the three Sabres over Garibpur, the successive Indian formations were now free to continue their advance towards Jessore.

Importance of the Battle of Garibpur

The Battle of Garibpur had many national and international repercussions. Gen Yahya Khan declared a National Emergency in Pakistan and complained to the UN Secretary-General U Thant about India's violation of the UN Charter.

The unique battle of one Battalion Group defeating a Brigade attack supported by armour and PAF will go down in history warfare as a classic example indeed. In the process, two Pakistani infantry battalions (6 PUNJAB and 22 FF) and 3 Independent armoured Squadron were badly mauled.

On the tactical level, the engagement compelled the Pakistanis to withdraw without resistance from Chaugacha. Later, in early December, when the war was fully engaged, our 9 Infantry Division marched into Jessore unchallenged, accomplishing its initial objective.

Casualties

Our losses, including those of the affiliated units, were 28 dead and 42 wounded, while four PT-76 tanks were destroyed. Whereas, 13 Chaffee tanks were neutralised on the enemy's side, including three captured in running condition. Three enemy aircraft were lost in the air battle, while 300 soldiers, including three officers, were killed and many wounded. Six enemy PoW were apprehended.

Honours and Awards

The Battle of Garibpur brought a total of 40 well-deserved gallantry awards to the battalion, its affiliated troops and the IAF. While Lieutenant Colonel RK

Image 2: 'Banglar Ronokhetro 1971' (The Battlefield of Bangla-1971)
The monument had been erected in the school premise which happened to be one of the biggest mango orchards bearing the testimony of Battle of Garibpur

Source: 14 Punjab.

Singh was awarded the MVC, the unit earned another MVC posthumously, two VrC and two Sena Medals (SM). The attached troops won one MVC (Major DS Narang) posthumously, two VrCs and two SMs. The three IAF Gnat pilots (Flight Lieutenants RA Massey, MA Ganapathy and Flying Officer D Lazarus) who shot down the Sabre jets were awarded VrC each.

The Battle of Garibpur was the first main battle of the 1971 War, and was a significant military victory that blunted the enemy's counter-attack capabilities and morale. This eventually paved the way for the Indian victory over Pakistan 50 years ago. Unfortunately, the unit was not awarded a well-deserved Battle Honour of 'Garibpur' Battle, since it was fought prior to commencement of hostilities on December 3, 1971. However, one of the Pakistani Chaffee tanks today occupies a place of pride in the Punjab Regimental Centre at Ramgarh Cantonment in Jharkhand.

9

Manoeuvre Warfare: Battle of Govindganj

JBS Yadava

One of the most significant battles fought during the Liberation of Bangladesh, from the point of achieving strategic objective within a strategic time frame, was in North Western Sector (NWS). This battle was a classic example of manoeuvre warfare, where both—the armoured Corps and the infantry exploited terrain, machine, and human ingenuity to the optimum. Regrettably, very little has been written about battle of Govindganj that was penultimate to the battles of Mahasthan and Bogra. Bogra, a strategic objective was captured in 9 days by a manoeuvre that covered approximately 250 to 300 kms.

NWS formed by the Ganga in the West and Bharamputra/Jamuna in the East was strategically important both to India and Pakistan for several reasons. Siliguri-Kishanganj Corridor and the Farraka Barrage on the Indian side were vulnerable to Pakistan's interdiction. It provided nearest point to the Chumbi Valley for a collusion action by Pakistan and China. Pakistan was sensitive to India, severing the neck at Hilli and thereafter either cross the Jamuna and dash to Dacca or roll down south to Bogra. A large number of rivers, and poor road and rail works imposed severe restrictions on movement of vehicles and troops.

16 Pakistan Infantry Division under Maj Gen Nazar Hussain Shah was deployed in NWS. It was divided in three sub sectors geographically. The northern sub sector consisting of Dinajpur, Saidpur and Rangpur ran close to Siliguri corridor and Chumbi valley. 23 Infantry Brigade with 29 CAV less one squadron and 48 Field Regiment under Brig Shafi was responsible for this area.

Map 1: North Western Sector (NWS)

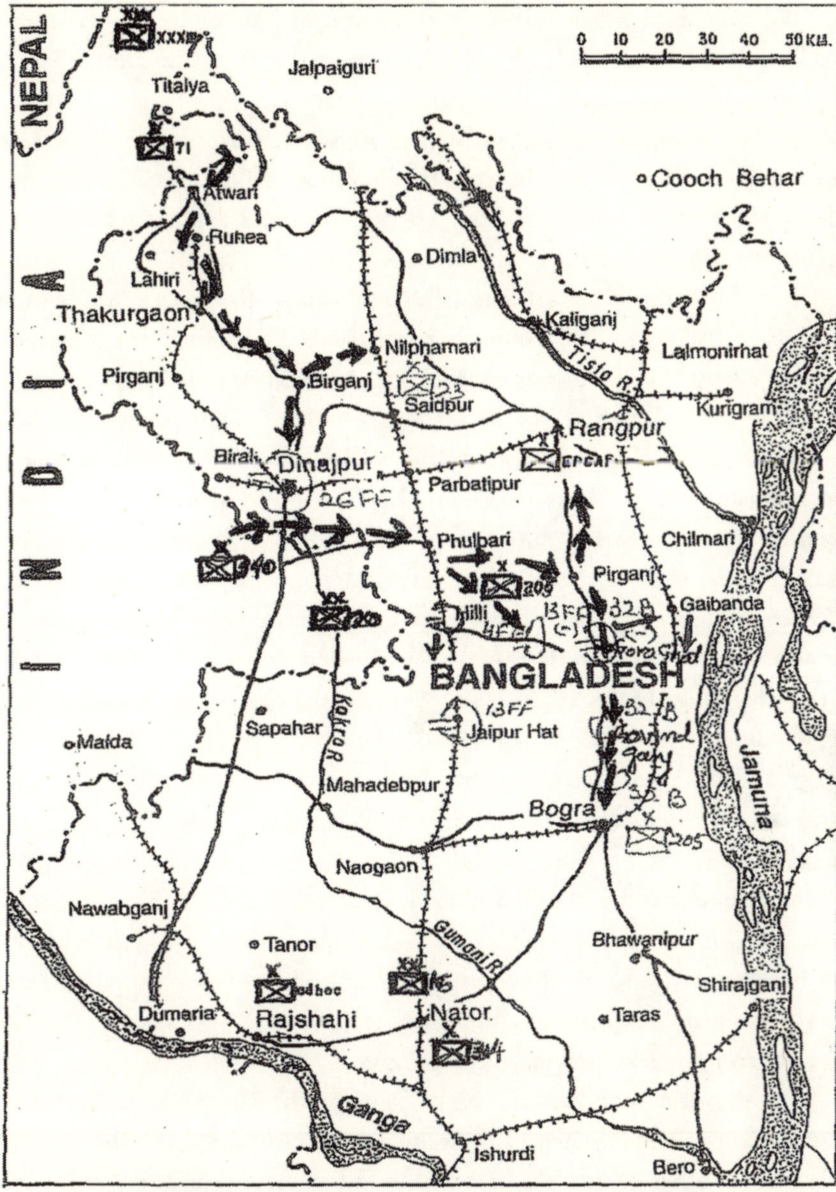

The external boundaries of India depicted in this map are neither correct nor authentic.

NORTH-WESTERN SECTOR

The Central sub sector consisted of the waistline Hilli- Goraghat- Palasbari and Gaibanda. Holding it was most important to prevent India severing the waistline. 205 Infantry Brigade was deployed with its entire compliment of infantry battalions, armour, artillery, and support elements.

The Southern sub sector consisted of Rajshahi, Bogra and Pabna. It was connected to Jessore and Khulna over the Hardinge Bridge and Dacca by Ferry at Bera. It was the shortest axis from Malda to Dacca. 34 Infantry brigade was deployed in this sub sector.

These brigades were not mutually supporting. The Sector was allotted 18000 East Pakistan Civil Armed Force (EPCAF) personnel. Each battalion was adequately stocked in rations, fuel, ammunition, and ordnance stores for four weeks, enough to hold the Indian Army with a shallow penetration.

Based on Pakistan's war doctrine, which stated that the defence of East Pakistan lay in West Pakistan[1], Lt Gen Niazi adopted the forward defensive posture. This would ensure that Indian Forces will not be able to capture enough territory to declare Independent Bangladesh on East Pakistan soil. His concept of Defence[2] envisaged unacceptable attrition on the attacking forces. Strong nodes were created as far as forward covering all the axes to delay the attacker as much as possible. No position was to be vacated unless a unit defending it had suffered 75% casualties. Niazi and the Pakistan Army were convinced that Indian Army was unlikely to resort to an all-out war[3] and would be content to nibble some territory in support of the rebel cause.

India may have had limited objectives in the initial planning, but as the magnitude of problem increased, it was evident that India's involvement may have to be deeper than imagined and nothing less than an independent Bangladesh would satisfy the Bengalis. Thus Dacca[4] was chosen the final objective and centre of gravity of the campaign.

Both countries mobilised for war by October. The Mukti Bahini [5]intensified their operations and targeted Pak lines of communications, ambushed convoys and attacked other vulnerable targets. The Indian Army launched preliminary operations at five places to test battle preparations, the Pakistani defences and create launch pads. The battle of Hilli from 22 - 24 Nov was one of them. A number of valuable lessons were learnt from these operations and plans modified accordingly.

The war commenced on 04 December and by 06 December, Dinajpur was contacted from North and South. 66 Mountain Brigade had reached Nawabganj but lost momentum thereafter. 202 Mountain Brigade failed to link up with 66 Brigade at Charkai. 340(I) Infantry Brigade was thus launched to resume advance to Gaibanda. The manoeuvre commenced on 07 December with 2/5 GR mounted on tanks of 69 Armoured Regiment (AR) while 5/11 GR speed marched on foot. Column of 2/5 GR and 69 AR interdicted Rangpur- Bogra High way by 1600 hours at Laldigi. They ambushed an enemy convoy at 1645 hours. It was revealed later that the convoy belonged to GOC 16 Pakistan Division who was returning to his HQ after a conference at Rangpur. The GOC managed to escape on foot to Rangpur under darkness. Orders to remove the road blocks immediately at Laldigi and Pirganj were given.

5/11 GR covered 39 Kms in 12 hours and relieved 2/5 GR at Laldigi by mid night. Immediately thereafter the enemy launched a furious counter attack supported by tanks. The attack was defeated and enemy withdrew. 5/11 GR consolidated at the Cross Road during night while 2/5 GR took defences at Pirganj. As the counter attack was launched by the Commanding Officer of 32 Baluch, without any reconnaissance or adequate information, it failed. The CO and along with 7 men was killed. After the war, it was revealed by Maj Gen Nazar Hussain that as per their appreciation Indian troops were unlikely to penetrate their defences up to Pirganj. The idea of a main Divisional thrust on this underdeveloped axis never occurred to them.

After analysing the terrain, enemy and crossings over the rivers, GOC 20 Mountain Division gave out his brief plan for capture of Bogra which was his main task. 202 Mountain Brigade was to capture Hilli and link up with 66 Mountain Brigade at Goraghat for operations towards Bogra. 66 Brigade to capture Bhaduria and link up with 340 (I) Brigade at Govindganj; and 340 (I) Brigade to capture Govindganj and advance to Bogra.

340(I) Infantry Brigade commenced advance to Govindganj on 09 December with 69 AR and 6 Guards. By 1100 hours, Palasbari was captured. Gaibanda was captured soon thereafter severing the waistline. The force in their enthusiasm destroyed the Jetty, an error that was regretted later when there was a need to reinforce the Northern Sector for the race to Dacca. 5/11 GR and 69 AR contacted Ghoraghat by last light 09 December defended by two enemy companies. Eastern Bank of Karotya River was captured by last light 10 December. During this operation 3 other ranks were killed and Maj N Bhasin with three other ranks wounded. The air and artillery had played a vital role in this attack. At 0800 hours 11 December the Battalion was asked to concentrate at Palasbari to assist 6 Guards in capture of Govindganj.

The enemy defences at Govindganj were well prepared based on the south bank of Karatoya. The bridge over the river had been demolished. Squadron 63 Cavalry (T-55) under Maj Bhaskar Nair that was leading the advance encountered anti tanks mines. Effective tank and RCL fire also engaged them. The GOC 20 Mountain Division[6] had expected both 66 and 202 Brigades to be at Govindganj by 10 December. Their move would have hastened 340 (I) Infantry Brigade operations. But this did not happen. A hasty assault on the enemy was fraught with heavy casualties with no guarantee of success. A deliberate river crossing would be time consuming allowing the enemy to reinforce Bogra. Therefore, it was decided to out flank Govindganj from the East by a manoeuvre and attack him from SE- a most unexpected direction. (Refer to Map 2).

A combat Command consisting of 5/11 GR and 69 AR was formed with artillery and engineers in support. Two enemy companies deployed on southern bank of Karatoya were effectively dominating the northern bank. Two companies were in depth. They were supported by tanks and artillery. 32 Baluch HQ was located at cross road. 'A' Company under me was grouped with 'C' Squadron under Major SC Mehra to lead the manoeuvre. We set off before mid-day along route Palasbari- Shahapara-Nakal-Kajla Ferry Crossing along west bank of the river to Sripatipur- Shahapura. From Shahpura our combat team was to peel off and establish a Road block at Kamar Track Junction. The reconnaissance troop with Mukti Bahini successfully secured the Kajla Crossing. An artillery observation post established with help of Mukti Bahini at Magura engaged the enemy effectively. We crossed the Karatoya River at Kajala at 1330 hours and reached Shahapura by 1500 hours. Thereafter while the Battalion and rest of 69 AR moved west to Govindganj, our combat team moved south west for road block at Kamar by 1600 hours. This manoeuvre of approximately 55 to 60 Kms was remarkable that exploited the capability of men and machines to the maximum in the battle that was to follow. The PT 76 tanks swam through the water obstacles wadded the marshes and negotiated soft ground at full throttle at some places.

Map 2: Battle of Govindganj

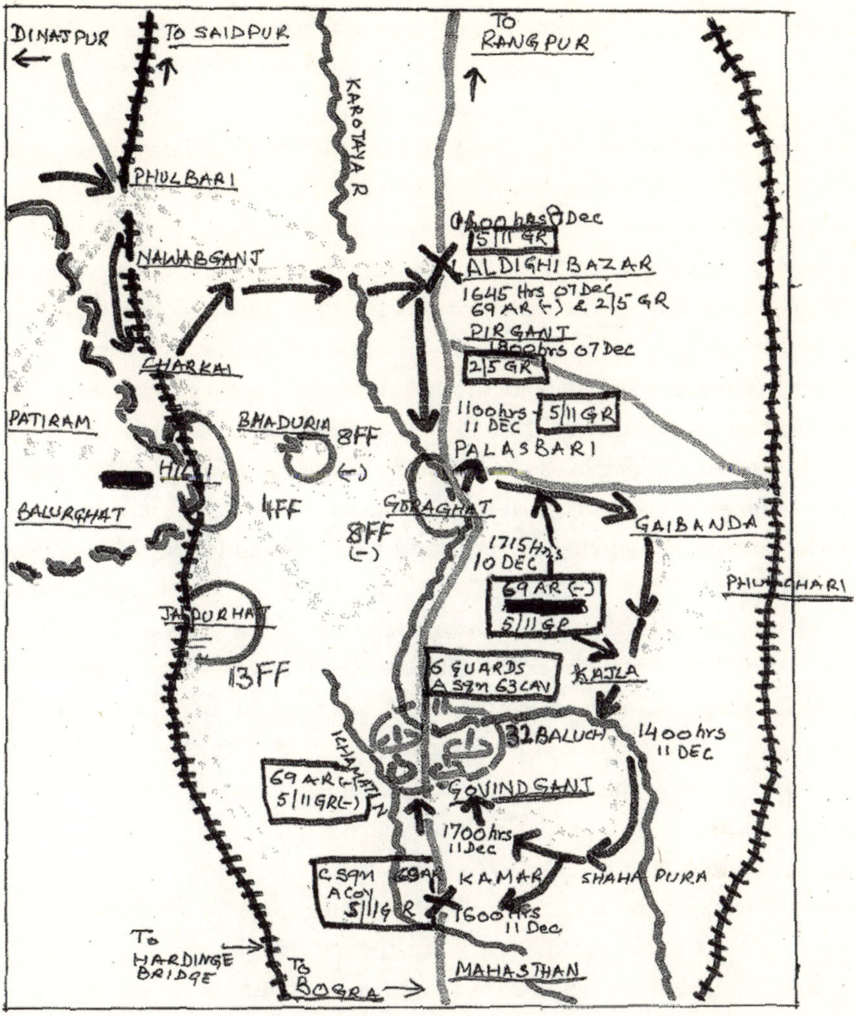

Not to scale

While this manoeuvre was executed, 6 Guards and 63 Cavalry under Lt HM Singh kept pressure on enemy from the North bank of Karatoya. When the attack by 5/11 GR went in from the rear with the tanks in support, the enemy was completely surprised and perplexed. However, his resistance wilted under the weight of our artillery and tank fire as well as determined assault by the infantry. He lost the will and abandoned his defences in confusion that followed. Command and control collapsed, and panic griped him. Road

Junction was captured by 1700 hours, but Captain PB Singh had been seriously injured. 'C' Company under Captain GS Pathania was also launched immediately thereafter. Area west and east of road was cleared quickly. Around 1800 hours, a convoy of enemy entered the killing zone of the road block. It consisted of tanks, artillery guns and many trucks. Suddenly hell was let loose on them both by our tanks and my company. We were deployed in shape of a horseshoe towards Govindganj and the enemy had no chance of breaking through. The enemy abandoned their tanks, guns and vehicles to make good escape on foot. One of the enemy parties trying to break through fired at me perforating my trouser. As darkness fell, the tanks were withdrawn in the inner circle while my company took up the defence in the outer perimeter. Lt Y Babu Rao, Battalion Intelligence Officer linked up with me.

As we were walking back after coordinating the defences, one of the enemy parties hiding in bushes fired at us. The automatic fire came right in my face and hit my helmet, grazing my neck and ears. My helmet rattled violently. I intuitively hit the ground for cover and thought for a moment that this was my end. After a while the firing died down gradually. When all clear was sounded, I got up but there was no trace of Babu Rao. After searching for a while, he was found in lying position some yards from us. We thought that he had not heard the all clear signal and one of the jawans shook him by the shoulder. He tried to get up, but his complete intestines fell out and he slumped to the ground face down dead. This was very sad. The enemy burst had caught him in the stomach before he could take position. We lost a very bold officer. I had also been wounded in the right forehead and right ear. The Nursing Assistant removed the shrapnel lodged in my forehead and after first aid injected morphine. In the morning, I realized my helmet had taken the burst at an angle that had saved me. The bullets had perforated the sides and the brim with splinters injuring me in the forehead, upper ear and lobe. My scarf and collar of the shirt had been perforated by bullets on both sides and smeared with dry blood. I had escaped death miraculously. The Regimental Medical officer evacuated me to the Advance Dressing Station, which were overflowing with casualties more serious than me. So, after treatment, I returned and re-joined my company. In this operation, one officer and three Jawans were killed and two officer, one JCO and seven jawans were wounded. We had killed approximately 80 enemy and taken 40 prisoners. Two Chaffee tanks were destroyed and four captured, two 105 mm guns destroyed and five captured. 60 troop carrying vehicles and 15 vehicles carrying ammunition and stores were also captured. Interrogation of prisoners revealed that the defences were held by 32 Baluch less two companies, one company 23 Punjab Regiment, two troops Chaffee tanks, 60 Field Company Engineers, one Field Battery 80 Field Regiment and 200 EPCAF personnel.

This was the boldest and longest manoeuvre of the war that resulted in capture of Govindganj at a low cost to us. The advance to Bogra was resumed in the afternoon of 12 December with Lt HM Singh of 63 Cavalry leading and 5/11 GR mounted on 69 AR behind them. Enemy opposition at Mahasthan resulted in attack by infiltration by 5/11 GR where 32 Baluch was annihilated by mid-day 13 December. Eastern Command was hard pressed to capture Dacca due to strategic time fame. They asked 340 (I) Infantry Brigade[7] to race to Dacca over the Gaibanda ferry on the Jammuna. Unfortunately, this had been destroyed by 6 Guards on 09 December. Thus, it became imperative to capture Bogra at the earliest.

The last manoeuvre took place for capture of Bogra, the final objective. Advance commenced in afternoon of 13 December, by 2/5 GR and 'A'Squadron 63 Cavalry isolating the town from the North and 6 Guards and 69 AR cut it off from East and South by a long encircling manoeuvre. Both the objectives had been achieved by first light 14 December, but the town could not be captured due to stubborn resistance by the defenders under Brig Tajummul Hussain Malik. 4 Madras and 5/11 GR were thus launched from the west and south to reinforce the assault. The town finally capitulated after two days of bitter and tough fighting at last light 15 December.

The Division had been allotted 3 Armoured Brigade with 63 Cavalry less one squadron and 69 AR. The initial bitter experience of Hilli and lessons learnt in a conventional employment of armour had been absorbed very fast. To optimize the potential of both PT 76 and T-55 tanks, the two had been mixed to form two composite regiments. Thus 340 Infantry Brigade operated with one squadron of T-55 and two squadrons of PT 76 under 69 AR. The advance was led by T-55 squadron and out flanking movements carried out by PT 76 squadrons with infantry mounted. 23 Brigade in north was isolated, 205 Brigade in the centre trapped leading to its destruction and 34Brigade in south made redundant by intelligently planned and boldly executed manoeuvres. Of the three manoeuvres, the one at Govindganj was classic with outstanding results. Once again, it was proved that success is achieved by bold manoeuvreswhichever theatre of war it may be.

Notes

1. Betrayal of East Pakistan by AAK Niazi, p. 103.
2. Ibid., pp. 83-84
3. Ibid., p. 87
4. Surrender at Dacca by Lt Gen JRF Jacob, pp. 60, 66–67
5. A Tale of Million by Rafiq Islam, pp. 302–305.
6. Indian sword Strikes in East Pakistan by Lachhaman Singh, p. 124.
7. Indian Sword Strikes in East Pakistan by Maj Gen Lachhaman Singh. pp. 135, 136 & 138.

10

The First Amphibious Assault by the Indian Army

ARK Reddy

The 11th Battalion of the Bihar Regiment was raised as war clouds were gathering and the strategic preparations were underway at the national level in early 1970s'. As an extension of that plan, 11 BIHAR was initially formed as a force for the protection of Vulnerable Areas (VAs) and Vulnerable Points (VPs). There were large number of highly technical and electronic warfare equipment that was procured and intended for deployment in the Eastern Sector. Barely two months after its formation, the unit received orders to move to Barrackpore/Zaffarpur for operational deployment.

11 BIHAR in Action: A 'Lucky' Surprise

The unit arrived with whatever equipment it had received and was deployed as follows:

- 'A' Company 'Adivasi' composition, was assigned the Dum Dum Airport.
- 'B' Company 'North Bihari' composition, at Panagarh, was to protect the Pakistani prisoners who had surrendered or was captured by Mukti Bahini.
- 'C' Company 'Adivasi' composition, was deployed for the protection of Zaffarpur air base and radar equipment.
- 'D' Company 'North Bihari' composition, was operationally deployed in Sundarbans – the riverine terrain.
- Support and Administrative Companies were appropriately orbatted.

During a social interaction with the Army Commander and the Chief of Staff of Eastern Command, it was conveyed that using a full-fledged infantry battalion to protect VAs and VPs was a waste of a force, and one full-fledged unit for the ceremonial and other duties in Fort William was also considered too luxurious during the war conditions. Therefore, the Senior Officers immediately ordered appropriate operational utilisation of these units.

I am not certain of the timings at this point, but perhaps in October 1971, the Battalion was reorganised for deployment across the Ichamati River near Barasat, opposite Satkhira (then East Pakistan). The operational task assigned was to provide flank protection to the forces tasked to capture Jessore and take offensive actions that would prevent any reinforcement to the Jessore garrison; thereafter dominate axis, Jessore – Khulna to facilitate speedy advance to Khulna. The unit was divided into two parts, with the Battalion HQ and two companies tasked for the capture of Satkhira and two companies for the capture of Jhodunga – both these were considered a threat to Jessore.

Mukti Bahini

The Battalion comprised certain Mukti Bahini personnel, who kept us informed about the strength, weapon systems, movements, minefields and other obstacles, as well as the deployment of artillery in support of the defences of Satkhira and Jhodunga. We were able to encircle both the objectives from three sides but were unable to approach them due to massive minefields that could have resulted in significant civil and battle casualties.

By December 1, 1971, we were completely aware of the enemy movements, capabilities and vulnerabilities. On December 3, 1971, we launched attacks on these garrisons and captured them by the next morning (December 4, 1971). The enemy fled, leaving everything behind. Since the objective was not active and the desired purpose was achieved, we did not get into Jhodunga, but the township of Satkhira was fully under our control. The locals gave us a very warm welcome. We reorganised ourselves to support the main attack on Jessore, and the entire unit's firepower and the physical deployment now aimed at preventing reinforcements or withdrawals from the Jessore garrison and establishing dominance along the Jessore-Khulna axis.

Ready for Action

On December 7, 1971, we received orders for regrouping of the unit and the two companies – 'A' and 'C' Companies – with the bulk of the Support Company weapons, were ordered to concentrate at the Khidirpur dock. The Gorkha Rifles battalion from Fort William, was also tasked for the same. Early on December 8, 1971, the Chief of Staff, Eastern Command, briefed us about the impending operations and the Army Commander dropped by. In attendance were also the Naval Commander in-charge of the entire operations in the Eastern theatre, the Air Force in-charge, some more Naval Officers, Naval diving teams, one captain of the merchant vessel 'Vishva Vijay' of the Shipping Corporation of India (maybe, he joined later after the operational briefings). If I recall correctly, a light field ambulance and one light Arty Battery was also deployed. The following instructions were given:

- The Force designated for amphibious landings at Cox's Bazaar was to operate under the Indian Navy (until the landing was complete).
- The Gorkha Regiment Battalion and 11 BIHAR were to move by sea to Cox's Bazaar with complete first-line ammunitions and two second lines plus mortar ammunitions to be loaded, but only weapon scales were to be disembarked. No tank threat per se was visualised. However, recoilless gun ammunitions on weapon scale were to be carried.
- Only 'one ton' and jeep vehicles, modified with exhaust pipes pointing upwards, to be carried.
- The troops and equipment to be carried in a merchant vessel.
- Two Landing Ship Tanks (LSTs) were earmarked – Guldar and Gadiyal.
- A host of Indian Navy war ships, of various classes, were part of the support systems.
- Indian Naval Ship (INS) Vikrant, equipped with all available aircraft, was to provide complete support for the landings.
- The exact landing zones to be selected by the Indian Navy Frog Men Team.

The broad operational tasks were assigned as under:

- To cut off all Pakistan Army withdrawal routes into Burma.
- To capture any area considered vital for the operations.
- To be tentatively prepared to advance to Dacca or Chittagong.

- The Force was designated as 'Romeo Force,' with a Brigadier ranked officer In-Command, who linked with us at Cox's Bazaar.

We had several difficulties in loading the personnel and the equipment, as the draft of 'Vishva Vijay' was extremely high and the gang was fragile. One officer of the Field Ambulance fell down and drowned – a bad start! Finally, the loading got completed and we sailed out on the night of December 9 through the Hoogly River into the Bay of Bengal. Winter month, war is on, high seas, threat of submarines, all led the ship to move in shallow waters and back again with reduced speeds.

The threat of American 7th Fleet heading towards East Pakistan to save them, as well as the USSR and other international pressure to complete the operations at the earliest – all increased the 'already high' anxiety level. On the intervening night of December 12/13, 1971, the Frog Men Team located and designated the landing/beaching sites. The troops and the equipment were to be transferred to the LSTs. The height difference was about 70 feet. Throughout the night we were engaged in transferring the troops and the equipment. The men were literally on their fours over the net that was spread linking both – the 'Vishva Vijay' and the LSTs. It was indeed very scary. Though the trans-shipment took time, however, we were able to commence landings before the first light of December 13, 1971 – the designated date.

The LSTs were supposed to land close to the beaches, but the shallowness of the beach and the low tide did not permit this. The Frog Men Team strung the ropes for the troops to hold and move towards the beach. Although the tide was low, it was high enough to drown us; however, none of the men of 11 BIHAR left the ropes and disobeyed the instructions. We had laid a sequence for the landing, that is, first six Light Machine Gun teams landed and they also carried the Medium Machine Gun detachments; they advanced, accompanied by intelligence elements from the units. Once the beaches were completely secured, the entire contingent of men relocated. Later, in the Second phase, the Gorkha Rifles Battalion also moved on the same beaches where 11 BIHAR provided the safety and a bridge head. The heavy equipment like the Battalion Mortars, Recoilless Guns and Vehicles could not be landed due to some technical reasons of the Navy. Even the

Artillery component did not land. We moved only with a small medical unit detachment.

The Ending

On December 13, we received orders to move to Chittagong and take surrender of a Pakistani Marine Battalion. Local transportation of various types, including a few light cars, were gathered. By the night of December 15, 1971, we had made our way across terrible roads, damaged, burned, wrecked bridges and hospitable people to Chittagong. We took surrender of a full-fledged Marine Battalion of Pakistan Army/Navy complete with Cook houses, kotes, transport, Quarter Guards, lines and so on. The command structure of the Pakistani troops were more than willing to surrender – the Commanding Officer, Second-in-Command, Adjutant, Quarter Master, the Company Commanders – a total of 36 Officers, 45 Junior Commissioned Officers and 850 Other Ranks. They appeared to be a select group of tall and handsome pathans. The process of separating the men from the leadership was done and the companies were dispersed towards the Port Trust, police lines and the airfield. The civilians of West Pakistan origin wanted to be taken by the Indian Army, as their lives were under threat – but we obeyed our own system.

Although the war was over on December 16, 1971, however, we were still struggling to mop up the township of Chittagong with other Indian Army units entering later on. We were allotted three sectors and confined ourselves to these sectors till December 23, 1971. The Battalion received orders to take the first set of Prisoners via ship to Andaman. The Marine Battalion, together with the Battalion HQ and one company, sailed off on December 25, 1971, and arrived at the same old Khidirpur Docks on the evening of December 31, 1971.

Unloading the Prisoners proved to be another challenging task. Additionally, one Pakistani soldier fell into the waves at this time period, but was immediately rescued by 11 BIHAR boys.

Some reflections after 50 Years

- The Battalion did not have sufficient time to integrate itself.
- The leaders barely knew the command and vice versa.

- The transfer of mindset from being a unit for the VAs and VPs to full-fledged operational role.
- There was no training whatsoever for the amphibious landing and the coordination with Navy.
- Almost the entire hierarchy experimented with the operation and obtained reasonably good results. The majority of people experienced the water for the first time. The morning nature calls were a misery and fraught with fear of a fall into the sea.
- Salute to the Indian Army soldiers, who just obey.

Mukti Bahini boys were of immense help in obtaining timely and correct intelligence about the terrain and Pak forces as well as logistical support throughout the operations.

11

Battle of Chatlapore: Reminiscences of a Subaltern

BM Daniels

I was commissioned into 10 MAHAR about 11 months before the war broke out. The Battalion (Bn) was deployed in a Counter Insurgency environment, requiring a different Operational orientation. Our Young Officers' course at Junior Leaders Wing Belgaum was curtailed and we missed the Tactics leg, with a farewell message, "Go to your units and learn tactics in actual battle, Best of Luck."

On reporting to the unit near Kailashahar (Tripura), I was impressed with the practical training levels of our subunits, platoons, support weapons and junior leadership that were oriented towards our upcoming task. Intelligence gathering and planning were underway for our first battle, i.e., capture of a well-fortified Chatlapore Tea Factory. Officer-led patrols, ably guided by Mukti Bahini (Muktijoddhas) personnel, had garnered enough intelligence regarding our objective, routes leading to it and area of influence beyond. Rehearsals for the attack were conducted in the wooded areas of Kailashahar to include house clearing drills, bunker bursting, blowing gaps in wire fences and navigation through 'Panji infested' tea gardens. The attack plan emphasised the importance of flexibility throughout execution. The preparations were akin to what we were taught at the Academies.

Deception, as a principle of war, was achieved by increased patrolling and firing/shelling on Chatlapore Border Out Post (BOP), but the actual objective was undisturbed, around 5 km from the border. For me, it was a good example of deception as was done in numerous battles in Burma, Africa and Normandy.

On D-Day, the excitement was palpable, and spirits were charged up with a motivational speech delivered by the Commanding Officer, Lt Col Har Rajinder Singh, replete with his customary expletives. The Mandir and Gurduwara prayers were inspiring. At the launch pad, the Commanding Officer and Subedar Major Dhanna Singh gave a final 'Thumbs Up'.

The border crossing was at last light. We crossed the dry Manu River, moved south of the Road Shamsher Nagar-Nomuja and encountered thick tea gardens, where the risk of losing direction and/or contact was possible. Our guides were the patrol leaders, Capt AK Datta and Capt A Banerjee, with Mukti Bahini personnel. Surprise of the attack was total and the execution flawless. Maj DA Paranjape, VrC, controlled the entire battle throughout, from marking of FUP (by Capt Datta) at 2300 hours on November 29 until the success signal at 1115 hours on November 30. When 'B' Company (coy), that was assaulting Manager's Bungalow, was held up due to intense enemy fire and excessive casualties, the reserve coy ('D' Coy) was launched through 'B' Coy that had firmed in. Here the coordination of troops crossing through was quick, despite continuous enemy firing.

Despite the gallantry honours (one MVC and three VrC) bestowed upon the Battalion's bravehearts, there were several valiant soldiers whose acts of bravery were no less praiseworthy. For example, Naik Prakash Singh of Pioneer Platoon, who crawled with a Bangalore Torpedo up to the 15-feet high fence around the Tea Factory, launching it and blasting a gap in the fence enabling troops of 'C' Coy to enter the well-defended complex. Next, Capt KL Gulati of 'D' Coy, who had to expose himself to enemy fire, personally fired three rockets of the 3.5 inch Rocket Launcher (RL) and 9 rounds of the 57 mm RCL at the Manager's bungalow. He sustained shrapnel injury in the process. Next, Havaldar Krishan Chander of 'C' Coy, single handedly eliminated a sniper, who was hiding on the first floor of the Drying Shed behind sandbagged flooring and walls. The sniper had chosen that spot so appropriately, that he was able to pin down almost the entire 'C' Coy. The staircase was blown up, so he climbed up the drain pipe at the rear of the Shed, crawled surreptitiously to the sniper and eliminated him. Krishan Chander was the team leader who was the first soldier to enter the Tea Factory through the gap made by Naik Prakash Singh. Havaldar Krishan Chander was awarded Mentioned-in-Despatches for his bravery. Next, Naik

Janak Singh of Medium Machine Gun Platoon was ingenious in the firing of Medium Machine Gun for the close support to 'C' Coy, by firing the weapon on the move, at the bunker, with the front legs of the tripod on the shoulders of Sepoy Phool Chand! These unsung heroes added to the glory of the unit in no less measure. The lessons I learnt as a subaltern, formed an indelible part of my battle experience. The battle of Chatlapore was a "unique" infantry battle (without artillery, air or mortar support) that has been used as a battle study in our training establishments since 1972.

The capture of Chatlapore BOP was accomplished with comparative ease, as depth areas were already captured, and so resistance was minimal. Maulvi Bazar (a Taluk headquarters) was captured with a more methodical and detailed attack plan. The assaults by companies were unconventional, as the targets were located in densely populated regions, necessitating a changed weapon systems application. It is here that the artillery (93 Mountain Regiment and 853 Light Battery) and our infantry mortars were utilised, in addition to bombing by Air Force, to soften the targets. The devastating fire assaults prior to Infantry assaults, destroyed a major portion of the defence works at the objectives and weakened the will of enemy troops to put up any resistance. The Infantry assaults were marked with boldness, swiftness, flexibility and ferocity, forcing them to execute a hurried withdrawal. However, house clearing operations were conducted over the next two days.

It was in Maulvi Bazar that we saw the horrible glimpses of genocide. The bunkers of enemy had women and children, most of whom were dead or near death. A heart wrenching reality of what Army personnel should not do. Here I realised the ethical reasons for our Country going to war to "sort out" Pakistan Army.

My Battalion (Bn) was chosen by 8 Mountain Division, for the onerous task of being Heli dropped at Dacca University (the HQ of Lt Gen AAK Niazi of Pakistan Army). The aim was to strike at the heart of the Pakistan Army in East Pak and apply pressure on them to surrender. The Bn was relieved on December 13 and concentrated at Kailashahar airfield by December 14, where it re-organised the fighting strength of subunits, prepared load tables for Heli-drop, redistributed arms and ammunition. This change in offensive mode, from standard infantry assaults to Heli drop, required flexibility in planning and execution of tasks in small teams and sub-teams without supporting arms. The Bn was airlifted in Dakotas to Agartala Airfield on December 15, 1971. Here, rehearsals of battle drills and small team actions were carried out. Due to the surrender of the Pakistan Army, our Heli drop plan was shelved.

As a subaltern, with theoretical knowledge of tactics and some knowledge of historic battles in Burma, Africa and Europe, the India-Pakistan War 1971 confirmed the highest standards of our glorious Indian Army, duly supported by the Mukti Bahini and the people of East Pakistan.

Image 1: Evidence of Rocket Hits on Bara Bungalow by Capt KL Gulati's Team

Image 2: Author (On The Right) with Capt VC Rajakumar, 10 Mahar at Maulvi Bazar College – In Front of Buildings Destroyed by Air and Artillery Shelling

12

Discard Pamphlet Teaching in War

Biren Borgohain

As a young officer, participating in the 1971 India-Pakistan War was a great opportunity for me. I'm nostalgic today – even after such a long time – as I relive those memories. From a tough field tenure in Jammu and Kashmir, I was posted to Assam Regimental Centre (ARC), Shillong – a beautiful Peace Station for training the recruits. As I had done the Weapons Course, I was posted as the Weapons Training Officer (WTO).

In 1971, the Pakistan Army had created a reign of terror in East Pakistan. One could see thousands of vehicles moving day and night on Guwahati-Shillong Road, carrying war materials – with half-on headlights at night. Given that Meghalaya and Assam were the worst affected states, and having witnessed the build-ups, all residents were understandably frightened and emotional. They unflinchingly supported and aided the soldiers in any manner imaginable. We also used to get curious questions from the people about the probability of a war, to which we gave vague answers.

Young Ideas

The refugees did not come alone; they were accompanied by young freedom fighters known as the Mukti Bahini, a band of Bengali Resistance Group who were directed to the ARC for the required Training. As a young WTO, and due to my ability to speak Bengali, I was put in-charge of their Weapons' Training, where I was to teach them minor tactics, long-range firing with an emphasis on stoppages in their weapons and quick rectification.

The boys were serious and committed, and continuously engaging with them was a great teaching and learning experience. The training was so important that the General Officer Commanding (GOC) himself came to the firing range, with the Commandant, to watch their firing. One day, while the boys were practicing firing the LMG at a distance of 500 yards, it started drizzling and I had to stop the firing, as per the teaching procedure, to protect the hot barrel from getting bulged. At that point, the GOC (Gen Gurbaksh Singh Gill) smiled and told me to continue firing and to forget about the 'pamphlet teaching,' saying that "these boys are going to fight a war and he will replace any number of bulged barrels," and thus the firing continued even in the drizzle.

It may be mentioned here that the Mukti Bahini boys travelled in foreign vehicles like Toyotas, Mercedes, Jeeps, and whatever vehicles they could get hold of – and all those were parked in front of my bachelor's room near our Mess. Two of these vehicles had bullet hole marks, which must have been fired at them by the Pakistan soldiers while fleeing. It's fortunate that no one was injured. In order to keep the car batteries in good condition, the cars were driven within the ARC campus on Sundays and I was given a joy ride. In fact, to my mind – with our Ambassador cars, it was indeed an interesting comparison. Those were the fond memories that I treasure till today!

The GOC's support was encouraging. Maj Gen Gill, GOC – 101 Communication Zone Area, Shillong – was a very adventurous and brave soldier. He wanted to fight the war on his terms – over and above his main Areas' Maintenance task. The GOC got the Area 'General Staff' Office converted into a war office and kept the staff extremely busy with updated information and maps marked ready for briefing. Our Centre Commandant, Col KS Brar, who was also the Station Commander, spent the majority of the time in Area HQ with the GOC, where they agreed to send a Company from the ARC to war. Therefore, an ad hoc coy was created from amongst the staff and sent under the command of Maj (now Col) YP Singh, the Officer Commanding Training of the Centre. The GOC, used to hop around in helicopters to various fronts to see the developments, but as luck would have it, during one of his operational trips he stepped into an enemy mine field and one of his leg was blown off. He had to be relieved of his command. What an irony of fate!

Bhupenda's Visit: Support to Army

In such a situation, prior to the war, famous multifaceted personalities like Dr. Bhupen Hazarika, then MLA, and subsequently recipient of Bharat Ratna, visited ARC to meet and encourage the soldiers. His visit was a spontaneous decision after our chance meeting in State Bank of India, Shillong, while I was in uniform collecting my salary. As per his wish, his visit to our mess was fixed on the same evening, after I spoke to the Commandant. Dr. Hazarika arrived in my room, duly escorted by our duty NCO at the gate. He addressed everyone and sang his famous songs, which he also sang at Kameng Frontier Division after the 1962 Chinese Operation, making the evening lively and memorable. I had the honour of singing alongside him.

The Indian Army fought war against Pakistan along with the Mukti Bahini and Dr. Hazarika instantly wrote and sang, "*Jai Jai Nabajato Bangladesh, Jai Jai Mukti Bahini, Bharatyo Xoinyor Hiote Rosila Moitrur Kahini …*," glorifying the joint co-ordination with both Mukti Bahini and the Indian Forces. He presented another beautiful song. "*Gonga Amar Maa, Podda Amar Maa, Amar Dui Chokhe Dui Joler Dhara Meghna Yamuna …*" – pouring his heart out. The lyrics, the meaning, the tune with his melodious voice, earned the best song award and he was honoured with the highest civilian award by the Bangladesh Government. Well, with the spirit of a soldier and a singer he was our pride of the nation!!

I had the privilege of witnessing and living all these moments firsthand in the Centre and on the War Front, and later in Sylhet following the surrender.

One particular incident made me feel sad and also proud of our young officers – a handsome 2nd Lt, was friends with a pretty girl who was the daughter of a Senior Officer, died in my vicinity, when an enemy mortar bomb landed near him; this left an indelible sad feeling in my heart …. Well, this is a part of a soldier's life. I remembered the caption … "*For Your Tomorrow We Gave Our Today*" … As the Operation area was not very far from Shillong, I frequently travelled to the front area with the Commandant, to visit our Company in action. We went to the Gorkha Rifles front on one such visits and saw casualties being evacuated in stretchers.

Leading a Convoy

I was leading a convoy to the front with logistical assistance. En route, I stopped the convoy to ensure that distances between two vehicles remained as planned, and that was the time when one of my next-door neighbour, from my village, saw me in battle dress and came up to me with a 'surprised and worried look'. I requested him not to talk about this at home or to anyone, as the family might get worried. He promised me he would not do so, but upon his return, he did exactly the opposite and informed the local villagers. Hearing him, many ladies came to comfort my mother, but my mother proudly said that "*my son has joined the Army for the safety of the country and he must do his job. We all should pray that they win and I am proud of my son*" – I bowed my head for my mother's brave attitude, having heard this on my return. Truly a great patriotic lady.

Following the surrender, I went along with the Commandant to Sylhet and en route noticed that all the bridges were heavily guarded and had positions dug in along with sharp fixed 'bamboo panjis', to act as obstacles for any enemy approach through the water. I also saw the great work done by IAF, who had destroyed the massive Meghna River Bridge, thereby completely disrupting the Pakistan Army's road movements. I took a photograph with my box camera. We also saw the bullet marks along the highway, as the IAF attacked the enemy convoy ... with precision!! The IAF had indeed done a great job during 1971. The news of capturing Sylhet and Dhaka, surrender ceremony and brave actions by the officers like Lt Gen Sagat Singh, who was instrumental in initiating the crossing of the Meghna River, and their Heliborne Operation with Gp Capt (later Air Vice Marshal) Chandan Singh, Vir Chakra – all these are exemplary stories now.

A Grateful Nation

We halted en route from Sylhet to see a large group of jubilant crowd waving and showing 'V' signs to us with their fingers. When the Commandant asked an elderly person as to how he feels about the action of the Indian Army, the grateful old man very humbly replied, "*We are eternally grateful to the Indian Army, so much so that we will not be able to repay even if we donate our skin to make their babies shoes.*" What a philosophical expression of gratefulness!

Assam Regimental Training Centre created history in the Indian Army by fighting a war in which the Company Commander, Maj YP Singh was awarded Sena Medal, and we proudly wore the 'Poorvi Star' Medal on our chests.

Image 1: Training of the Mukti Bahini

Source: news 18.com

Image 2: Mukti Bahini in 'Salda Nodi' Area

Source: moddb.com

13

The Belated Battle Honour: Raghupratap at Shyamganj

Ghanshyam Singh Katoch

Prior to the outbreak of the 1971 war, 1 JAK RIF was part of 350 Infantry Brigade, 9 Infantry Division located East of Kolkata. The brigade comprised of 1 JAK RIF, 4 SIKH and 26 MADRAS. The brigade was supported by PT-76 tanks of 45 Cavalry and a squadron of 63 Cavalry with T- 55 tanks.[1] As tensions rose before the 1971 War, 1 JAK RIF was involved in several operations on the border, as each side tried to improve their tactical postures. The most significant of these were the beating back of a Pakistani incursion across the border in pursuit of the Mukti Bahini on November 3, 1971, seizing a Pakistani Border outpost at Maslia on November 12/13, 1971, and defending it against five counter attacks by the Pakistanis (where the Pakistanis suffered 83 casualties).[2]

1 JAK RIF in Action

After the war was declared on December 3, 1971, the 9 Infantry Division attacked Jessore using 42 and 350 Infantry Brigades. Jessore was a designated fortress and cantonment town assigned to be defended by Pakistan's 107 Infantry Brigade.[3] The 2 Corps was operating against the Pakistani 9 Infantry Division – it's mission was to capture Jessore and Khulna, which would contribute to the success of the overall campaign.

The 350 Infantry Brigade at that time was being commanded by Brigadier HS Sandhu of the Punjab Regiment (who ironically was a classmate of the opposing brigade commander Brig Muhammad Hayat of 107 Brigade, who had 15 Frontier Force, 4 PUNJAB and 12 PUNJAB under his command). 1 JAK RIF was commanded by Lieutenant Colonel Surinder Kapur. The Companies were commanded by Major (later Brig) HD Pant, Major (later Brig) KK Khajuria, Major KHS Billauria and Major Sarwan Singh during the war.

Map 1: Plan of Advance of 9 Infantry Division

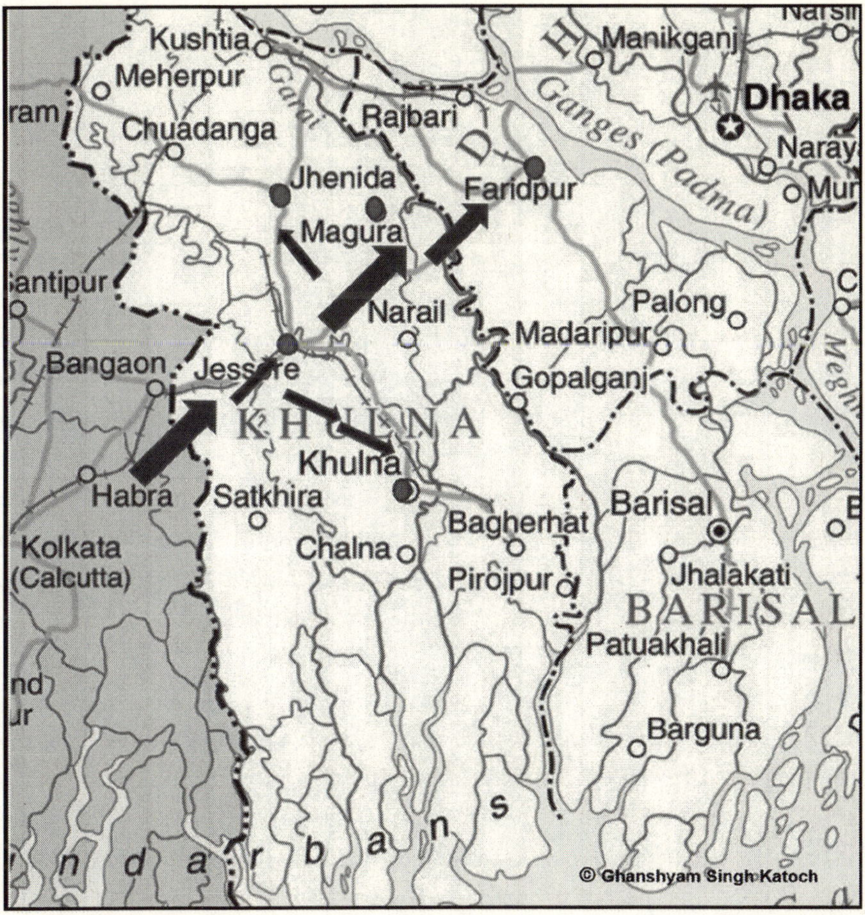

Map not to scale

Source: Annotated by the Author

The mission assigned to 9 Infantry Division was to capture Jessore by D-plus 7, followed by the capture of Khulna with a brigade group. Thereafter, the division was to be prepared to capture Jhenida or Magura and then secure the ferries in the Goalundo Ghat and Faridpur areas; Goalundo Ghat was a ferry point for Dacca and had been a major transportation hub for travel in eastern parts of Bengal and Assam before partition. A railway line was connected from Calcutta, and steamers departed from there for Dibrugarh in Assam. The divisional commander planned to launch a brigade on either side of the main Bangaon-Jessore axis. The weight of the advance was on the left flank that aimed to tackle Jessore from the 'unprepared' North. The 1 JAK RIF was tasked to advance to Jhingargacha, as a diversionary force from the South.[4]

The Pakistanis recognised that this was the shortest route and the most dangerous, and therefore destroyed the road/rail bridge on it. The General Officer Commanding (GOC) of 9 Infantry Division sent 42 and 350 Infantry Brigades on the central and northern approaches with 32 Infantry Brigade as reserve. Due to heavy resistance, 42 and 350 Brigades were stuck at Arpara and Burinda – although the 350 Brigade seized Burinda on December 5, the advance slowed.

Meanwhile, the Pakistanis misjudged that they were being attacked by an armoured brigade on seeing the dust raised by APCs of 7 PUNJAB (Mechanised), which was part of 32 Infantry Brigade, and vacated Jessore.[5] The Commanding Officer (CO) of 1 JAK RIF, advancing up from Jhingargacha and seeing no opposition, rushed 'hell for leather' along the road in a commandeered autorickshaw with his Forward Observation Officer (FOO), Intelligence Officer (IO) and four men for protection. After sometime, on hearing a loud bell of a fire engine from behind, the slow-moving rickshaw moved towards it. To his astonishment, Col Kapur saw that the fire truck was being driven by his Mechanical Transport Officer (MTO) – Captain Rajinder Chauhan and the truck was loaded with as many men as could clamber aboard.[6] The motley group continued and reached Jessore, which they found had been abandoned. Lt Col Kapur reported his progress to the brigade commander and was instructed to halt till they entered from the North. Major General MH Ansari, GOC Pak 9 Infantry Division, shifted his HQ to Magura while Brigadier Muhammad Hayat Khan, Commander of Pak 107 Infantry Brigade, moved towards Khulna.

After a planned withdrawal of 60 km, 107 Infantry Brigade had occupied a compact defended sector in the general area of Daulatpur on the outskirts of Khulna, astride the road and railway line between Jessore to Khulna. To the east, the defences rested along the Bhairab River, and 10 km to the west on interconnected marshes. Three battalions were defending the frontage – 6 PUNJAB was deployed to the east from Bhairab River up to the railway line; a Company of 15 Frontier Force Rifles (FFR) was deployed to the west of 6 PUNJAB and 12 PUNJAB, less two Companies, was further deployed to the west of 15 Frontier Force (FF). These battalions were supported by elements of 21 PUNJAB, Reconnaissance and Support, two tanks that had survived the battle of Garibpur and one artillery regiment; 22 FF was deployed in depth for counterattack.[7]

Map 2: Enemy and Own Deployment prior to the Attack

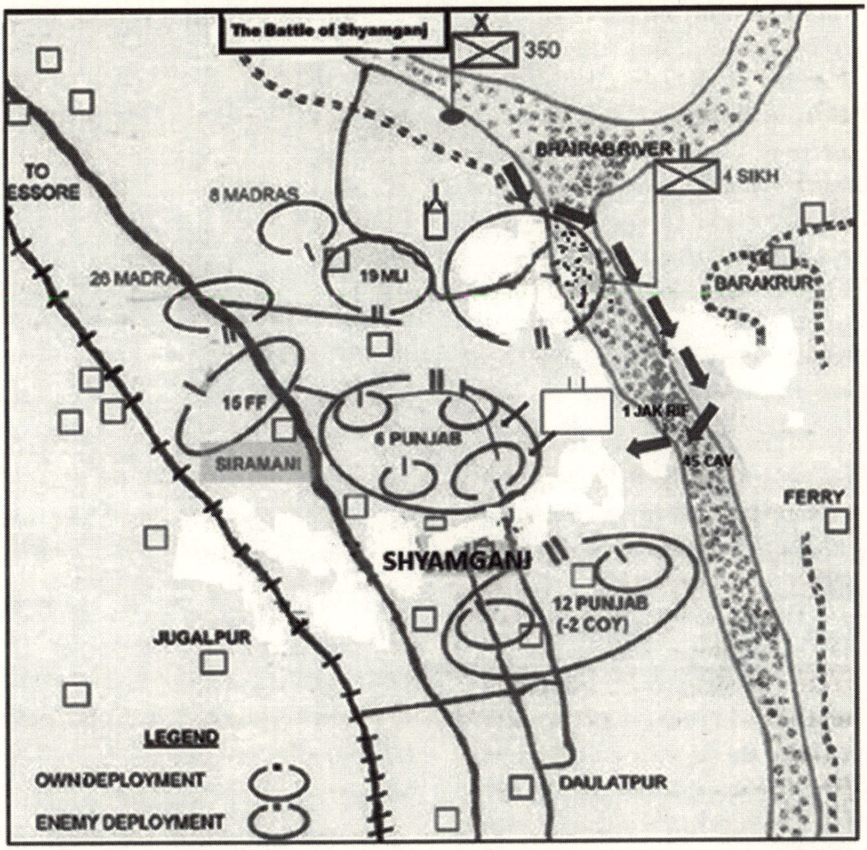

Not to Scale

Source: Derived and modified based upon map from article by Lt Gen RS Sujlana (Retd) "The Saragarhi Sikhs at Siramani"

The Daulatpur defences were based on the villages of Siramani, Shyamganj and the Road-Rail axis to the rear, which was a strategic position. As mentioned previously, to the east ran the Bhairab River with large stretches of marshy land towards the west, and the sea to the south. The defences were very well sited and could not be bypassed. On December 12, 1971, 9 Infantry Division launched a division level offensive on the Daulatpur axis. The attack failed to make much progress except establishment of a roadblock by an infiltrating column of 4 SIKH to the South of Siramani.[8] Thereafter, two battalions – 1 JAK RIF and 13 DOGRA were assigned the mission of capturing Shyamganj and Siramani. The Dogras captured Siramani in an attack launched at 0930 h on December 16, 1971[9] on the intermingled defences of 15 Frontier Force and 6 PUNJAB.

On the Shyamganj side, the earlier attack on 6 PUNJAB in an attempt to secure the Shyamganj ferry had floundered, with 19 MARATHA LI suffering significant casualties.[10] 1 JAK RIF was then tasked with the job of seizing Shyamganj by December 14, 1971, which was reorganising at Jessore. A troop of PT-76 tanks of 45 Cavalry were deployed to cross over the Bhairab River and provide enfilade fire support to 1 JAK RIF from the flank.[11] The defences, included concrete bunkers, well-built and organised. A dense undergrowth added to the difficulty of capturing the 300 yards × 600 yards objective. A two-phased attack was planned with two companies up.

The COs of 1 JAK RIF and 19 MARATHA LI (Lt Col Shamsher Singh), accompanied by the battalion IO 2/Lt UC Gupta, carried out a reconnaissance of the objective and collected information of enemy defences from close quarters. 19 MARATHA LI was in contact with the enemy and in the thick undergrowth, on orders, would give their battle cry of "*Chhatrapati Shivaji Maharaj ki Jai*" to jitter the Pakistanis to open fire and disclose their positions (which was successful). However, the enemy spotted the COs party among the thick betel leaf plantation and opened fire. Lt Col Kapur recounts that Lt Col Shamsher on his left shouted, "*I am hit;*" though the bullet grazed only his earlobe, he bled a great deal. Lt Col Kapur's radio operator asked him for a first field dressing. Col Kapur thought that it was for the CO of 19 MARATHA LI and told the operator that the Maratha CO was 'okay' with a graze wound. The operator then informed him that it is for the 'IO *sahib*' who appeared to be seriously injured. When Col Kapur looked to his right 2/Lt UC Gupta was dead on the ground in a kneeling position. A chance bullet had hit him in the centre of his forehead.[12] 2/Lt Gupta was posthumously awarded with a Mentioned-in-Despatches.

1 JAK RIF had established itself on a narrow strip on the Western bank of the River – from here they moved to their Forming Up Place.

Map 3: Plan of Attack by 1 JAK RIF

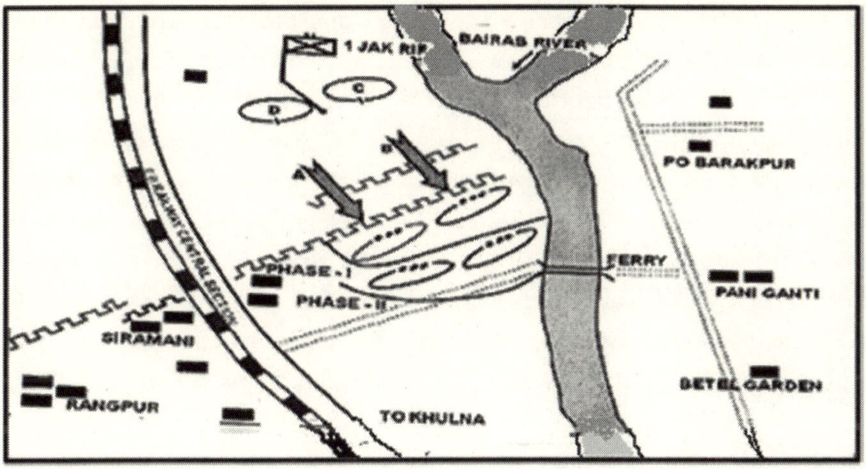

Not to Scale

Source: JAK RRC

The attack was scheduled to begin at dawn but was delayed due to the time required for the PT-76 tanks to swim across the fast-flowing Bhairab River, under their intrepid troop commander Capt Sharma.[13] At 0645h on December 15, 1971, the Battalion got into position for the attack. Preparatory fire support started at 0645h – 19 MARATHA LI provided the fire base. The CO of 1 JAK RIF had also created his integral firebase, by concentrating all 36 Rifle Grenade launchers at one place. The troops went across the Start Line at 0700 h in broad daylight.[14] Unfortunately, there was a line of eight to ten brick toilets with their doors towards the village and ventilating windows towards the attacker's side. The Pakistanis used these as makeshift bunkers to fire upon the advancing troops.[15] Bravo company – the left forward company – led by Major KK Khajuria came under intense fire immediately on crossing the Start Line, including Medium Machine Gun (MMG) fire. The company commander, who was leading from the front, was struck in both thighs by an MMG burst and fell incapacitated near the objective. The Regimental Medical Officer (RMO) Capt AL Sharma did an exceptional job in coordinating the evacuation of the Company commander and other wounded for which he was awarded a Sena Medal. After fierce fighting that resulted in numerous losses, the objective was finally seized and a foothold established.

Alpha company – the right forward company – led by Major HD Pant came under intense enemy fire as well, and the entire company had to crawl practically the entire distance to the objective. Thereafter, it just took 40 minutes of intense fighting to clear the enemy's forward line of defences. Charlie company – the reserve – leapfrogged forward to press on the attack. The enemy then retreated, occupying previously prepared positions in depth with concrete bunkers. By 0715h, Delta Company was also involved into the attack. The objective was finally captured by the afternoon of the same day. The RAGHUPRATAP had captured Shyamganj, after suffering heavy casualties; the route to Khulna now lay open. Orders were received for a ceasefire at 1500h on December 16. By this time, the attack at Siramani was also over.

The Winning Day and the Final Honour

In a brief ceremony held next day at Khulna, almost 5000 Pakistani troops, including Brigadier Muhammad Hayat, surrendered to Major General Dalbir Singh, GOC, 9 Infantry Division; the CO of 1 JAK RIF was involved in the pre-surrender negotiations and later in the acceptance of the surrender.

The Commanding Officer – Lt Colonel Surinder Kapur – was awarded the Mahavir Chakra in the 1971 war. The battalion was also awarded three Vir Chakras (Naik Rajinder Singh and Posthumously Lance Naiks Megh Raj and Magar Singh), four Sena Medals (the RMO Capt AL Sharma, posthumously, Naib Subedar Sukhdev Singh, Naik Inderjit Singh and Lance Naik Baldev Singh) and one Mentioned-in-Despatches to the handsome and dashing IO, late Second Lieutenant UC Gupta. The bulk of the awards, including the CO's Mahavir Chakra, were for the operations before December 3, 1971. In the tumultuous and fast-paced days following the events of the surrender, the Battle of Shyamganj got overshadowed as far as a battle honour or theatre honour to 1 JAK RIF. For this action 1 JAK RIF had paid a heavy price of 28 martyred and 72 wounded! They had, however, killed 68 and wounded 167 on the enemy's side.

In 1979, Army headquarters established an Appeals Committee, to evaluate cases of units that may have been overlooked for battle honours. Lt Colonel Surinder Kapur (who had taken premature retirement for personal reasons in 1978), was called to Army Headquarters to present the Battle of Shyamganj before the Committee. The Committee under Lt General KP Candeth heard the case, which was a summation of all that the Battalion had done before the outbreak of the war at Maslia and after December 3 at Jhingargacha and Shyamganj. The long-overlooked Battle Honour Shyamganj and Theatre Honour East Pakistan 1971 was finally awarded to 1 JAK RIF. It was a belated but well-deserved honour to the RAGHUPRATAP, for which the battalion had paid the ultimate price in blood. It had lost 49 men in total, including one officer and four JCOs, as well as a considerable number of injured.

Notes

1. Lt Gen RS Sujlana (Retd), "The Saragarhi Sikhs at Siramani," Mission Victory India, December 3, 2020, at https://missionvictoryindia.com/the-saragarhi-sikhs-at-siramani/. Accessed on April 24, 2021.
2. Lt Col SK Kapur MVC (Retd) narrated to the author on April 26, 2021. He said this figure was confirmed from the Mukti Bahini sources who got it from Chaugacha hospital.
3. Col JK Achutan (Retd), 'Deep Operations' Theory: 1971 Bangladesh Liberation War' IDR, at http://www.indiandefencereview.com/news/deep-operations-theory-1971-bangladesh-liberation-war/
4. Lt Col SK Kapur MVC (Retd), n. 2.
5. Lt Col KRS Jaswal (Retd) of 13 Dogras narrated to the author on April 26, 2021.
6. Lt Col SK Kapur MVC (Retd), n. 2.
7. Lt Gen HS Panag (Retd), "Why 1971 Battle of Khulna's outcome made me respect Pakistan Army Brigadier Muhammad Hayat." *The Print*, December 12, 2019, at https://theprint.in/opinion/why-1971-battle-of-khulnas-outcome-made-me-respect-pakistan-army-brigadier-muhammad-hayat/333930/. Accessed on April 25, 2021
8. Ibid.
9. Brig HS Lamba (Retd), "The Battle of Siramani," *The Tribune*, December 9, 2018, at https://www.tribuneindia.com/news/archive/column/the-battle-of-siramani-695672. Accessed on April 27, 2021.
10. Lt Gen Satish Nambiar (Retd), "Marathas In The 1971 Indo-Pak War," *Salute*, October 29, 2015.
11. Some accounts state that 1 JAK RIF crossed the Bhairab River and attacked from the Eastern flank. However, Lt Col Kapur the CO, whom the author interviewed, stated that the battalion did not cross the river and that was done by the troop of 45 Cavalry.
12. Lt Col SK Kapur MVC (Retd), n. 2.
13. Ibid.
14. Ibid.
15. Ibid.

14

First Artillery Unit of Bangladesh

OS Goraya

Between March and June 1971, Pakistani Forces launched many operations to suppress the rebel East Bengal Rifles (EBR) and East Pakistan Rifles (EPR), which had seized important communication centres. Though the Bengali units fought tenaciously, but they were severely handicapped due to lack of artillery support and requested the Indian authorities to raise a few of their own artillery units. The suggestion received a positive response. Two units of our Brigade (59 and 65 Mountain Regiments) were inducting newer equipment into service, that is the 75/24 Howitzer. Rather than back loading the old guns (18 x 105 Italian guns and 18 x 3.7 inch Howitzer) and ammunition to depots, they were put to a better use by being transferred to the Border Security Force (BSF) to boost the firepower of selected Border Out Posts (BOPs). Small units called 'Post Groups Artillery' were raised with four guns each, consisting of BSF personnel trained by instructors from artillery units. The remaining equipment was used to lay the foundation of future Artillery of Bangladesh.

The mantle to raise the first artillery unit of Bangladesh Forces was vested with the 59 Mountain Regiment. I issued comprehensive guidelines for this task, on behalf of my Commander. The training was to commence in the beginning of July and would involve live firing practices with an aim to make the unit ready for war in barely two months. Lt Col AC D'Silva – Commanding Officer of 59 Mountain Regiment – renamed this unit as 'Mujib Battery' and assigned the responsibility to 'Q' Battery commanded by Maj Ashok Kumar. The 'Q' Battery was operationally deployed at Harihardola, in support of Mukti Bahini holding the liberated salient of Salda Nadi, southwest of Agartala. It was decided to train the new unit there only. The training team was formed under Capt K Mahadevan assisted by 2/Lt Pradeep Kapoor, 2/Lt NS Rana and a few JCO instructors. The trainees consisted of 120 spirited Bengali youth, mostly raw civilians and few deserters from the Pak Army units, but no one was a gunner. In the normal course, it takes about six months to condition a raw recruit to an ordinary foot soldier and a year more to teach him different trades of gunnery; raising a unit from untrained civilian youth and making it fit for war in just two months necessitated the adoption of few shortcuts.

Language was a challenge, but the eagerness of the young trainees to study, removed this barrier. The trainees were deployed on each gun detachment with regular Indian gunners and learnt the trades on the job. The facilities and training conditions were far from satisfactory – it was both amusing and impressive to observe barefoot gunners doing gun drill in *Lungis* in the monsoon slush. Nonetheless, they learnt fast and within six weeks were ready for the first 'course shooting' with live ammunition. An Observation Post (OP) was established atop a commanding hillock overlooking the railway line from Kasba to Comilla through Mandabhag station under Pakistani control. The guns were deployed behind the same hill inside India. What added realism and excitement was the freedom to engage live targets like Pakistani static posts, moving patrols or defence works that were visible from the OP. The Pakistanis were in no position to retaliate. In a matter of two months Mujib Battery was declared 'fit for war'.

In the first week of September 1971, the operational responsibility of Salda Nadi salient was handed over to Mujib Battery in situ at Hariharkhola. During active war, the Battery formed part of 'Kilo Force' along with a Post Group Artillery of BSF and an Indian mountain regiment. This force operated in the area of Fenny and Chittagong from December 6 onwards. Mujib Battery also had the unique honour of firing the first ever gun salute to welcome Bangabandhu Sheikh Mujibur Rahman on January 10, 1972, when he arrived in Dacca from captivity. After the war, another Battery named 'Roshanara Battery' was formed with the Italian guns shed by 92 Mountain Regiment in April 1972, before they left for Talbahat; both these batteries were later merged to form 1Field Regiment of Bangladesh artillery.

15

Scintillating Saga of Sagat Singh

Probal Das Gupta

It was on December 9, 1971, that Lieutenant General Sagat Singh, the General Officer Commanding (GOC) of Indian Army's 4 Corps, stood at the precipice of history. The mammoth Meghna river was flowing as a barrier between an advancing Indian Army and a probable victory. The Pakistani Army, having destroyed the Ashuganj bridge, had 'supposedly' effectively ruled out the advance of the Indian Army over the 4,000 feet wide river, only to realise later that how wrong they were. The General, on the other hand, used heliborne operations to take a brigade across the river – an unprecedented action that would alter the course of the war overnight.

During the 1960s, Sagat's career ran parallel to the revival and rise of the Indian Army after the debacle in the 1962 India-China war. As tensions between India and China built up at Nathu La in Sikkim, Sagat set the tone by rebuffing China's aggressive stance in the period leading up to 1967. Five years after the Indian army had suffered substantial setbacks against the Chinese in the war, Sagat restored the nation's pride by inflicting two crushing defeats on the PLA, thus shattering the Chinese myth of invincibility.

Several times throughout his career, when confronted with difficult decision-making situations, Sagat behaved with unflinching faith in achieving extraordinary goals. In Sikkim, he knew the limitations of the Indian Army against the PLA and thus understood the importance of dominating the Himalayan watershed: especially since any lost ground could never be won back (he was proved right since Nathu La remains with

India whereas China occupied Jelep La – a feature India withdrew from under Chinese pressure).

In East Pakistan, Sagat was aware of the position, role and support of the Muktijoddhas and the people. The crossing of Meghna, against all odds, was one of the pivotal moments that decisively swung the advantage in India's favour, which resulted in India establishing a strong foothold in Dhaka. The initial objective laid out by the Army leadership for 4 Corps was to secure the area east of river Meghna. The political situation, however, had changed. US President Richard Nixon, a staunch ally of Pakistan, threatened to interfere in the war using USS Enterprise and the Seventh Fleet in the Indian Ocean. As a result, India wanted to end the war fast to avoid a lengthy conflict. Lt Gen Sagat believed that the capture of Dhaka was critical to win the war. Military commanders that challenge the status quo await thankless prospects of either inviting a proverbial Damocles sword to hand over their heads in case of failure or of leaving behind an envious, grudgingly appreciative fraternity in the event of success. Sagat was perpetually at odds with his seniors throughout his career.

By the end, several generals and military leaders contributed towards India's remarkable victory. However, in the context of its final outcome, Lt Gen Sagat's decision to cross the Meghna and surprise the Pakistani Army was of critical significance. The war was over by December 16 – a week after Meghna was crossed by Sagat's forces.

Noted political scientist John Mearsheimer termed the war as India's blitzkrieg. Sensing the importance of Dhaka, Sagat discussed the tasking for its capture with Lt Gen JS Aurora, the Eastern Army Commander, and was told that it depended on the progress of the offensive.[1] Lt Gen HS Panag writes that Indian Army's attrition style of warfare meant that Dhaka would be captured only after other places held by the enemy had been taken.[2] Sagat found the plan disagreeable but cleverly kept his cards close to his chest.

Sagat's mission throughout the war's planning stages was to secure the Meghna river line and isolate Sylhet. Therefore, no allocation was made for provision of inland water transport.[3] Before the war, Sagat did a reconnaissance of his launch pads and bases in Tripura. He invested significant time in war scenarios, investigating and pushing his field commanders to think about various plans and approaches. He maintained constant contact with his battalions in the area and quickly gauged the morale and mettle of his troops.[4] Sagat was quick to learn about the ability of Pakistani troops to dig in and display resilience to hold off attacks. He sensed that protracted war was a possibility that could engage Indian Army for months. Therefore, his conviction about the criticality of capturing Dhaka was reiterated. These aspects played a big role in shaping his aggressive thinking in the war, as events progressed.

By the time he arrived in Meghna, the importance of Dhaka appeared proverbially clearer to him than to any other lay observer on the 'far unseen bank' of the mighty river. Before the heliborne operation across Meghna, Sagat undertook a perilous helicopter reconnaissance of Bhairab Bazaar and adjoining Pakistani areas. His helicopter was targeted by machine guns, shattering the windshield and injuring him. However, he narrowly escaped death. While under treatment, the doctors advised Sagat a day's rest, but he was determined to achieve his mission; hence, he continued with the planning of the heliborne operation. On hearing the news that the Indian Army, under Lt Gen Sagat, had landed on the west bank of Meghna and was on its way to Dhaka, an elated Prime Minister Indira Gandhi ran through the corridors of her office, beaming with joy[5] – Sagat had swung the war in India's favour. Undoubtedly, Indian Armed Forces, supported by the Mukti Bahini and the population of East Pakistan, had worked together to set the stage for the decisive victory.

One of the determining characteristics that stood out in Sagat's career was his clarity of purpose. As the general's Aide-De-Camp (ADC) during the 1971 war, Maj Gen Randhir Sinh believes, *"His (Sagat's) knowledge of operational war was perhaps without parallel."* For a military leader who had never lost a war, Randhir Sinh says, *"He can be compared with the best generals of the first and second world wars."*

In 1971, Sagat sensed at an early stage of preparation that there was an inherent flaw in theatre plans and understood the importance of going for the jugular, which was Dhaka. In this case, his audacious sense of timing was a lesson in military leadership.

Sagat had constant professional differences with seniors throughout his career. Whether during the Goa operations or during his interactions with Lt Gen (later COAS) GG Bewoor over decisions at Nathu La, or while differing with Lt Gen Aurora's plans in 1971, Sagat believed he had a steadfast understanding of the situation developing on ground. More importantly, he acted on his military instincts and beliefs, sometimes defying expected protocols.

Could he have worked on repairing his relations with his bosses? What would have happened if he had decided to stick to the brief and hadn't crossed the Meghna river in 1971? History would have turned out to be different. Sagat thus proved that brilliance in war is a function of having the courage to act on one's belief and explore the unanticipated.

The story of Sagat serves as an inspiring beacon for general readers, students of history and leadership, military strategists, officers and troops. Why have we not produced more generals like him? (Barring a few exceptions). The answers could be many. One of which could be that though physical courage is rare, moral courage in military leaders is rarer. The credibility of this virtue rests in the words of a war veteran who is quoted in Randhir's biography on him: *"(Sagat's) His leadership was not only on the battlefield but over the minds and will of the people he commanded."*

Notes

1. Maj Gen Randhir Sinh, *Talent for War*, p. 126.
2. theprint.in/opinion/dhaka-pakistans-psychological-defeat-how-indian-military-commanders-won-1971/163216/.
3. Maj Gen Randhir Sinh, n. 1, p. 127.
4. Ibid., p. 136.
5. thedailyguardian.com/the-forgotten-general-who-never-lost-a-war/.

SECTION 3

Power of the Muktijoddhas and the Local Populace

16

Attack: Kalachara Tea Garden

M Harun-Ar-Rashid

Under cover of darkness on the night of March 25, 1971, the barbarian Pakistan Army launched its military might against the unnamed civilian population. The Father of the Nation gave the final message of Independence and for all-out resistance against the Occupation Forces until the last soldier was defeated. The entire Bengali Nation rose to the occasion and initiated the resistance phase of the War. After the massacre of civilians by the Pakistani Army on the 25th night, we, the Bengali officers and soldiers, knew in our hearts and mind that it was now or never to liberate the motherland. This overwhelming drive helped us to disregard military oath and protocols. We were fully aware of the consequences of staging such a revolt, which could result in court martial and subsequent death sentence. However, there appeared to be only one calling in the soul, and nothing else seemed to matter except "Freedom" at any cost. Through careful planning and much deliberation, troops of "C" company and my company of the 4th Battalion of the East Bengal Regiment successfully revolted under the leadership of Major Shafayal Jamil (Later Colonel) at Brahman Baria at around 0830 hours on March 27, 1971. Other companies and platoons located in far-flunged areas joined the unit by end of the day. Major Khaled Musharaf, Bir Uttam (Later Major General) joined the unit from Sylhet in the afternoon, and took over the command of the unit.

Immediately after the revolt, I was assigned to defend the southern side of the city on the home bank of river Titas, to stop any Pakistani move from Kumilla (Comilla) Cantonment side. The rest of the unit moved to Teliapara in Sylhet.

After defending Brahman Baria up to April 12, 1971, I was tasked to move forward and take up defence South of Akhaura in line Gangasagar-Ujanisar area. Pakistani advancing column contacted my defence at Gangasagar on the night of April 13, 1971. Since then, we fought a series of defensive battles at Akhaura, Kharampur, Azampur and Singerbil area. By end of first week of May 1971, I had crossed over to Narsingar (three kilometres North of Agartala Airport) Tripura, India, opposite Singerbil of Bangladesh, with remnants of my company.

By the end of June 1971, the strength of my company rose to about 300 men. Though the number of Freedom Fighters multiplied, we were severely lacking in weapons and equipment. Additionally, we faced a severe ammunition shortage due to our reliance on Chinese weapons. Until then, the Indian Army did not have any Chinese ammunition to help us. Due to these constraints, as well as the onset of the Monsoon season, the situation was not very congenial for launching any operation deep inside Bangladesh. At that time, our primary mission was to train and deploy volunteer Freedom Fighters and send them to Bangladesh for guerilla/minor operations. However regular forces also carried out limited operations like fighting/domination patrols, raids and ambushes close to the Border areas. During this period, operations of freedom Fighters more or less remained limited to "hit and run" actions against fixed defenses and other locations of Occupation Forces. By having extensive patrolling in Akhaura, Kharampur, Rajapur and Sigerbill area, we regained some control over the area. At this time enemy restricted their operations to day time only. From Narsingarh camp site it was easy for the Freedom Fighters to infiltrate into Bangladesh, as the bordering area was thickly vegetated and sparsely populated. Additionally, after crossing about a few thousand yards of land stretch, the great "Kalia Bill" east of Akhaura-Brahmanbaria rail line, which was not controlled by Pakistani forces, provided great flexibility to the Freedom Fighters. In fact, by June, Narshingarh corridor had developed into a very safe and popular crossing point for the Gono Bahini members of Number 2 as well as Number 3 Sectors.

As a result of the large number of Mukti Bahini members infiltrating through Narsingarh corridor and successfully carrying out operations in Dhaka-Kumilla (Comilla)-Brahman-Baria area, Pakistani authorities started taking action to close the gap. By mid-July, a Pakistani Battalion (31 PUNJAB) was deployed in the area and they deployed two companies with Battalion Headquarters at Akhaura. One advance company at Rajapur-Singerbil-Merashani area and another advance company was deployed at Kalachara Tea Garden factory area. These deployments were supported by a battery of Artillery based at Kodda area west of Akhaura. The enemy effectively controlled the area through these deployments and link/domination patrols. Mukti Bahini infiltration virtually came to standstill. On the other side, Indian authorities also imposed strict restrictions on us to undertake any operations from Indian territory, in fear of retaliation against Agartala Airport as well as Agartala Township.

By this time due to serious shortage of logistic support like accommodation, food, ammunition, communication equipment, etc., the morale of the Mukti Bahini was sagging. A few soldiers and Freedom Fighters deserted the camp. Only training activity at camps could not keep the fighters happy. As such, I felt a pressing need to conduct an operation that would boost the morale of my own troops, while also shattering the confidence of Occupation Forces located in the area. After the initial thoughts and appreciation, we decided to attack Kalachara Tea Garden area, as it was isolated from rest of the defended locations. The Tea Garden is located about 12 km North of Akhaura Railway Junction and on the East of Akhaura-Sylhet Railway line within the area protruding inside Indian Border. The South and East of the Garden was thickly vegetated with 3-4 feet high tea plants and other trees. The area is undulated, with heights varying between 15 and 20 feet. Capturing the area would reopen the previous route of infiltration for Freedom Fighters. After detailed patrolling and thorough reconnaissance, we established that a full company of Pakistan Army with one additional platoon of East Pakistan Civil Armed Forces (EPCAP) was deployed in circular fashion to cover the whole factory area. The location was logistically supplied from Akhaura and also supported by Artillery Battery located at Kodda west of Akhaura.

Planning

As per standard military equation, an attack on the company position would require more than a Battalion strength. Though I had about 300 men in my camp, but only one company strength weapon and another platoon strength equipped with assorted weapons from East Pakistan Rifles (EPR), Mujahid and Ansars. I also needed additional troops to establish blocking positions to stop any reinforcements to the area from Akhaura in the South as well as Mukundapur on the North. Significant constraints included scarcity of small arms ammunition for our Chinese weapons and the complete absence of indirect fire (Artillery/Mortar) support. Furthermore, an attack would require authorisation and coordination from Indian Army Authority which was very unlikely to be approved. This type of situation can result in the loss of morale among troops. In light of the overall situation, I was adamant about launching an attack against all adversities. My main strength was the urge of rank and file to undertake some operation that would shatter the confidence of the Occupation Forces in the area. Through extensive patrolling and other operations in the area over the last few months, we had also gained some familiarity with the terrain. Moreover, the population of the area was on our side. To compensate for the weapons shortages, I sought assistance from my neighbouring camp Commander Captain (later Major General) Golam Helal Morshed, Bir Bikrom. Captain Morshed was generous and loaned me two Light Machine Guns, two 2" Mortars and a thousand rounds of 7.62 (Chinese) Light Machine Gun ammunition. Captain Morshed also agreed to establish a blocking position at Mukundapur area, to block any reinforcement from the North. This support gave a tremendous boost to the zeal of my troops for the attack. Before launching the attack, we carried out extensive reconnaissance of the defensive area. We found out that three sides facing the Indian Border were extensively mined with anti-personal mines. The mines were also covered with low wire entanglement and bamboo spikes (*punjis*). In view of these obstacles, attacking the position from South, East and North was a difficult proposition. Moreover, Indian authorities also barred us from undertaking any operation from the Indian side.

With these factors in mind, we were left with only one option: launch the attack from the west, which was the rear side of the defence. The only approach route available to the objective area was the supply route followed by the Occupation Forces. Still, we decided to launch the attack from the West following the supply route. As we did not have any Artillery/Mortar support we decided to launch the attack at night during the hours of darkness. To overcome the shortage of men power, weapons and equipment we greatly emphasised on achieving surprise over the enemy. For achieving surprise, I also decided to break away from conventional rules and not lay any marked Forming Up Place (FUP), which is an essential organisation for deliberate attack. After evaluating all these factors, I decided to launch the attack on the morning of Tuesday, August 3, 1971. On that morning, moon rising time was around 3:30 am and we fixed the attacking time (H hour) at 3 am. The final plan was for one company plus platoon strength to launch the main attack from the west under my leadership. A section, led by Havildar Halim (Shaheed) was to establish a blocking position on the home bank of the canal facing Merasani, covering the railway bridge and block any reinforcements from the South. Captain Morshed was to establish another blocking position at Mukundapur to ward off reinforcements from the North. We left a section under command Subedar Rezaul at the base camp as reserve. This group was tasked to help either Havildar Halim's group or the main attacking group in case of emergency. As stated earlier, to avoid any loss of surprise we did not go for conventional marking of FUP. However, in the camp, we spent a lot of time practising how to form up before an attack. The local guides proved to be extremely valuable for reaching the objective on time and without much difficulty.

After briefing all the subordinate commanders, I felt that everyone was excited about the attack. I also addressed the Company, emphasising the value of surprise. Following the address, I felt that everyone was not only enthusiastic, but also very eager to accomplish the task. I was really overwhelmed and also surprised to see that no one was concerned about the shortage of weapons and ammunition. Everyone felt confident that the job could be done. However, I was certain that I was taking a significant risk. If anything goes wrong and we become trapped at any point during the process, extrication would be extremely difficult and we would have to suffer heavy casualties. However, I was determined to launch the attack and achieve success.

The Attack

Everything began moving according to plan on the evening of August 2, 1971. At approximately 2300 hours, we departed from the Narsingarh base camp and infiltrated into Bangladesh via Qasimpur. We took a lengthy detour and travelled via Akhaura-Qasimpur-Bishnupur-Ganeshpur-Shejamura-Ikartali - Kalachara.

Every platoon group had a local guide and they played a pivotal role in taking the group to their designated area. Fortunately, everything went smoothly, and we reached assembly area Shejamura at around 0145 hours, which was half an hour earlier then the schedule. However, our reorganisation for the attack took a little longer then schedule, as a result time was adjusted. We moved out of the assembly area in time and proceeded towards the objective. At this time, we faced a serious problem as we could not see the objective area through the under growth of tea plants and thick fog. As a result, we failed to locate the designated FUP. To our good fortune, we could hear the sound of sentry changing and some people talking in low voice. We were only 15-20 yards away from the objective at that moment. We instantaneously shouted "Joy Bangla". As planned, soldiers formed an assault line on the run and in no time they were on the objective. The enemy defence was taken completely by surprise. They could not even call for Artillery support, as the telephone line was cut off at the first instance. Few minutes later, enemy Artillery fired few shots, which fell on the eastern side of the objective. Perhaps it was their appreciation that the attack would come from the Indian side that prompted the Artillery to fire in that direction. My company soldiers overran the whole objective area by 0345 hours. It was too quick and resembled a peacetime attack exercise, as the enemy did not have any time to react. However, the position towards the East (enemy left forward platoon) opened up, but they failed to realise the direction of attack. As such, these fires were also not very effective. As the enemy platoon realised that rest of the defence had been abandoned by their colleagues, so they also abandoned the area after a few minutes.

LAYOUT OF KALACHARA TEA GARDEN AREA

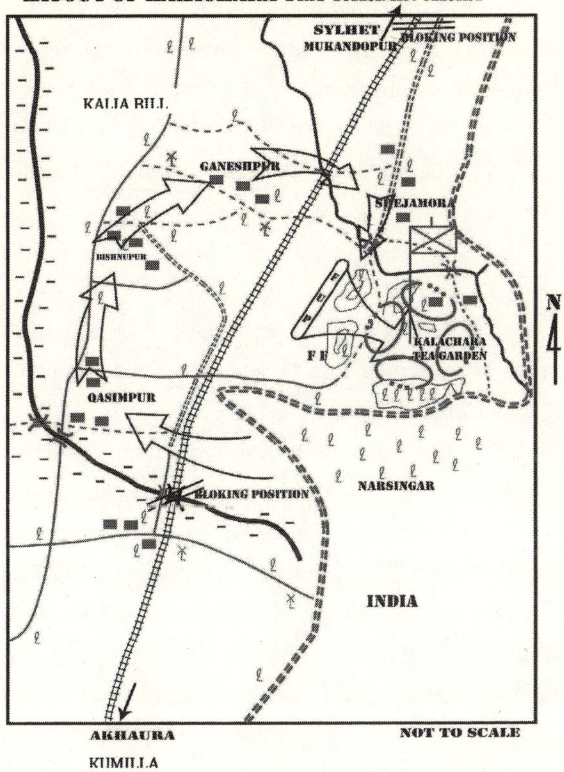

Reorganisation

After capturing the whole area, we realised that the area needs mopping-up, as most of the bunkers remained intact. By around 0530 hours, it was quite clear light and we could see the whole area. Lots of dead bodies and injured persons were scattered around the area. Our priority was to clear up all the bunkers. Unfortunately, we had to suffer some casualties during the mopping up process. Some of the enemy soldiers of the defence could not escape during attack and they remained inside the bunkers. While mopping up, enemy soldiers emerged from these bunkers, causing confusion among the attacking troops. The confusion lasted for about an hour or so. At this time, I also lost my runner who was also my wireless operator Sepoy Md Tajul, due to enemy fire. Nevertheless, by about 0630 hours, we were firmly in control and re-established command and control. Both the blocking positions at Mershani Railway Bridge and Mukundapur were subjected to intense enemy reinforcement pressure, but they held their positions until the end. Havildar Halim displayed extraordinary courage in holding the reinforcement group which was approximately the size of a company, with only one section. Four members of the attacking group were injured, and Sepoy Md Tajul, Freedom Fighter (FF) Rafiqul Islam Samir and FF Abdul Aleem were killed. Havildar Halim's group suffered two serious injuries.

Outcome

By all standards, the attack was a complete success. Not only did we capture the entire Kalachara Tea Garden area, but we also seized a large quantity of weapons and ammunition including 2 × MGIA3, 4 x (7.62 mm) LMGs, 15 × Rifles and approximately 22,000 rounds of ammunition including 2,000 grenades. We also captured a reasonable amount of rations, blankets and clothing. We captured 12 Prisoners of War (POWs), seven of whom were regular soldiers and five of were EPCAP members. The senior JCO (Junior Commissioned Officer) of the Enemy Company was also captured as an injured person. According to standard military equation, attacking one company strength position with only one company plus troops is impossible. Particularly with such shortage of arms and ammunition and no indirect fire support. More so, the defensive locations were located on higher ground than the attacking troops. If the attackers lost surprise and the enemy opened fire before reaching the objective, the result could have been catastrophic for the attacking troops. The determination of all ranks and their courage played significant role in achieving the success against all odds. The courage and valour shown by few soldiers was unprecedented, particularly by Havildar Halim (Later Shaheed during Chandrapur attack), Naib Subedar Gias, Naib Subedar Rezaul, Havildar Monir, Civilian Mizan, Abul Khair, Dhan Mia and Jasim (Gorilla). Sepoy Md Tajul, FF Rafiqul Islam Samir and FF Abdul Aleem were all elevated to the status of *Shaheed.* We also had a few injured persons. One of the injured soldiers had 3 to 4 bullet hits in his abdominal area and was bleeding profusely. Unfortunately, we had no medical support with us, as such were trying to shift him to Agartala Hospital as soon as possible. He was unwilling to leave his companions and die in an unknown environment. To achieve this, we broke a door of an abandoned house nearby and made an improvised stretcher to carry him. While leaving, he held my hand firmly and said, "*Sir last few months I fought under you with other colleagues, but you are now sending me away. I am certain that I will die either on the way to hospital or in hospital. My earnest request to you is that I should be buried in my own land for which I am shedding this blood.*"

I promised him that I would do everything possible to fulfil his final wish and bury him in his own free motherland. It is unimaginable to think how a mere soldier could love his motherland so dear. He was finally handed over to Bangladesh Admin Headquarters Agartala, for admission to Hospital and subsequent follow up. Unfortunately, due to service requirement, I had to move out of that area during the first week of September 1971. I am not sure whether he survived or died. It pains me tremendously that, due to my Unit's obligations and the circumstances of the war, I was unable to ensure a valiant soldiers' dying wish. It was also my great misfortune that I failed to record his particulars due to my consistent need of command attention following the attack. I will never forget that moment of bonding with him and my appreciation of his valour and ultimate sacrifice for an independent motherland.

Bangladesh Nation owes a lot to these valiant fighters for their selfless and gallant contribution in achieving freedom for the Nation. The success of the attack gave tremendous boost to the morale of my troops. Pakistani forces never tried to reoccupy the Tea Garden area, as such the area remained liberated till the end of the War. Following the area's capture, the route for infiltration of "Gono Bahini" into Bangladesh was reopened and remained so till the end. We also got valuable information from the captured POWs on the deployment of the Pakistani troops in the area and also state of their morale. The captured soldiers informed us that they had no idea that they were fighting against Muslims. The authorities always briefed them that they were fighting against Indian Hindus. Indeed, they were taken aback when they heard the sound of Azan (Prayer Call) in the camp upon their arrival at the base camp. The captured soldiers expressed their regret for fighting a false and unjust war. We turned over the POWs to Indian Authorities for subsequent disposal.

Though I did not intimate anyone in the hierarchy about the attack earlier, yet the news of the success spread to all concerned within no time. The Indian authorities were very alarmed, as the fire fight broke out at the dead of the night. However, as nothing was happening from their territory, they felt comfortable. After learning of the success, Number 2 Sector Commander Major (later Major General) Khaled Mosharrof, Bir Uttam along with "D" Sector Commander (Indian) Brigadier Shah Beg Sing visited the base camp in the afternoon of August

4, 1971. Brigadier Shah Beg Sing expressed dissatisfaction for launching the attack without consulting Indian authorities, but congratulated every one for the success. On August 4, 1971, Headquarter Number 2 Sector issued a special Situation Report (SITREP) to Bangladesh Forces Headquarters' at Kolkata highlighting the success of the operation (Annexure 'A').

Annexure 'A'

SITREP of HQ No 2 Sector to BDF HQ dated 04 August 71

UNCLASS

~~SECRET~~

SPECIAL SITUATION REPORT

OPS IMMEDIATE

HQ No. 2 Sector
Bangla Desh Forces
BD/0002/G
August 71

To: Control Room

Info: HQ Bangla Desh Forces - 2 copies. 1 copy may please be sent to C-in-C.

Subject: Over the Dead Bodies

1. The enemy defence position at Kalamchari tea garden near Northern Comilla was a headache for the 'Mukti Bahini' and the fire fight between the 'Mukti Bahini' and the West Pakistani intruders was a regular feature in that area for over a month. To save them from regular harassment by 'Mukti Bahini' the enemy fortified their defence by making bunkers and pill boxes with over head cover without gauzing the courage and dash of the 'Mukti Bahini' who can storm any fortified defence of the enemy even with 303 Rifle and hand grenade.

2. At about 2100 hours on 02 August 71 a small troop of 'Mukti Bahini' without any fire support attacked that enemy position occupied by a coy. Fierce fighting for about 3½ hours continued. Enemy used her artillery and mortar besides the heavy automatic weapons to keep the 'Mukti Bahini' at bay. But the 'Mukti Bahini' with sheer courage, valour and with dogged determination drove the attack in and destroyed ten bunkers with hand grenades to flush the sacred soil of Bangla Desh from the occupation army. The fleeing enemy left behind 50 dead bodies and numerious injured to polute the pure air of Bangladesh and to be happy feast for the vulture and jackels. Those few who ran away from the defence must have been slain by the locals. The 'Mukti Bahini' captured many weapons including MG1A3, automatic rifles and over twenty thousand ammunition. Other captured items includes every thing issued to Pak Army with few maunds of food etc. The Mukti Bahini also captured 2 prisoners. Our casualty is only 2 dead and 4 injured.

Comd
(Khaled Musharraf)

17

Calculated Brutality: The Ordeal

Shamsher M Chowdhury

In 1971, I was a Lieutenant in the Pakistan Army and was posted in 8 East Bengal Regiment located at Chittagong (now Chattogram). This allowed me to experience the various events at ground zero, which eventually culminated in the birth of Bangladesh as an Independent State.

Where it All Started

It was midnight March 25, 1971, and as usual, I was on road patrol duty near the Chittagong Cantonment along with my 12 sepoys and four rifles. As I approached the Cantonment area, I clearly heard sounds of tremendous firing coming from inside the Cantonment; thereafter, I got out of my vehicle to assess the situation. Sensing something wrong, I immediately called my Unit and briefed Duty Officer Captain Oli Ahmed about the assault. Soon after that, Havildar Moniruzzaman, from the East Bengal Regimental Centre (EBRC), came rushing to me. Trembling in shock, he said that 20 Baluch Regiment of the Pakistan Army had attacked EBRC and killed the Chief Instructor (CI) – Lieutenant Colonel MR Chowdhury, who was a Bengali Officer. Along with the CI, some JCOs and innumerable recruits, who were all sleeping in their barracks had also been killed; several Bengali Officers had also been arrested. Moniruzzaman had managed to escape with five sepoys. On hearing this, I immediately rushed to my battalion that was located at Solashahar Market near the city and passed the information to Captain Oli Ahmed. Soon afterwards, Major Ziaur Rahman, the Second-in-Command of our Battalion, mutinied against the Pakistan Army and assumed command of the battalion – he arrested the Commanding Officer and four others of the Pakistan Army. They were eventually eliminated by our rebellious soldiers.

Realising that we were badly outnumbered and were vastly under equipped to face an attack by the Pakistan Army, it was decided to move the battalion to a safer place outside the city. Accordingly, 8 East Bengal under Major Ziaur's command, left its lines and marched on foot throughout the night and reached Kalurghat area – a few miles outside the city limits on the Chittagong-Cox's Bazar road. On the way, we were joined by Captain Harun Ahmed Chowdhury of the East Pakistan Rifles (EPR), who had come from Kaptai after having revolted there. We established our base camp in a village called Payiya. The other officers with us were Major Mir Shawkat Ali, Captain Khalequzzaman Chowdhury, Captain Sadek, Captain Oli Ahmed, and Lieutenant Mahfooz. We had 300 men with us, including JCOs, NCOs and sepoys, all Bengalis. On the afternoon of March 26, Major Ziaur Rahman made us all take an oath to *"fight for the independence of Bangladesh and be prepared to sacrifice our lives, if necessary"*.

Operation Ready

My first major operation was on March 29 – when I led a platoon into the heart of the city and took up position at Ispahani Hill near Askar Dighi, which was within small arms and mortar range of the Chittagong Circuit House – the Headquarters of the Pakistan Army. We had a heavy exchange of fire with the Pakistan Army from Ispahani Hill; I shelled the Circuit House with my mortars. In the evening, the Pakistan Army tried to surround us; however, since we were running out of ammunition, we had to retreat and return to Kalurghat. The fact that we fought right inside the city, shaking the Pakistan Army, without suffering any no casualties, was a big victory for us. Subsequently, we heard from Radio intercepts that at least four Pakistan Army men were killed and about a dozen more injured.

Our next objective was to build up defences at Chowk Bazar to obstruct the only route which the Pakistan Army could use for reaching Kalurghat.

At Chowk Bazar

The following morning, I heard gunfire in a nearby village. Locals came and informed us that two Pakistan Army commandos had entered the Boalkhali village nearby and were killing the villagers indiscriminately. I took ten of my men and went there. Soon we located the Commandos and in the exchange of fire that followed, both the commandos were killed. We seized a map, weapons and a piece of paper from them, which showed that they were from the 3 Commando Battalion of the Pakistan Army – the commandos were part of a force commanded by Major Mannan, a Bengali Officer. Next day, Captain Harun joined us at Chowk Bazar with a platoon of EPR troops and plenty of arms and ammunition, including Second World War vintage 'Vickers' Heavy Machine Gun.

On March 31, the Pak Army tried to break through our defences but failed to breach our strong defences. However, the Pakistanis were not ready to surrender so easily. On April 4, the Pakistanis launched an attack with two companies, this time supported by tanks. We were left with no other alternative but to get into a street fight. Fortunately, at that moment our mortars came to our rescue. In the street fight, some casualties were inflicted on the enemy. We suffered no casualties. Being outnumbered and the impossibility of defending, we had to withdraw from Chowk Bazar and return to Kalurghat.

At Kalurghat

At Kalurghat, our Battalion defended the bridge by establishing defensive positions on both sides. With such a small number of troops at our disposal, we could not afford to launch frontal offensive operations and it was decided that we would follow the tactic of 'hit and run'. At the same time, we built a strong defence at Kalurghat bridge. Our hit and run tactic worked extremely well!

On April 7, we saw some men of the Pakistan Army occupying an under-construction cinema hall near Ispahani Jute Mill, not very far from Kalurghat bridge. Without losing time, Major Mir Shawkat and I launched a joint operation against them. He fired on the enemy with his automatic weapon from a close range, inflicting major casualties on them. I fired three 83 mm Blendicide rockets into the room that the army was occupying – the rockets rocked the room! Not a single man of the Pakistan Army managed to escape alive. I lost my sepoy Naeb Ali in this operation; he died a hero, one of the first *shaheeds* of the Bangladesh Liberation war. The local people accorded him a befitting funeral.

On April 5, the Pakistan Army tried to attack our position at Kalurghat. Captain Harun with his force beat them back. They withdrew by four miles and took up position near a tannery factory on the Kaptai Road.

The Ordeal Day(s)

Things took a dramatic turn for me on April 11!

It was a bright morning. Captain Harun, Shawkat Hussain (a student of Chittagong University), Shawkat Alley (of Dhaka University), Fazlur Rahman (a local student) and Mustafa Hashmi (a cadet from the Marine Academy) were all with me. These young boys had been with us from the beginning. We had given them basic training on weapons and they had taken part in all the actions we had fought till then.

It was about 8:00 am when we heard heavy firing somewhere quite close. Suddenly, we saw a large number of Pakistan Army troops advancing towards us. I ordered my troops to open fire and take defensive position inside a bunker – Captain Harun was positioned inside a guard room and was firing on the advancing enemy. The Pakistan Artillery was also shelling our positions heavily and Captain Harun got hit; he fell on the bridge; I asked my troops to move him to the rear immediately. I was providing cover fire for Harun as he was being evacuated. Soon after, I realised that we could not stay there much longer and asked my troops to start retreating. I informed them that I would join them soon.

After my men withdrew, I exited my bunker and began firing at the enemy while standing in the open. It was at this point that I was hit. I collided with the bridge. I initially had no idea where the bullet had struck me, but soon discovered that it was on my left thigh. I was bleeding profusely. I tried to get up but could not due to lack of strength in my right leg. There was nobody to evacuate me, as all my men had withdrawn by then. I braced myself for death as the Pakistanis approached. Surprisingly, the Pakistanis chose to take me as a prisoner rather than kill me. I was subjected to kicks, blows and the worst possible verbal abuse. Army troops picked me up and took me to the Martial Law Headquarters at Chittagong Circuit House. The authorities decided to give me some basic medical treatment. I was then sent to the Naval Base Hospital at Chittagong. There the doctor discovered that the bullet had entered through my left thigh, pierced right through my stomach and lower abdomen and crushed my right hip bone. In fact, it was still lodged on my right hip. The same night I was operated and the bullet was taken out.

I was shifted to the Chittagong Combined Military Hospital (CMH) three days later. On the way to the CMH, two Sepoys of the Pakistan Army tried to choke me to death. They had also been wounded in action and were being transferred to the CMH. God bestowed His mercy on me once more, and I survived.

The same night, while I was lying on my bed at the CMH, Major Meher Kamal of the Pakistan Army attacked me and stabbed me repeatedly with a bayonet. He stabbed me on the chest and on my cheek right below my left eye, all the time calling me a traitor. On this occasion, a Nursing orderly came to my rescue.

Around April 24, I was flown to CMH Dhaka and was left there without any treatment except for changing the dressings.

After a few days at Dhaka CMH, I was taken to the Field Interrogation Centre (FIC) for interrogation, where I was subjected to ten sleepless nights. Their contention was that we had planned this whole mutiny over a long period of time in connivance with the Awami League leadership and with India. Finally, I asked for paper and pen and wrote down my ninety-page confessional statement. I admitted that we did had some meetings with local Awami League leaders in Chittagong, but never had anything with anyone from India.

On May 19, I was shifted to the Prisoner's Camp Number 1, located inside the Cantonment. This place was a scene of 'brutality beyond imagination.' People were being mercilessly tortured by the Pakistan Army. I was subjected to the same treatment, even in my wounded condition. I was beaten so badly that I could not have my food for a couple of days. This was standard procedure. There were many prisoners in that camp. However, I was the only officer taken prisoner from the battlefield. The rest were arrested either from their houses or from their places of work. No one was spared the brutality unleased by the Officers in-charge of the Camp – a top Bengali civil official was actually beaten to death inside the camp. The food that we were given was of minimum subsistence level; however, we needed to eat to survive.

Around mid-July, all the officers were shifted to the Sher-e-Bangla Nagar prisoner's camp. Here, the living conditions as well as the quality and quantity of food, were much better. We were also allowed to have food brought from our homes, and even our families were allowed to visit us once in a while.

The Final Leg and India's Intervention

At the end of August, the Pakistani authorities offered me a chance to become a State Approver, in return for which they would not award me the death sentence, although they would still try me in a military court for waging war against Pakistan. However, I flatly refused. On September 1, I was issued with a charge sheet, containing six charges, the first of which was Mutiny, meaning a 'death sentence'!

I, then mentally prepared myself for the worst, but was never afraid. I knew what I had done was right. On November 19, my parents were allowed to see me in the prisoner's camp. In the course of the meeting, my father said that he had been approached by the Pakistani authorities with a suggestion, that I accept my guilt and seek mercy from the President of Pakistan and pledge my loyalty to Pakistan. If I agreed to this, I will be spared the death penalty. I explained to my father that I had committed no wrong for which I should seek mercy. I stood firm in my decision and was prepared to face the consequences. My parents must have been pained at my decision but they respected my resolve.

On November 28, I was moved to solitary confinement in preparation for my trial in a Military Court – however, the trial never occurred!

Everything changed on December 4, when India joined the war in our support. From early morning, Indian Air Force aircrafts were playing havoc in and around Dhaka. After the second or third day of the war, the Pakistan Air Force was barely operational.

I anticipated that it would only be a matter of time before the Pakistan Army laid down their arms and Bangladesh Mukti Bahini proudly marched towards the city of Dhaka. My dreams came true on December 16. At that time, I was in the Cantonment; we were all shifted there after our building in Sher-e-Bangla Nagar had been hit by the Indian Air Force on December 9 and caught fire.

We received the news of the surrender of the Pakistan Army on December 16 with 'jubilation beyond description'. The false pride of the Pakistan Army, their sadistic ego and the war mania they were nursing had come to an end. Rarely in Military History one can find such disgrace and shame which the Pakistan Army had to suffer.

On the December 17, I proudly walked out to freedom and set foot on a liberated and an Independent Bangladesh. The damage done to me by the Pakistani Army on April 11 never healed. My right hip was shattered and shortened as a result of the lack of treatment. I still have to walk with some support. For me, however, my physical disability is a source of pride because it embodies the history of our glorious Liberation War!

18

Operation Kilo Flight

Shamsul Alam

I graduated from Pakistan Air Force Academy, Risalpur in July 1967. I escaped from West Pakistan on June 3, 1971, while serving in No. 6 Squadron Pakistan Air Force (PAF) Base at Chaklala, to join the Bangladesh freedom struggle. While escaping, I was captured upon landing at the Dhaka Airport and was sent to military concentration/prison camp at Dhaka cantonment, where I was subjected to severe physical torture during the interrogation process. After prolonged interrogation, a charge sheet was issued against me in July 1971; if I was found guilty by Pakistan Military Court, then I would have been awarded death sentence for treachery! In mid-August 1971, I made a second attempt and successfully escaped from the Pakistan Military Prison Camp, by crossing over to Agartala, India, and finally reported to the Bangladesh Government in exile in Kolkata. The rest of the story of the 1971 War would be shared during this deliberation.

I was one of the pioneering officers in the formation of Bangladesh Air Force in India named as "KILO FLIGHT", which was inaugurated on September 28, 1971, at Dimapur, India, and comprised of three ex-PAF officers and six licensed civilian pilots from the Ex-PIA and Pakistan Plant Protection Department. The Kilo Flight was inaugurated by Air Chief Marshal PC Lal of the Indian Air Force, in the presence of Group Captain AK Khondker (Second-in-Command of our Armed Forces/Mukti Bahini during liberation war), Sqn Ldr Sultan Mahmood, Self, Flt Lt Badrul Alam, Capt Khaleque (Ex-PIA), Capt Sattar (Ex-PIA), Capt Muqueet (Ex-PIA), Capt Shahab (Ex-PIA), Capt Akram (Ex-Plant Protection Pilot), Capt Sharfuddin (Ex-Plant Protection Pilot) plus 58 airmen of various technical trades of PAF.

Training for Action

Kilo Flight started its journey with one DC-3, one DHC-3 Otter and one Aluettee-3 helicopter. The aircraft was assigned to the following flying crews for conversion training:

- **Otter:** Self, Capt Akram (Late), Capt Sharfuddin (Late) and Flying Instructor Flt Lt Ghoshal (IAF).
- **Aluette-3:** Sqn Ldr Sultan Mahmood, Flt Lt Badrul Alam, and Capt Shahab and Flying Instructor Flt Lt Singla (IAF)
- **DC-3:** Capt Khaleque (Late), Capt Sattar, Capt Muqueet and Flying Instructor Flt Lt Chowdhury (IAF).

Otter conversion flying training began immediately upon completion of brief technical training in early October 1971. After completion of solo stage flying and long day and night navigation training, sorties were flown and was concentrated on long low-level night flying missions covering a flying duration of 7-8 hours.

By the first week of November 1971, the Otter aircraft was fully modified with the following armaments: Two Under Wing fixed Rocket Pods each carrying 7 Air To Ground Rockets – the right Door was removed where twin barrel 303 browning guns were installed; at the tail end the floor was cut open to install 3 bomb racks – each rack carrying 4 x 25 pounds incendiary type bombs (a total 12 bombs).

Without wasting much time, our live armament training mission started and I had to achieve almost 90 per cent Rocket Hits within the inner circle of a Parachute target during both day and night training missions. This was accomplished using 'trial and error method' without any gun sight. This had to be accomplished following a lengthy navigation flight of approximately 8 hours at very low-level night flying, identifying the Parachute as dummy target spread over various hill tops and firing rockets at them in pairs at the end of each long night navigation mission. Night after night, these missions were flown to achieve the highest level of accuracy, safety and timely arrival at the targets.

Time for the War

Around mid-November 1971, both Otter and Helicopter crews were called in by Gp Capt Chandan Singh, Base Commander, IAF Base (Jorhat), to announce the D-Day and assign our targets. The D-Day was November 28, 1971, and the Otter aircraft was tasked with destroying Chittagong Fuel Refinery Storage Tanks of Eastern Refinery, while the Alouette Helicopter was tasked with destroying Godnail Aviation Fuel Storage Tanks, Narayangonj. The Time Over Target (TOT) for both aircraft was fixed at 05 past midnight, with Otter aircraft night recovery at IAF Kumbhirgram Airfield. Full intelligence briefings were given to us with target pictures and Chittagong Airfield pictures. During our intelligence briefing, we were assured that there were no anti-aircraft (Ack-Ack) guns positioned at Chittagong Airfield and we would experience 'no blackout' of Chittagong City and Port areas. This simplified our night attack planning, as our targets, the fuel storage tanks of Eastern Refinery in Chittagong were located very close to Chittagong Airfield.

As per our final briefing, the Otter aircraft under my command, was to be positioned at Koilash Shahar— a 3,000-foot plant protection airstrip, and the Helicopter was to be positioned at Teliamura for the final mission. Both the aircraft left Dimapur Airfield on November 26, 1971, for their respective staging posts.

Working backwards, I prepared my flight plan to reach my Target at 05 mins past midnight, with a start-up time of 7:45 pm. The aircraft was fully manually refuelled at Koilash Shahar by the IAF contingent. We passed the uneventful nights of November 26 and 27, and had a hearty breakfast on the morning of November 28 living in tents. While I was giving the final briefing to my crew for our night mission on November 28, at about 4:30 pm, an IAF Flying Officer entered my tent and handed me a copy of a typed signal which read "Operation Kilo Flight Mission is Postponed till further order. Remain at your Station" – this came as a shock to us!

Our long wait was over, when on December 3, 1971, the same IAF Flying Officer entered my tent at about 5:30 pm and handed me another Signal copy which read, "Operation Kilo Flight Mission is 'On' Tonight – All other briefings are as before."

On the targeted date, we got airborne at about 8 pm in the darkness of the night initially flying at 1,000 feet. The route planned was simple during the outbound journey. Till we hit our first outbound check point at the Bay of Bengal shoreline, I shared the flying segment with Akram in order to jointly monitor our flying parameters. We were depending on our only navigational instrument, Directional Gyro (DG) and standby Compass, maintaining our plan under accurate heading, speed and height. During this journey we had no ground check point to compare our route to our map, and our passage was obscured by winter fog and passed through jungle hilly terrain. We flew due south until we hit the coastline of Bay of Bengal. We kept on lowering our altitude from 1,000 feet to 500 feet to avoid PAF radar detection and by the time we hit the coastline we were about 100 feet, turning left for Chittagong. Upon hitting the coastline, I took over the control and turned left heading towards Chittagong Port lowering our height further to about 50 feet. Contrary to our intelligence briefing, we found that no city lights were visible. On our right, we noticed few ocean vessels berthed/tied together at outer anchorage point emitting some lights. Now I was maintaining my heading, speed and height and monitoring my elapsed time!

I began gradually pulling up after crossing our Zero Hours, and Chittagong Airfield was clearly visible against the shinning moonlight. Just few seconds later, I was able to see the shining fuel storage tanks of Eastern Refinery, Chittagong! Identifying my first attack target, I pulled up the aircraft with full power and went into dive for my first attack, clearly aiming for the Fuel Storage tank with a steady attack dive and firing my first pair of rockets. As I arose from the dive, I could clearly see our pair rockets hitting target. There was no explosion! I came in for second attack, fired the second pair of rockets, hitting the targets and pulled up for the third dive. Again, there was no explosion. As I was preparing for the attack, my co-pilot Akram was distracted by streaks of light gushing past our right wing. We were under fire from deadly "Ack-Acks" from Chittagong Airfield. To our utter surprise and horror, the entire Chittagong Airfield was fortified with AD guns which were now continuously firing at us.

Crossing my finger, I launched my third attack, dodging the "Ack-Ack" fire and aiming at fuel storage tanks, firing pair of rockets, hitting the tanks directly. As I pulled up, I heard a thunderous explosion. As I was progressing with my 4th attack, a huge ball of fire lit our entire cockpit. Thrilled with joy we pressed on with our 4th, 5th and 6th attacks hitting our targets persistently and finally headed towards the sea making few orbits to see for ourselves from afar, the towering inferno of Eastern Refinery fuel storage tanks. During the course of our rocket attacks, I did not hesitate to command my bombardier to drop bombs in pairs and asked my gunner to continuously strafe from his side guns at random during every recovery from our dive. We accomplished our given mission successfully. As we headed on our return journey, both our gunner and bombardier came to our cockpit to watch the fireball on our right, which still lighted our entire cockpit as we flew west to our next turning point for Kumbhirgram Airfield.

After hitting our inbound checkpoint, we turned right to our planned heading for IAF Kumbhirgram Airfield. The easy part was over, now we had to get back to our home in Kumbhirgram! By this time, we had already flown over 0430 hours. The mighty Otter had just destroyed a major enemy target at night taking the enemy by surprise which neutralised the entire fuel supply of Pakistan Army, Navy and Air Force. We were flying back home with a bare Directional Gyro (DG) and Standby Compass, and the Almighty's blessings! We had no ground reference points to compare our map to during this pitch-dark foggy night of hilly jungle terrain, other than simply flying on track, speed, height and hoping God would take us back home safely! In 1971, the seven sister states of eastern India did not have adequate electricity supply. So, on our inbound route we did not experience any lighted city or township.

As we were approaching our Expected Time of Arrival (ETA) at Kumbhirgram Airfield, I kept on looking out and giving calls on my Crystal radio set switching on to pre-set VHF frequency of Kumbhirgram Tower, but I did not receive any response – this worried me. Suddenly, I heard a 'God sent faint voice' in my earphone, "*Kilo Flight!! This is Kumbhirgram Tower.*" For the second time I screamed with joy. I requested Kumbhirgram to switch on their Pundit Light (*this is a powerful rotating light on top of a tower that shows the visual location of an airfield at night for pilots to home to*). As it flashed in a second, I saw we were about 5 miles right on track. I put a left bank and headed for the Pundit Light, which continues to flash in my heart to this day! I made a beautiful landing after orbiting the Kumbhirgram Airfield for approximately 20 minutes, until the Goose Neck lamps were laid on the runway. It was a mission lasting over 8:15 night flying hours, beating the RAF's Dam Buster night mission during World War II!

As I first disembarked from the aircraft with my sweat soaked overall, I was received by Group Captain Chandan Singh, Base Commander, IAF Jorhat who literally picked me up from the ground saying, *"Oh Boy Oh Boy You Have*

Done It." I asked him, *"Sir, how did you know I had done it!"* He said that, they all heard a news report from BBC Radio a few minutes back reporting about one unidentified aircraft destroying Chittagong Fuel Refinery on the midnight of December 4, 1971. Group Captain further lovingly scolded me by saying, *"Bloody Man you even delayed our Prime Minister from declaring her war speech announcement against Pakistan, which she declared at 00:23 hours on December 4, 1971 in All India Radio. She agreed to do this, to maintain our element of surprise at the request of Air Chief Marshal P. C. Lal."* We are all indebted and grateful to the Late Prime Minister Indira Gandhi and the Indian Air Force.

Note: For this mission Capt Akram and I received the highest living Gallantry Award "BIR UTTAM" of Bangladesh and Bombardier and Gunner received the Gallantry Award "BIR BIKRAM". After this mission, both Otter and Helicopter flew over 48 operational missions destroying vital targets of military importance.

19

My Brother Naseem Mohsin: A Freedom Fighter

Selina Mohsin

Unforgettable Days

It was a bright and sunny day on March 25, 1971, as my younger brother, Naseem Mohsin ran down the stairs of our two-storey house in Dhanmondi residential area in Dhaka, then East Pakistan. A first year Dhaka University student of the English Department, he was an exceptional student, a born leader, astute debater, witty, intelligent and full of life. He found the repressive situation imposed by the West Pakistani Army intolerable, and the rousing speech of Sheikh Mujibur Rahman on March 7, 1971, was a catalyst. It inspired the Bengalis to fight for independence, as Pakistan refused to transfer power to Mujib, although his party, the Awami League, gained majority in the National Assembly of Pakistan. Naseem realised this injustice and was furious at the ruling West Pakistanis.

"Where are you going and where is your team of friends that you lead?" I asked smiling.

"I am driving to the University to pick them and then we shall return for some very serious discussions and lunch."

A natty dresser, he was wearing a dark well cut tweed jacket and tan trousers. It was still cool. He took out his driving gloves from the pocket of his jacket and dashed to the red Toyota car numbered 'Chattogram Kha 100' that our father had bought a few years ago while serving as Deputy Inspector General of Police in Chittagong. It was essentially Naseem's car, as he was the one who used it the most. We used other vehicles.

He got into the car and drove away at breakneck speed. "Be careful," I shouted behind him.

"I will try," he laughed as the car flashed by. Naseem's room was next to mine, and I could hear the record player playing a Tagore song. He had forgotten to switch it off. On his writing table was a copy of Faulkner's 'Sound and Fury.'

Naseem was expected to bring his friends for lunch and tea. I could imagine the vibrant analysis of the current situation of East Pakistan and Sheikh Mujib's rousing speech. My mother prepared lunch for Naseem and his friends. Morning passed and it was late afternoon, but there was no sign of him or his friends. An ominous silence fell over us as my parents, cousins and I sat down to lunch, but could hardly eat. No one seemed to have any appetite. As the afternoon turned to evening, the sun's rays streaked the sky blood red. Perhaps a symbol of what was to happen or had already begun.

The late dinner was a totally silent affair as Naseem had not arrived. No one spoke as we were all immersed in our own thoughts. They were not happy thoughts. These were uncertain times with the West Pakistani army all round us. For some months, the West Pakistani soldiers had created a sense of fear and unease among the Bengalis. There was a curious uncertainty in the air with a feeling of restlessness. I was a Lecturer in Jagannath College and when I went to teach, the army 'jawans' stopped my car to question me as to where I was going. I usually answered in Urdu, which I had had learned as a child through listening to the language. The Jawans would smile and let me go, not noticing the disdain in my eyes.

That day, March 25, we waited for Naseem's arrival after dinner. The roads were dark and empty, lifeless and totally silent. Then spurts of gunfire filled the air, which must have caused consternation among the people inside their homes. We stood with fear in our hearts and prayers on our lips. The night was long and for us, it was too long. Sleep had left our eyes as we scanned the road for Naseem's arrival. Baba (our father) picked up the telephone to call a friend but the line was dead.

Finally, at 1 am, Naseem's car screeched in and he got out. All of us rushed downstairs to meet him. His clothes were dishevelled; his hair dirty and his eyes spoke silently of horror. "*My son is back, my son is back,*" cried my mother hysterically. "*Calm down, let the boy rest and eat,*" said our father calmly. His voice had the desired effect, and all stopped.

Naseem was breathing fast, "*This cannot be tolerated,*" Naseem burst out. "*The army are killing thousands of people. The university campus is dotted with dead bodies. 'Operation Searchlight' is taking place by the Pakistani Army.*" There was intense shock in his eyes. "*I don't want to eat, just a cup of tea and then I shall go to bed.*"

"*How is that possible, you must eat,*" my mother said persistently.

"*Let the boy do what he wants. Don't press him,*" said Baba and continued regretfully, "*I wanted to send him to the UK to study at Christchurch College in Oxford, and should have done it earlier. It was a mistake to let him stay in East Pakistan at this dangerous time.*" He turned to Naseem, "*Don't leave the house,*" Baba ordered.

Early next morning Naseem was again going out of the house. I was up early too, feeling restless. "*Where are you going my darling brother,*" I asked.

He smiled sadly at me. "*Just for a walk and shall be back in an hour.*" Naseem came back in an hour with a brown bag in his hand and left it on his writing table and went to the bathroom for a shower. I peered inside the packet and found a rough '*lungi,*' which is usually worn by rural farmers and by servants at night. I thought to myself, this must be a gift for one of the servants. My cousin Juicy saw it as well and was surprised.

After some time Naseem came to my room and held my hands, "*We had some great times together and I love you so much my darling sister,*" he said in a soft voice. "*I do not know what I would do without you,*" he murmured.

He then said, "*I have a box in my dressing room table. Please keep it with you.*"

"*Why?*" I asked in surprise, "*Are you going away?*"

"*No,*" he replied after some hesitation. "*But I like to think it is with you.*"

"*I shall certainly keep it safe and give it back to you when you return,*" I said.

He smiled and said, "*You are an adorable sister.*"

Late at night on March 26, he knocked at my door, "*Are you asleep? I want to say something important.*"

"*Can you wait for a while? I am taking a hot bath as I am not feeling too well, but I shall be with you in a few minutes.*"

"*Unfortunately, I can't stay. So, I shall see you when I see you,*" he said in a forlorn voice.

"*Wait, wait I am coming.*" I dressed as quickly as possible. But when I came out Naseem was gone.

It was 12:45 am in the morning. I ran out to the gate where the gateman said ominously, "*Naseem Bhaiya has left.*"

It seemed that I could not breathe. A heavy weight was on my chest. I knew now he would be in the midst of the Liberation War. 'Operation Searchlight' was the final straw in his decision to leave us. A hater of injustice and a lover of peace and all that was good, my brother Naseem could not tolerate the current situation. He was gone, surrounded by danger on all sides.

As I entered his dressing room and took the box, I found myself suddenly alone. It read, "*If I do not return, then please give the box to the girl I care for. You know her.*" Tears filled my eyes. I knew they were letters from his girlfriend, whom he intended to marry after a few years.

Soon the family knew that Naseem had left the house to do something useful in the Liberation War. Now, I realised why he bought the lungi. It was for him to wear and mingle with the villagers.

His friends, particularly his closest friend Fakrul, came enquiring for him repeatedly, but Naseem was not at home. His record player was switched off. Several books sat on his writing table, and the empty room was filled with wind.

The atmosphere of the house altered. Naseem's smiles, laughter, wit, and hordes of friends were gone. Everybody was saddened. However, as his elder sister, I was constantly in grieving for my brother. To me, he was a bright light in my life and that light had gone. I did not know when he would return.

A Traumatic Ending

My brother Naseem Mohsin, who had so unexpectedly left home after 'Operation Searchlight' during the Liberation War of Bangladesh did not return for weeks and months. He was my mother, Ammu's beloved and youngest child, and she was engulfed with a peculiar restlessness in his absence. Every day, she would spend hours on the front balcony of our two-storey house, looking out expectantly.

The liberation resistance had taken a vicious turn. The Pakistan Army's repression and violence prompted millions of people to flee from villages and towns to seek shelter in neighbouring India. The Pakistan Army swept over villages killing and raping women. None were safe. The stench of blood attracted birds of prey to villages, and rivers were strewn with dead bodies. Their blood floated with the currents. The smell was almost unbearable. In a bid to fight back, Bengali youths formed the 'Mukti Bahini', Freedom Fighters. They were untrained but were joined by Bengali army officers and other ranks.

Dhaka was a city under siege. We were three young girls in the house and I was the eldest, around 20 years old. My two cousins were younger. Due to the possibility of untoward incidents, my parents placed a ladder at the back of the house against the back wall, so that we could climb the ladder and jump on the other side where there was a small patch of land with trees and then another house.

Now my regular trips to Jagannath College to teach became unsafe. I would go sometimes but not regularly.

Our only reliable source of news was the BBC Bangla service, which we heard on a transistor radio in a closed room at night. We heard of the atrocities perpetrated on the Bengalis by the Pakistani Army. A large number of Urdu-speaking people from Bihar and many pro-Pakistan Bengalis took the side of the Pakistani Army and formed groups called "Razakars", "Al Badr" and "Al Shams". They acted as spies, and identified freedom fighters and pro-Bengalis to the Pakistanis, who brutally shot them. There were mass murders and genocide all over the country. The screams of women being raped and men killed reverberated in the air of numerous villages and towns.

Through the BBC, we heard that a provisional government had been formed in Mujibnagar and then moved to Calcutta in India. Sheikh Mujib was still in jail in West Pakistan awaiting trial. Soon, the Prime Minister of India began to assist East Pakistan, and the Soviet Union was on our side. My mother was full of hope. The very first benefit concert took place in New York, when Beatle George Harrison sang a song titled 'Bangladesh'. The name Bangladesh became popular. The USA was on Pakistan's side and called for ceasefire twice in the UN Security Council. But the resolutions were vetoed twice by the USSR.

According to BBC Radio, both India and Pakistan accepted the 'existence of war between the two countries following a Pakistan Air Force attack on India's western front on December 3, 1971.The Indian Army quickly overran East Pakistan and Indian aircraft flew over our house. On December 16, 1971, the Pakistan Army was forced to surrender by guerrilla attacks by the Mukti Bahini and a concerted attack by India.

All of us were jubilant. Ammu resumed her vigil on the front balcony to watch for Naseem's return. Hordes of Freedom Fighters came to Dacca carrying Light Machine Guns and firing in the air with joy and gusto. Many young men passed through Road Number 18 in Dhanmondi where we lived, but Naseem was not amongst them.

Towards the end of December my father, Baba, was forced to seek help to find Naseem. He went to the Indian Army Headquarters and met Major Onkar Singh Goraya and Captain Sharma. Since Ammu was prostrated in grief, Baba requested the young officers to come to our house to meet my mother and help her in her distress.

Ammu greeted the two Indian Army officers with visible relief. She still had hopes of Naseem's return and now there were Indian Army officers to assist Baba. Hospitable by nature, Ammu entertained them with variety of sweets and requested them to come regularly and also help to find her son. To assist in finding my brother, the officers wrote a letter and gave an escort for Baba to visit camps of Freedom Fighters in Agartala, as Indian Officers had found Naseem's name in a list. The search was fruitless. But Ammu invited the two Indian Officers to her house and addressed them as "beta" (son). She piled them with Bengali delicacies and was always pleased to see them. After a few weeks the Indian Officers went back to India.

My mother again went back to her place on the balcony assuring everyone, "*My son will surely come. He cannot leave me. He is my most beloved and the best. I love him with my life.*"

A month or so later Major Onkar Singh Goraya came to visit Dacca. My mother insisted that he stay in our house and in Naseem's room. I called him Onkar Bhaiya and my mother seemed to find some relief in his genial presence. She cooked delicious Bengali food for him and taught him to eat rice with his fingers. He was handsome, interesting and a very affectionate man. Soon he became an integral part of our family. Early in the mornings we would all have tea together, talk and discuss numerous things.

Finally, Baba learned of a young man fitting Naseem's description who had been killed by a Pakistan Major on the Comilla border. He went there in our jeep with Naseem's best friend, who is now Dr. Fakrul Alam, and others. They discovered the grave in a small village following a police search. The grave was opened, and Baba identified Naseem's body with the help of a dental chart he had brought with him from Naseem's dentist.

A gory story was revealed by the locals. On December 16, the day of the Liberation of Bangladesh, a Razakar informed the Pakistani Area Major of a Freedom Fighter crossing the border to India. The Major arrived in his vehicle and caught Naseem who was wearing a lungi and who could not hide himself. The villagers were in their homes trembling with fear. The Major in a vicious mood told Naseem to say his last prayer and with a rifle he shot him through the heart! Naseem screamed in agony from the impact of the bullet and fell inert. The villagers were unaware that Pakistan had surrendered and were fearful of burying Naseem's body. The body, once that of a vibrant and extraordinary character, lay in the open, under the winter days and nights. Once a smart dresser, now Naseem lay dead in a dirty lungi. Weeks later when the locals heard that Bangladesh was liberated, they took the body and buried it near a farmer's front yard.

After identification by Baba and photographs had been taken, the body was reburied after Muslim Janaza. Hundreds of people, police and civil officers crowded the village. Baba prayed as tears trickled down his cheeks. Then after thanking all those present, Baba turned towards Dacca. Fakrul Alam, Naseem's friend, was traumatised. No one could speak; all were in a state of shock. At last Baba returned home.

When he narrated the events, I collapsed. When I could get up, I said, "*It cannot be true, it cannot be true.*" I sobbed silently to myself and could hardly breathe. A stone seemed to have landed on my chest. Naseem was not only my brother but also my friend and half of my being. For me, the world appeared to have come to an end.

Ammu became hysterical and kept screaming, as she narrated incidents of Naseem's life, his academic achievements, his habits, his effervescent presence, making our grief and pain more unbearable. She talked on and on refusing to stop and hardly ate anything. We were now concerned for her sanity. She refused to see a doctor, and as people poured into the house to offer condolences, Ammu repeated herself over and over again. What could we do with her? Baba, silent in his pain and agony could not reason with her.

Then, suddenly, after a month she stopped crying, washed herself and changed her clothes. She began to resume her normal activities but never mentioned Naseem's name again. It seemed as if Naseem had not existed in her life. Perhaps it was God's way of healing her.

But my life changed forever. We, Naseem and I, had very close bonds and had shared many joys and hilarious moments that will never be forgotten. I could not come to terms with his death. My life would have been so much richer and happier with him alive. Little things came to haunt me. His jokes, his gifts his early morning knocks on my door to get up, his analysis of events, including when he played Willy Loman in the play "Death of a Salesman". He was unusually brilliant in life, and his death was unusually traumatic. I remembered part of a verse from Shakespeare's Romeo and Juliet, "Take him and cut him out into little stars and he will make the heaven so fine that all will be in love with night...."

Naseem reminded me of a constellation of sparkling stars one can see on a dark night.

For many years my mother would ask me, "*Where is your Indian brother Onkar? Do look for him. I so want to see him*". I, too, wanted to meet Onkar Bhaiya and asked several Indian diplomats about his whereabouts. None could help and soon Onkar Bhaiya became a cherished memory. Suddenly, a couple of years back a defence Attaché of the Bangladesh High Commission in India called me. He said Onkar Bhaiya was looking for me and gave me his contact number. I was amazed and utterly surprised. I called Onkar Bhaiya, and he has since become my Onkar Dada. At last, after many decades, I found my favourite Indian brother.

Many changes have taken place in over four decades. First my beloved father passed away in a small operation. I have two sons. My mother, Ammu, so full of life, so very social, so hospitable and so beautiful is now almost 102 years old. She is blind and quite deaf. It's hard to believe that this woman who was such an excellent conversationalist, so fashionable, so charming, and so full of life is now nearly lifeless and exhausted. But she endured all the pains and lives on.

Decades have passed and I worked and studied in many countries, but there was always a void in my heart as I remembered Naseem almost every day. Throughout the years, Naseem was alive in my being. I did not want to remember his death. It was a painful truth I wished to forget.

My elder son Towheed, who had never seen my brother Naseem but had heard stories of him from me and Naseem's friends. Towheed wrote in the newspaper about his brave uncle he had never known. An uncle who was outstanding, extraordinary, kind and vibrant, who desired to live life to the fullest and bring sunshine to those around him but was unable to do so due to his brutal assassination at a young age by a Pakistani Major. To my son Towheed, Naseem mama (uncle) is a symbol of all that is good and great.

Naseem is no more, yet for me he is everywhere.

20

An Overview of Bangladesh Liberation War

Ishfaq Ilahi Choudhury

The year 2021 is of particular significance for Bangladesh, for it will mark the two Golden Jubilee Celebrations. On March 26 the Nation celebrated 50 years of Bangladesh's emergence as a free and sovereign state, and on December 16 the nation will mark the 50th anniversary of our Victory Day, which commemorates the surrender of the occupying Pakistani forces to the Joint Command of India-Bangladesh Forces. The Victory Day this year will be celebrated by both the countries with even greater zeal and enthusiasm. The year 1971 tied Bangladesh and India in a relationship that is drenched in martyrs' blood, which can only grow from strength to strength. The 50th anniversary of our special relationship is also a time to reflect on the gains and constraints of our relationship, as well as to explore new avenues of mutual cooperation to face the emerging challenges of the 21st century.

Anti-Colonial Movements

Bengal, over the centuries, had developed a syncretic culture that assimilated Animists, Hindu, Buddhist and later Muslim traditions. Diverse communities coexisted in peace and harmony. It began to change, however, as a result of the British policy of "Divide and Rule."[1] Their aim was to sow the seeds of discord among the people, so that they do not stand unitedly against the British rule.

In 1793, Governor General Lord Cornwallis introduced Permanent Settlement[2] in Bengal that reduced millions of rural farmers, mostly Muslims, into tenants of the Zamindars (Landlords), who were mostly upper caste Hindus. On November 19, 1831, a Bengali peasant leader known as Titumir was assassinated by the British in a fortification he built in Barasat, not far from Kolkata. Titumir is hailed as a hero who stood up to the oppression by the Zamindars.[3] In 1835, Governor General William Bentinck replaced Persian with English as the official language in India. While the Hindu population accepted the change, a section of the Muslim clergy issued a "*Fatwa*" against learning English language. As a result, the Muslim community soon fell behind in every sphere of economic, social and political life.[4]

Since the beginning of the 20th century, Bengal has been a hotbed of secret revolutionary organisations committed to armed struggle against colonial forces, alongside the open political movement led by the Indian National Congress (INC).[5] Bengali freedom fighters, such as Khudiram Bose (1889-1908),[6] Bagha Jatin (1879-1915),[7] Surya Sen (1894-1934)[8] and Pritilata Waddedar (1911-1932)[9] sacrificed their lives for the cause of Indian freedom. While Congress claimed to represent all Indians, a large section of the Muslims felt that they needed a separate political platform. In 1906, a new political party, called All India Muslim League (AIML), was formed in Dhaka.[10] The Bengal wing of the party, named Bengal Provincial Muslim League (BPML), won popular support calling for an end to the atrocious Zamindari system and usurious money lenders who had pauperized the farmers. Between 1940 and 1947, the BPML formed government in Bengal. On March 23, 1940, in the Lahore session of the AIML, Sher-e-Bangla A.K. Fazlul Haque, then Prime Minister of Bengal, was chosen to move the resolution that came up to be known as "Pakistan resolution."[11] Leaders like A.K. Fazlul Haque, Hussayn Shaheed Suhrawardy and Khawaja Nazimuddin spearheaded the Pakistan movement. In the 1946 election, Bengal was the only province where Muslim League won a huge majority, whereas in all other Muslim majority provinces Muslim League fared badly.[12] Thus, when Pakistan was born on August 14, 1947, the Bengali Muslims expected that they will enjoy their rightful shares in the political and socio-economic life of Pakistan.

Political Struggle During the Pakistan Period

The Bengalis soon realised, however, that they merely succeeded in displacing the British colonial masters with a new power élite from West Pakistan. Although 56 per cent of the Pakistanis spoke Bengali, Pakistan's founding father Mr. Jinnah declared in Dhaka, in March 1948, that "Urdu and only Urdu will be the state language of Pakistan."[13] This sparked the first popular movement throughout the province that led to police firing on demonstrating students on February 21, 1952.[14] Although Bengali was declared as one of the two state languages of Pakistan in 1956, the issue remained at the core of discontent. In the first provincial election in March 1954, the combined opposition (*Jugto Front*) led by Suhrawardy, Fazlul Haque and Maulana Bhasani completely routed the ruling Muslim League. Out of 303 seats, the Muslim League won only 9. However, the popular Jugto Front ministry was dismissed in less than two months by the Centre, depriving the Bengali people of their democratic rights. When finally, a Constitution of Pakistan was framed in 1956 and the date for a new national election was announced, the Army Chief General Ayub Khan seized power in a coup in October 1958.

Gen Ayub ruled Pakistan until 1969, under martial law or a quasi-martial law administration. The period saw a widening economic divide between the two wings and a virtual political isolation of the Bengali people from the policy making bodies.[15] For example, although 60 per cent of the central budget used to go for defence, the share of East Pakistan was too negligible. There was one infantry division in East Pakistan in 1948, which remained the same till March 1971. One fighter squadron arrived in Dhaka in 1962 and remained until the war's conclusion on December 16, 1971. There was no Navy in East Pakistan except few riverine patrol crafts. Bengali representation in the military was around 5 per cent. Inter-wing disparity was acute in higher administration and policy making bodies. Leading politicians who opposed Ayub Khan's undemocratic policy were put in jail and were barred from entering into public office.[16] The period was marked by major political upheavals that resulted in a mass upsurge in 1968-69, forcing Ayub to once again declare Martial Law on March 25, 1969, and hand over power to the Army Chief General. Yahya Khan. Yahya promised to hold a free and fair election on the basis of 'one man one vote'. In the general election held on December 17, 1970, Awami League (AL), led by Bangabandhu Sheikh Mujibur Rahman, won 161 out of 300 seats in Parliament.[17] Despite securing absolute majority, President Yahya conspired not to hand over power to the Awami League, under pressure from Mr. Zulfiqar Ali Bhutto and senior military leaders. As the agitation in East Pakistan mounted, Yahya launched a massive military crackdown called "Operation Searchlight"[18] on the night of March 25-26, 1971.[19] Meanwhile,

Bangabandhu declared independence of Bangladesh in the early hours of March 26, 1971, before his arrest by the Pakistan Army.

Liberation War 1971

Pakistan's military crackdown was aimed to terrorise the Bengalis, especially the Hindu minority. Their aim was to eliminate Bengali political leadership and the pro-Liberation students and intellectuals. People had no option but to cross the border and seek shelter in India. Bengali elements of Pakistan Army, police and paramilitary forces rose up in arms in opposition to the attacking Pakistani Army wherever they could. However, against well-organised, pre-planned military operations, the scattered and desperate resistance by the Bengalis did not succeed. By the beginning of April 1971, a massive exodus of Bengali refugees into India began.

While the Indian Government had to quickly organise camps for millions seeking refuge, India was concerned about the inflow of armed military, para military and political cadres, particularly the leftist elements. It was a period when Maoist Naxalite movement was at its peak in West Bengal and Bihar.[20] Also, there were insurgencies raging at that time in the North East states of India. Bangladesh crisis had put the Government of India in jeopardy. Prime Minister Mrs. Indira Gandhi took a bold political decision at the time to stand beside Bangladesh, despite all the risks involved. She called the senior AL Leadership in exile headed by Mr. Tajuddin Ahmed for a meeting in New Delhi on April 4, 1971. She gave a patient hearing to the delegation and then advised them to form an interim government so that India's political, economic and military assistance could be channelised.[21] Accordingly, on April 10, 1971, the Provisional Government of the People's Republic of Bangladesh was proclaimed in a place now known as *Mujibnagar*.[22] This opened the door for assistance to Bangladeshi forces fighting the Pakistani occupation. Guerilla training camps were opened, regular forces were organised into fighting units with adequate arms, ammunition and personnel. At the same time, thousands of youth were trained in guerilla warfare in various camps set up close to the border. These highly motivated boys, popularly known as *Mukti Bahini*, kept on harassing the Pakistani forces inside Bangladesh. Mukti Bahini guerillas severely disrupted internal rail and road communications, thus forcing the Pakistan Army to confine themselves in built-up fortifications.

There was a huge global outcry against the genocide being committed by Pakistan Army. Unfortunately, despite popular support, there was not enough external support forthcoming. Muslim majority countries, other than Egypt, Syria and Iraq, continued to support Pakistan financially and militarily; so were the USA and China, which sided with Pakistan for their own strategic reasons. At this juncture, strong Soviet support for India came as a vital plus point. Indo-Soviet Treaty of Friendship and Cooperation signed in August 1971 further bolstered India's position vis-à-vis Bangladesh policies.[23]

Towards the end of November 1971, the position of Pakistani forces in Bangladesh were precarious. Although the army had formed four divisions on paper, at least two of them were ad hoc formations, a hotchpotch of various irregular forces brought by air from West Pakistan. Army lacked adequate armour and artillery, while air power consisted of only one squadron of ageing F-86 Sabre jets deployed in Tajgaon, Dhaka, which had a single runway. Only a few riverine gunboats were available to the navy, and they were completely unsuitable for sea operations. Afraid of Mukti Bahini's harassment, the army chose to remain static in their fortified positions. Pakistanis lacked discipline as a result of their involvement in arson, rape and plunder. Morale was low as a result of the forces being cut off from their homes and forced to operate in a hostile environment.

By November 1971, India had massed about seven full-fledged divisions with massive armour and artillery support, about two dozen modern fighter, bomber, helicopter and transport squadrons against these forces. The Indian Navy had deployed their Eastern naval fleet led by an aircraft career. Regular Bangladesh forces, which had grown to three brigades strength by that time, were closely integrated with the Indian Army. It was an overwhelming force that was designed for a quick victory. Yet, Mrs. Indira Gandhi desired to avoid a full-scale war until the very end. However, when the PAF launched air attacks on the IAF airfields on the afternoon of December 3, 1971, she ordered an all-out retaliation by land, air and sea.[24]

The Indian retort to the Pakistani air attack was swift and sure. By December 5, the PAF in the east was grounded when the single runway in Tejgaon was cratered by repeated IAF attacks. With complete air supremacy achieved, the IAF was free to bomb Pakistani army's positions round the clock. Meanwhile, the Indian Army, supported by the Mukti Bahini bypassed Pakistani strong points and raced towards Dhaka. While the main Pakistani forces were still holding on to various fortress positions, an Indian para brigade was dropped on December 11, in Tangail, 40 km north of Dhaka. These forces, accompanied by Mukti Bahini, were at the northern gate of Dhaka by December 14. Another combined Indian and Mukti Bahini forces advancing from Agartala, bypassed Pakistani positions on the bank of river Meghna and reached the outskirts of Dhaka within a few days. Meanwhile, Lt Gen Niazi, the Pakistani commander who boasted of a last-ditch battle of Dhaka was left with no fighting forces at his disposal and his forces were cut off in tiny packets along the border. As the collapse of Dhaka become imminent, US President Nixon ordered a Task force of 7th Fleet, headed by the Nuclear career *USS Enterprise* into the Bay of Bengal. To checkmate any US move, the Soviet Union too ordered a task force with nuclear submarines to shadow the 7th Fleet; thus, countering any US attempt to change the fait accompli. Niazi realised that the game was up and surrendered all his forces to the joint India-Bangladesh Command on the afternoon of December 16, 1971, following a brief negotiation.[25]

The swift victory was possible mainly because the Mukti Bahini destroyed the morale and fighting spirit of the Pakistani forces in their nine months of operations inside Bangladesh. Road, railway and riverine communications were severely disrupted due to guerilla operations. Indian generalship was superb, in that they never allowed the Pakistani commanders to guess what would be their main line of thrust. While the Pakistanis were deployed all along the border in tiny packets, the allied forces had reached Dhaka. It should, however, be noted that wherever Indian forces tried to take the Pakistani positions head-on, they met with stiff resistance and both sides suffered heavy casualties.[26] India's total control of air and sea ensured that the Pakistanis were cut off from any external assistance as well as an escape route. The Pakistanis paid the price for years of neglect in defending the Eastern wing.[27] The most important lesson of this war is, however, that no army can fight without the support of the people. When the Paksitanis lost the "hearts and minds" of the Bengali people, their defeat was inevitable.

India-Bangladesh Relations in the Early Days

As the new government of Bangladesh settled down in Dhaka, several pressing bilateral issues came up for discussion. Bangabandhu, in his first official meeting with Mrs. Indira Gandhi in Calcutta on February 6-8, 1972, raised the issue of the withdrawal of Indian troops from Bangladesh. Bangabandhu wanted the troop withdrawal by mid-March before Mrs. Gandhi arrives on a visit to Dhaka. Numerous obstacles had to be overcome – a sizable contingent of Indian troops had been deployed, and thousands of Pakistani troops remained in POW camps in India. With lines of communications still poor, it was a huge logistic challenge. Yet, Mrs. Gandhi acceded to the request. The Indian Army started withdrawing almost immediately. Thus, when Mrs. Gandhi arrived for her historic visit to Dhaka on March 17-19, 1972, the last of the Indian troops had already left Bangladesh. This was a significant event that speaks of the high statesmanship and far sightedness of both the leaders. Both leaders signed the historic "25-year Treaty of Friendship, Cooperation and Peace" on March 19, 1972, during Mrs. Gandhi's visit to Dhaka.[28] The treaty laid the groundwork for future bilateral relations.

Land Boundary Agreement (LBA). During Bangabandhu's first official visit to India, the two Prime Ministers signed India-Bangladesh Land Boundary Agreement (LBA) on May 16, 1974. This was a historic agreement that sought to eliminate some of the anomalies and absurdities in the India-Bangladesh borders that was a legacy of the partition in August 1947. It was unfortunate that the treaty could not be fully implemented for nearly four decades. On June 6, 2015, during Prime Minister Sheikh Hasina's visit to India, a new LBA was signed, resolving long-standing issues regarding issues of enclaves, adverse possessed lands and undemarcated portion of the border. A task that could not be done in 68 years was completed within few months, a remarkable achievement in inter-state relations. [29]

Sharing of Waters of Common Rivers. In his first meeting with Mrs. Gandhi in Calcutta in February 1972, Bangabandhu brought up the issue of water sharing. There were few short-term agreements between the two governments till 1982, but after that India withdrew water without any communication with Bangladesh. Finally, on December 12, 1996, a 30-year comprehensive treaty was signed that guaranteed a minimum water flow for Bangladesh.[30] Despite repeated assurances, the Teesta River water sharing agreement reached between the two governments in 2011 remained unsigned. The two countries share 54 common rivers, including massive Brahmaputra. China, meanwhile, is unilaterally constructing series of dams and other structures on the Brahmaputra that worries all the lower riparian. Equitable share of common rivers continue to bedevil the inter-state relations in the region.

Border Security Management. Bangladesh-India border cuts through towns and villages, along roads and rivers, markets and homesteads. Frequent killings of civilians on the border as a result of cross-border firing, has been a sore point in India-Bangladesh relations. While there have been efforts by both the countries to curb smuggling and human trafficking, which are the main reasons for these unfortunate incidents, much more needs to be done to bring the border killings down to zero. Border situation often reflected the relationship between the two countries. However, as the relationship has warmed over the last decade, both countries have forsaken the policy of meddling in each other's internal matters. There is a growing realisation that 'pin pricking' each other does not pay.

Increasing Trade and Investment. Bangladesh is India's biggest trading partner in South Asia, while India is Bangladesh's second largest trading partner in the world. India-Bangladesh trade had been growing rapidly. Our mutual trade in 2019 was in access of $10 billion, with Bangladesh export to India reaching over a billion dollar. The huge trade imbalance in India-Bangladesh trade is often cited by the Bangladeshi critiques as an example of Indian exploitation. The fact, however, is that much of what Bangladesh imports from India is again processed here for export to the West. Thus, Indian imports contribute to Bangladesh's export basket's value addition. Recent years have shown growing Indian investment in Bangladesh's manufacturing industry. Bangladesh has offered India an exclusive Indian Export Processing Zone (IEPZ) where Indian manufacturers will set up plants to produce goods for export to India. India has extended $7 billion of credit lines to Bangladesh to build and improve communication infrastructures, power plants and manufacturing industries.

Improving the Connectivity. Over the last two decades, there has been steady progress in restoring and bettering the connectivity between the two countries. Old railway lines are being restored and, in some cases, new lines are being laid. Between the two countries, an increasing number of direct train services are being established. The roads are being widened and strengthened to facilitate direct transshipment of goods from the ports of Chattogram and

Mongla to NE India and Himalayan states of Nepal and Bhutan. The two nations signed delimitation of maritime boundary and the Exclusive Economic Zone (EEZ) on July 7, 2014, opening up the immense potential of "Blue Economy" for peaceful exploitation. Visa regimes have been relaxed to ease human connectivity. The goal should be seamless movement of goods and people within the region and beyond.

India-Bangladesh Relations into the Future

There are immense opportunities to further develop the relationship between the two countries. Security forces of both the countries are closely working to track down criminals and terrorist who operate across the borders. Defence cooperation is another arena that is just opening up. On the strategic level, the defence forces' goals could be so tailored as to provide mutual cooperation when needed. The whole process will augment mutual trust, which is important for a long-term relationship. However, for these to develop we need to avoid political rhetoric that could harm our relationship. The issue of National Register of Citizen (NRC) in Assam and National Citizenship Act (NCA) across India was played up by a section of the political leaders as an election ploy, but it has been exploited by the communal elements in both countries to terrorise the minorities. The rise of communal forces does not help any country. Unfortunately, the minorities have to become the scapegoat.

Bangladesh is well positioned to graduate from a LDC to Lower Middle-Income economy status.[31] Bangladesh recovered well from COVID-19 Pandemic and is well on its way to reach full recovery by 2022. Our performance in combating the pandemic has been acknowledged by the WHO as a "Star Performer". India, too, is emerging as a major regional power and a major player in the geopolitics of the region. A cordial India-Bangladesh relationship is essential for the well-being of billions of people in the region. As we commemorate the golden jubilee of India-Bangladesh relations, a cordial relationship between India and Bangladesh is our insurance for the future.

Notes

1. https://www.aljazeera.com/opinions/2017/8/10/the-partition-the-british-game-of-divide-and-rule, accessed on February 2, 2021.

2. http://en.banglapedia.org/index.php/Permanent_Settlement,_The, accessed on February 2, 2021.
3. https://en.wikipedia.org/wiki/Titumir, accessed on February 2, 2021.
4. Deobandi schools had been urging Muslims to shun modern western education. One of the Chief protagonist of this school, Maulana Ashraf Ali Thanvi had written extensively on why learning English, even wearing English suits, trousers or ties are *Haram* (Prohibited) in Islam. Deobandis had, and continue to have, a large following in Bengal as in other parts of the sub-continent, accessed on February 2, 2021.
5. http://en.banglapedia.org/index.php/Revolutionary_Terrorism, accessed on February 2, 2021.
6. http://en.banglapedia.org/index.php/Basu,_Kshudiram, accessed on February 3, 2021.
7. http://en.banglapedia.org/index.php?title=Bagha_Jatin, accessed on February 2, 2021.
8. https://en.wikipedia.org/wiki/Surya_Sen. (One of the students' Hall in Dhaka University is named after Surya Sen), accessed on February 2, 2021.
9. http://en.banglapedia.org/index.php?title=Waddedar,_Pritilata (One of the female dormitory in the Chittagong University is named after Pritilata), accessed on February 2, 2021.
10. http://en.banglapedia.org/index.php/Muslim_League, accessed on February 2, 2021.
11. http://en.banglapedia.org/index.php/Lahore_Resolution, accessed on February 2, 2021.
12. In the 1946 election, the BPML won a majority of 114/250 seats in the Bengal Legislative Assembly, compared to 28/60 in Sind, 75/175 in Punjab, 17/150 in the North-West Frontier Province, 54/228 in the United Provinces, 34/152 in Bihar, 31/108 in Assam, 30/175 in Bombay Presidency, 29/215 in Madras Presidency, and 4/60 in Orissa.[2] The result in Bengal, with 45% of seats won by the BPML, was among the largest mandates for the League *Jalal, Ayesha (1994). The Sole Spokesman: Jinnah, the Muslim League and the Demand for Pakistan. Ca*mbridge University Press, p. 162, accessed on February 2, 2021.
13. "Let me make it very clear to you that the state language of Pakistan is going to be Urdu and no other language. Anyone who tries to mislead you is really the enemy of Pakistan. Without one state language, no nation can remain tied up solidly together and function. Look at the history of other countries. Therefore, so far as the state language is concerned, Pakistan's shall be Urdu." Muhammad Ali Jinnah in a public meeting at the Race Course Maidan, Dhaka, on March 21, 1948.
14. The day is observed since then as Language Martyrs' Day and since 2000 as the International Mother Language Day, as per UNESCO direction. It is a public holiday in Bangladesh.
15. https://en.wikipedia.org/wiki/East_Pakistan, accessed on February 12, 2021.
16. Elective Bodies Disqualification Order (EBDO) - An ordinance proclaimed by Ayub Khan, the first military president of Pakistan, in August 1959. In this ordinance he disqualified 75 elective politicians of the assembly. Most of them were from East Pakistan. This ordinance was abolished in December 1966.
17. Awami League fought the election on the basis of its 6-point charter. For details: https://en.wikipedia.org/wiki/Six_point_movement, accessed on February 12, 2021.
18. https://www.thedailystar.net/opinion/perspective/news/remembering-the-barbarities-operation-searchlight-1719859, accessed on February 2, 2021.

19. https://www.dhakatribune.com/bangladesh/2017/03/25/operation-searchlight-genocide-unleashed, accessed on February 12, 2021.
20. https://www.efsas.org/publications/study-papers/an-introduction-to-naxalism-in-india/, accessed on February 14, 2021.
21. An interesting story of how the meeting took place is narrated here: https://thefinancialexpress.com.bd/national/indira-gandhi-acknowledged-bangladesh-leaders-on-april-4-1971-1585999264, accessed on February 14, 2021.
22. http://en.banglapedia.org/index.php/Proclamation_of_Independence, accessed on February 14, 2021.
23. https://mea.gov.in/bilateral-documents.htm?dtl/5139/Treaty+of, accessed on February 14, 2021.
24. Ms. Gandhi was addressing a public rally in Kolkata when the PAF aircraft started its preemptive against the Indian airfields. She flew back to Delhi immediately, called an emergency meeting with inner cabinet and the services chiefs and then went on the radio and TV to announce massive retaliation. For Indira Gandhi's speech: https://www.nytimes.com/1971/12/04/archives/mrs-gandhis-statement.html, accessed on February 14, 2021.
25. For a detailed story: http://www.uplbooks.com/book/witness-surrender, accessed on February 14, 2021.
26. Battles of Hilli, Kamalpur or Ashuganj, for example.
27. In order to deny the then East Pakistan of its rightful share of defence spending, the usual Pakistani rhetoric was, "Defence of the East lie in the west; before the Indians can reach Dhaka, we shall reach Ambala." War in 1971 clearly debunked these boastful utterances.

21

Unheard Voices: Revelations by Bangladesh Citizens

(Excerpts from Personal Interviews)

Jyoti M Pathania

A Brave Woman's Perspective: Dr. Naila Zaman Khan

Dr. Naila Zaman Khan, a Dhaka based Professor of Child Neurology and Development, is presently the Director of the Clinical Neurosciences Centre, Bangladesh Protibondhi Foundation. Her entire family fought alongside the Mukti Bahini in the Liberation War of 1971 – "*There are layers after layers of horrors and genocide.*" She says "*It's like peeling the layers of an onion; as you peel one, tears start rolling, and another, and so on.*"

Her father – late Lt Col Quazi Nooruzzaman, Bir Uttam (retired) – had resigned from the Pakistan Army before 1971; but when the freedom movement began, he told us, "*I am a trained soldier and my Nation needs me; and so I am leaving Dhaka in search of any armed struggle,*" she recalls. "*He eventually found Bengali officers and soldiers who had defected from the Pakistan Army and eventually founded the Mukti Bahini,*" she explained.

"*In April 1971, we heard on Indian radio, my father's name was announced among those preparing a resistance movement. We were all quite proud of him, but also worried for his safety. Meanwhile, we, along with our extended family of over 50, had fled to a village in the northern districts to escape the genocide being perpetrated in Dhaka. Eventually most of them returned to Dhaka, but as our father was already named as a Mukti Bahini officer, we were sent deeper into the countryside, for our own safety – where we remained till May 1971. I witnessed horrific crimes, torture, and raids on villages by the Pakistani Army, which spared no one, including women and children. I remember my mother entering a Pakistani bunker after the battle finished in December 1971 and seeing blood soiled saris, shattered bangles.... Even now, as I am recounting this to you, I can feel the brutality unleashed by the Pakistani Army."*

Image 1: A Photograph of Dr. Naila Khan and Dr. Moazzem, a doctor who fled Dhaka for India and a medical student from Rajshahi Medical College, both of whom had joined the Advance Dressing Station in the Mukti Joddha camp in Mohdipur

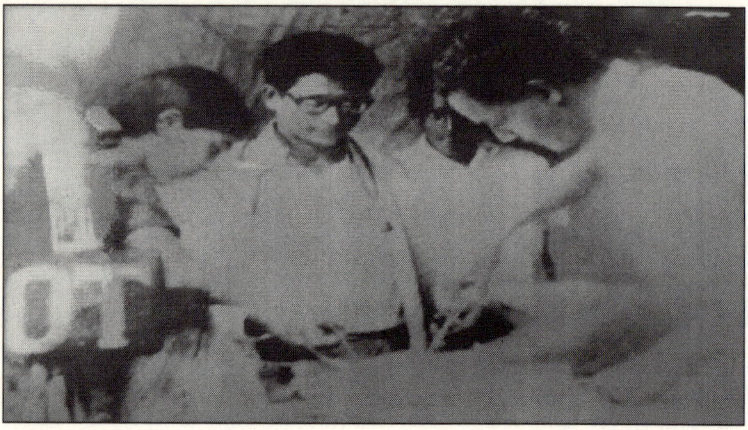

Source: Personal Collection of Dr. Khan

In May, members of the Mukti Bahini assisted them in crossing the border into Agartala and relocating to Kalyani, a university town in West Bengal close to the Jessore Border. This area was home to one of West Bengal's largest refugee camps, which housed several lakhs of refugees, including children, expectant mothers, old people and civilians. Among them were many children of various ages who were without a guardian or family, having been separated from them during their lengthy journey to India. With the assistance of Maitrayee Devi and Gauri Ayyub from Kolkata, Naila's mother founded an orphanage 'Khelaghar,' where she, her sister Lubna and their friends – the Uddin sisters (Rehana, Zarina, Shamim and Bilquis), whose father was also a retired army officer, tried to provide shelter, food, safety and education to over 50 children from the camps. As Naila was also a trained singer, she would travel to Kolkata to perform with a troupe called the 'Bangladesher Mukti Shongrami Shilpi Shongstha,' which was founded by eminent cultural activists Sanjida Khatun and Wahidul Huq (both of whom were also Dhaka refugees). The troupe served as morale boosters and aimed to educate the people about the ongoing struggles. The troupe performed extensively across West Bengal, Delhi and also travelled in buses and trucks to refugee camps and Mukti Bahini camps; their songs were recorded by an American documentary film maker named Lear Levin, and eventually some parts of the footage was restored after 20 years by the late Tareque Masud and his wife Catherine Masud into a documentary titled 'Muktir Gaan.' The documentary extensively covered the participation of Naila and her sister Lubna.

In September, her mother received a letter from her father, who was fighting in Sector 7 (Rajshahi, Rangpur, Bogra and Pabna) as the Sector Commander, requesting assistance in caring for the massive number of wounded soldiers and civilians in the *Muktijoddha* Camps bordering these areas. With the help of the International Red Cross in Kolkata, Naila's mother, along with her two daughters, carried truckloads of medical supplies to set up an Advanced Dressing Station (ADS) in the Mohdipur Shonamasjid sub-sector in Chapai Nawabganj district of Rajshahi – just inside the territory of Bangladesh. Their fifteen-year-old brother, Nadeem, too joined the Mukti Bahini in the same sub-sector.

From October till mid-December Naila and her family witnessed Pakistani Army's cruelty towards civilians in the Chapai Nawabganj area. It was an area of mangroves, where the Army planted hundreds of mines, and villagers, especially children playing there were brought in with mutilated limbs blown off by the mines. Taking a long pause, she further elaborated that it was extremely traumatic to speak about the 1971 war, as she lost many friends and many never recovered psychologically from the horrors they had witnessed. She became a doctor because of the inspiration she derived from witnessing people's sufferings in the combat zone. Finally, she exclaimed, "*Women were the main source of information for intelligence in the Liberation battles and for the guerrillas who infiltrated deep into Bangladesh. They also bore the brunt of torture, rape and systematic abuse by the Pakistani Army and their local partners, the Razakars. The courage and bravery of the majority of the women of Bangladesh still remains unvoiced.*"

SECTION 4

Pakistan's Miscalculations in the Western Sector

Most Befitting Response

22

The 1971 India-Pakistan War: Through a Captain's Eyes

Zameer Uddin Shah

I was one of several hundred officers from the 'Battle Axe Division' seated on tarpaulin sheets on the desert sands of the Jaisalmer sector in late October 1971, awaiting the address of the Chief of the Army Staff (COAS) – General (later Field Marshal) Sam Manekshaw. There was a table covered with an Army blanket, chair and a microphone set up in front. We heard the COAS' helicopter land. He walked in, brushed aside the microphone, climbed on the table and stood facing us with his hands on his hips. His address was short and crisp – "*Boys, I am sending you across. Victory must be ensured! I want you to remember three things, firstly, prisoners of war will not be ill-treated; secondly, there will be no plunder or booty hunting, and, lastly, keep away from the 'Begums' (Pakistani women).*" He jumped off the table, joined us for a cup of tea in an enamel mug, and flew off. His speech was short, crisp and left no doubts in our minds. He was not a verbose individual. He exemplified all the characteristics of a leader: effective oratory that was succinct, and to the point to 'fire' the imagination of the listeners. Sam Manekshaw's address left us spellbound. He had incomparable charisma, which is a strange alchemy of inner spirit, energy, fire, radiance, enthusiasm and spontaneity. This charisma was genuine, not staged. It was like a 'spark' that 'ignited the fire within us'.

The Desert Force in Action

For several months we had been rehearsing our role of breaking through the Pakistani defences, with our objective being the town of Rahim Yar Khan – a rail and road communication centre in Pakistan. My Regiment abandoned camels in favour of motorised transport. Our shortfall of vehicles, equipment and manpower were compensated for when our three Batteries were allotted as direct support to three Infantry Brigades. Another battery of the Regiment, which I subsequently commanded, was deployed to support the Longewala post. This post was established to check any out-flanking attack by Pakistan during the Battle Axe Division's thrust to Rahim Yar Khan (RYK) planned for December 4, 1971. RYK was our objective in the desert. We had to traverse very rugged and inhospitable terrain.

The Sadewala and Longewala posts protected the western flanks of our formation. We also did not expect the Pakistanis to take the approach via Longewala. They surprised us by surrounding our post on the night of December 4/5, 1971. This was preceded by massive pre-emptive strikes on our airfields in the West, including Jodhpur. We were concentrated further East at Tanot, preparing for our divisional thrust on December 4, 1971. The Pakistani armour surrounded the post, comprising Chinese T-59 tanks of 22 Armoured Regiment. For some unknown reason, the Pakistani armour paused awaiting the arrival of their infantry, which they had overshot. They were probably also inhibited by the wire fence which they mistook as markers of a minefield; it was 'really' meant to keep out stray dogs and cattle. The post commander, Major Chand Puri, and his Commanding Officer Lt Col Khursheed Hussain, at Sadhewala, maintained their composure. Unfortunately, the movie 'Border' depicted the latter in ambiguous light, probably to add grist to the mill.

Time for Action

There was widespread confusion hat night, December 4/5, 1971. We were asked to move West from our Assembly Area North of Tanot and head for Longewala. The single road artery was clogged and we were like 'sitting ducks' for the Pakistan Air Force (PAK). On December 5, 1971, we called in the Indian Air Force at dawn. We saw our Hunter aircraft dive and play 'merry hell' into the Pakistani Armour and neutralise the bulk of PAF; 40 Pakistani tanks were destroyed or abandoned. We seized five field guns and three anti-aircraft guns. The blazing tanks cast an eerie glow across the night sky. Each artillery piece within range delivered a barrage of fire and contributed significantly to the defence of Longewala. Without the IAF, our armour, comprised of obsolete

AMX-13 tanks buttressed by a few Russian T-54 tanks, would have been no match for the Pakistani Armour.

The Pakistani plan was audacious. They planned to outflank us and head for Jaisalmer, which was their ultimate objective. They, however, made the cardinal error, in execution, by not allocating enough air resources for their thrust to Longewala and allowing their armour to overshoot the Infantry. The destruction of the Pakistani Armoured Regiment gave us respite, and it took another day to stabilise the situation. According to reports, Pakistan's Divisional Commander (18 Infantry Division) was relieved of his duties following this incident.

The Pakistanis therefore, had no option but to fall back with us in hot pursuit. Our movement encountered difficulties due to difficult terrain and logistics. Our vehicles could only move on 'duck board' tracks made of wooden planks linked together. Water was strictly rationed. Three khaki clad figures staggered into the gun position with their hands above their heads one night during a lull in the firing. They kept shouting "*Don't shoot, we're Bengali Officers*"; they were actually deserters from the Pakistan Army. As a precaution, we took their weapons, but took good care of them. They were promptly dispatched to Higher HQ where they were debriefed and then dispatched to the East to join the Mukti Bahini. Several POWs were taken, interrogated and sent to POW camps – Sam Manekshaw's instructions were scrupulously observed.

During a raid on a Ranger Post one night, our artillery observation Officer with the raiding party attacked a village fort called 'Islamgarh,' which was involved in a cross-border movement. Our men were adept at such moves and the raid came as a surprise to the enemy. In the morning, the JCO, who was part of the raiding party, handed me a cloth bound Koran that he had retrieved from the village mosque. He felt that there was a likelihood of it being desecrated and that it would be safe in my custody. I still have it and will return it to its rightful place at the appropriate time!

Despite our overall superiority, we made only limited progress, about 15 km, till the ceasefire was declared. We spent the next six months in the blistering heat of the Thar Desert in Pakistan, Sindh. Temperatures touched 50 degrees and snakes and scorpions were a hazard. Swarms of flies were a nuisance and mosquito nets had to be used to keep them at bay, even during the daytime siesta. The one vivid memory I have was of a 'flag meeting' we had with our Pakistani counterparts after the ceasefire. Only I was allowed, in disguise as a jeep driver. Whilst we waited at the appointed place, a corpulent Pakistani colonel emerged with a soldier holding an umbrella for him. I was appalled – such a non-soldier-like practice would be unacceptable in the Indian Army.

In 1977, General Jacob, the hero of the capture of Dacca and the then Army Commander, Eastern Command, selected me as his personal staff in the Military Secretary's Branch. He had his own distinct style of informality and did not hesitate to walk into the office, punch me in the stomach and enquire about postings that had been received and other officer's management matters. He was dreaded by the senior staff officers because of his penchant for unpredictability. Several books have been written on the liberation of Bangladesh, but Lt Gen Jacob's – *An Odyssey in War and Peace* is the most authentic. The book makes for interesting reading but is also highly controversial. Before its publication, Lt Gen Jacob had handed me the draft and asked me to edit and offer my comments. I was shocked by his references to and write-ups about a few senior officers. I had been privy to the private correspondence between Lt Gen Inder Gill (Director General Military Operations during the 1971 war) and Lt Gen Jacob – both were close friends who shared the same views on the war and the twisted half-truths being bandied about.

The Lessons

The most significant lesson learned was that, 'military leadership' is subordinate but not subservient to political leadership. The Army resisted the pressure to launch operations in 'East Pakistan' prematurely in the summer of 1971. Had it not been for this resistance then, the government would have steamrolled its decision to go in for an offensive in the summer of 1971, since the pressure of Bengali refugees was a huge burden on the fragile economy of our country. This was despite the fact that we were inadequately prepared and the Mountain Passes on the Tibetan border were open, making it possible for a Chinese riposte, to support Pakistan.

The decision to delay the operations was taken in the Operations Room of the Army HQ sometime in April 1971. The reported story of Sam Manekshaw's aside to Mrs. Indira Gandhi, "Madam, you don't stick your big nose into my business, and I won't stick my big nose into yours," was definitely in jest of the forte of the Field Marshal. Second, given the Prime Minister's iron grip, it is doubtful that anyone could have taken the liberty of addressing the domineering Lady in such a casual and jocular manner. Gen Jacob, who was responsible for logistical preparations, undeniably played an important role in ensuring that the Army's point of view was taken seriously by the national leadership. The second issue that emerged was the importance of media management. Despite its initial condemnation, the world community supported India's stand because of the unbiased reporting made possible by the access given to the media and its 'embedding' with troops in the field.

Gen Jacob maintained that the initial aim was 'salami slicing' of Bangladesh, i.e. capturing terrain in the proximity of the border. He deserves credit for the plan that bypassed towns and the thrust to Dacca, bypassing pockets of Pakistani resistance. The Indian Army was fully aware of the support received from the Mukti Bahini and the people of East Pakistan. Taking troops and artillery resources away from the India-China border for the offensive was undoubtedly risky. This was undoubtedly a violation of orders, but in battle, the adage "the ends justify the means" applies!

23

1 Corps Operations: A Critical Appraisal

PJS Sandhu

India's 1 Corps was the main instrument for executing the strategy of offensive defence in the Western theatre of operations in 1971. Undoubtedly, Indian 1 Corps had by and large achieved the missions assigned to it; however, military thinkers have expressed the opinion that the Corps could have achieved much more. There may also be a few lessons that can be derived from the operational point of view. It is with these aims in view that a critical analysis of Indian 1 Corps operations during the 1971 War has been undertaken.

Geostrategic Importance of Shakargarh Bulge

The bulge is surrounded on three sides by Indian territory, providing multiple avenues of ingress. Pakistan benefited from interior lines of communication, which gave her greater freedom for manoeuvre within the bulge. The Bulge also provided Pakistan a good launch pad for offensives against the important towns of Gurdaspur and Pathankot, as well as the Pathankot-Jammu highway, which runs very close to the northern periphery of the bulge. Hence, the security of this highway has always been the prime concern of the Indian high command. However, the terrain configuration of the bulge provided multiple options to India for offensive operations.

Force Level: Pakistan

Pakistan's 1 Corps comprised three Infantry Divisions, an Armoured Division, an Independent Armoured Brigade and two independent armoured squadrons. The 15 Infantry Division was deployed for defence of Sialkot Sector, while 8 Infantry Division was responsible for defence of the remainder Shakargarh Bulge. The 8 Independent Armoured Brigade was the Corps Reserve to be used for launching counter attacks or for carrying out counter penetration. The 6 Armoured Division and 17 Infantry Division, though part of 1 Corps, were essentially strategic reserves and were located in Area Pasrur-Daska-Gujranwala. The 20 Lancers was the Corps Reconnaissance Regiment that was assigned to the Covering Troops under 'Changez Force', an ad hoc force created to delay the enemy.[1]

Planning Imperatives: Pakistan

Though Shakargarh Bulge provided a suitable launch pad to Pakistan for offensive operations towards the Pathakot-Jammu highway at many points, it was also a defender's nightmare. Since Pakistan was forced to move additional forces to East Pakistan, it did not have enough forces to undertake a meaningful second offensive in the Shakargarh Bulge, even more so after launching a major offensive in the Chhamb Sector. Hence, Pakistan thought it prudent to remain on the defensive in the Shakargarh Bulge.

Force Level: India

The Indian 1 Corps, commanded by Lt Gen KK Singh, comprised 36, 39 and 54 Infantry Divisions, 2 and 16 Independent Armoured Brigades, two independent reconnaissance squadrons, two independent artillery brigades and two engineer brigades. The infantry divisions lacked integrated armoured regiments. The 16 Independent Armoured Brigade was equipped with Centurion tanks that were nearing obsolescence.

Planning Imperatives: India

Though Indian 1 Corps was a strike corps meant for offensive operations, it had been given both defensive and offensive roles in the area of Shakargarh Bulge. This had happened at the instance of Lt Gen KK Singh, who, as the Director of Military Operations at the Army HQ before assuming the appointment of Corps Commander had drafted the 'Operational Instruction' for the Corps. In the event, it proved to be a disadvantage, as the responsibility to defend the periphery of the Bulge against a Pakistani offensive kept on diluting the forces available for offensive operations. This dilemma was to impact his decisions throughout the operations.[2]

Pakistan 1 Corps' Likely Pattern of Operations and Operational Plan

Pakistani plan for employment of 1 Corps was essentially reactive rather than proactive. Pakistani Corps Commander decided to wait and watch what India would do regarding the Shakargarh Bulge. Pakistan had correctly anticipated that the main Indian offensive would be launched in the area between Degh and Bein rivers. Hence, Pakistan planned to employ its 1 Corps as under:[3]

- To eliminate an Indian enclave on the Pakistan side of the River Ravi in area Narowal and to simulate offensive actions in order to draw enemy forces into the Shakargarh area.
- Shakargarh, Narowal and Jafarwal were to be developed into fortified strong points to act as pivots for manoeuvre.
- An ad-hoc force known as the 'Changez Force,' comprising two armoured regiments and a reconnaissance and support battalion, was to act as Covering Troops and fight delaying actions, thereby creating conditions for launching counterattacks. The 6 Armoured Division and the 17 Infantry Division were to remain as GHQ reserves.

Indian 1 Corps' Battle Plan for the Offensive

Map 1: Indian 1 Corps Offensive: Shakargarh Bulge – December 1971

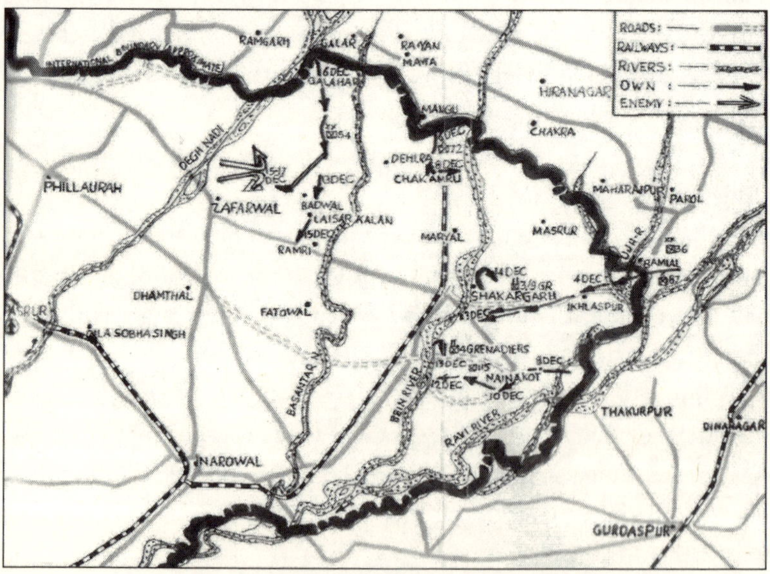

Source: *The India-Pakistan War of 1971*, SN Prasad & UP Thapliyal, 2014.

Indian 1 Corps was tasked with launching an offensive into the Shakargarh Bulge, South of Degh River, and capturing territory up to the line of Jafarwal-Dhamtal-Narowal; it was then tasked with expanding operations towards the Marala-Ravi Link Canal and capture Pasrur. The Corps Commander felt that it would be best to draw out the Pakistani Strategic Reserves into an area East of Degh River and bring it to battle in the Area Zafarwal-Dhamtal-Narowal. Once this reserve was degraded, it would open the way for developing operations into the hinterland towards the Maral-Ravi link canal, as also for capturing Pasrur. With this in mind, he planned to launch his offensive on the following broad front:[4]

- 54 Infantry Division with 16 Independent Armoured Brigade, less 16th Light Cavalry to advance from general area Mawa-Galar southwards and capture Zafarwal - Dhamtal complex.
- While holding a divisional defended sector, the 39 Infantry Division was allotted 72 Infantry Brigade (four battalions) ex 36 Infantry Division and 2 Independent Armoured Brigade, less 14 HORSE, and was tasked to advance from general area Londi-Mangu Chak southwards and capture Shakargarh.
- The remainder of the Corps, namely the 26 and the 36 Infantry Divisions, with two regiments and two independent reconnaissance squadrons of armour, were to remain on the defensive.

Thus, it would be seen that out of nine infantry brigades available to Indian 1 Corps, five brigades were to be used for defensive, leaving only four brigades for the offensive. As regards armour, out of six armoured regiments available, only four regiments were to be used for offensive operations. It was a very cautious plan, with the primary objective of defending the area of responsibility against an offensive by Pakistani 1 Corps.

An Overview of the Operations

The war commenced with Pakistan launching an offensive in the Chhamb Sector on December 3. Indian 1 Corps, which was already in its concentration areas launched its offensive into the Shakargarh bulge at last light on December 5. The 54 Infantry Division advanced with two infantry brigades up, each supported by armour with the third brigade in reserve.

The advance was slow and cautious but determined. By December 8, it had crossed the first belt of minefields and was in the process of attacking across the second minefield. This alarmed the Pakistan high command enough to despatch a Brigade of 33 Infantry Division (a reserve division) to 1 Corps on December 9, as also alerting 11 Cavalry to be ready to move from Chhamb to Shakargarh.

Due to Pakistan's failure to launch an offensive from the Bulge, the Corps Commander decided on December 8 to develop a thrust towards Shakargarh by deploying 36 Infantry Division (two brigades) with 14 HORSE across the River Ravi through Thakurpur ferry. Nainakot was captured by December 10. Thereafter, the Division commenced their advance on the Nainakot-Shakargarh Axis on December 11. Meanwhile, 87 Infantry Brigade along with a squadron of 16th Light Cavalry, which had been holding a defended sector in the general area of Bamial-Parol, also commenced their advance along the Ikhlaspur-Shakargarh Axis on December 10.[5]

However, the advance by 72 Infantry Brigade and 2 Independent Armoured Brigade, less one regiment under 39 Infantry Division, had been rather slow and the eastern flank of 54 Infantry Division was getting exposed. Hence, 54 Infantry Division was tasked to capture Chakra-Dehlra complex, which initially were the objectives for the 39 Infantry Division.[6] Though this was done successfully by the 54 Infantry Division during the night of December 10/11, it had the effect of slowing down the overall Corps operations. By now six days had elapsed since the launch of the offensive but neither Jafarwal nor Shakargarh had been contacted, leave aside capturing the same.

As the 39 Infantry Division was not making much headway, Lt Gen KK Singh decided to rehash the Corps plan and do some regrouping on December 12, which in essence included the following:[7]

- HQ 39 Infantry Division was given the responsibility for defence of the area West of Basantar river.
- 72 Infantry Brigade assumed responsibility for the Sector between Karir and Bein rivers, and in turn came under command 54 Infantry Division as the fourth brigade.
- HQ 2 Independent Armoured Brigade with 1 HORSE was moved eastwards and placed under command the 36 Infantry division, thus increasing the armour component to two regiments.

- 87 Infantry Brigade with the squadron of 16th Light Cavalry advancing on Ikhlaspur-Shakargarh Axis was also placed under command 36 Infantry Division.
- The responsibility to capture Shakargarh was now given to 36 Infantry Division.

Battle of Basantar (December 15-16, 1971)

No appraisal of 1 Corps operations would be complete without a mention of the Battle of Basantar. By December 13, the leading elements of 16 Independent Armoured Brigade were dominating the Road Jafarwal-Shakargarh, while the 47 Infantry Brigade had closed in with the Basantar river in area Lagwal on the East bank. The plan was to establish a bridge head across Basantar river in general area Sikandarpur-Lalial-Barapind and by a turning move tackle the Supwal Ditch cum Bandh defences, between Degh and Basantar from the rear, thereby creating conditions for 39 Infantry Division holding this area to go on to the offensive, allowing 1 Corps to advance further towards Jafarwal.

The bridge head across Basantar river was established by the 47 Infantry Brigade during the night of December 15/16 and 17 HORSE was inducted during the night itself without waiting for the safe lanes to be fully breached. The decision by Lt Col (later Lt Gen) Hanut Singh, Commandant 17 HORSE, to induct his regiment without waiting for the minefield safe lanes saved the day. Commencing with the early hours of December 16, Pakistan's 8 Independent Armoured Brigade launched a series of counter attacks against the bridge head during the next 36 hours. All the counter attacks (at least four of them) were beaten back, with Pakistan suffering heavy losses.

Pakistan had lost 43 tanks and captured ten, against Indian losses of two tanks.[8] The 47 Infantry Brigade and 17 HORSE had covered themselves with glory.[9] The ceasefire that became effective from 2000 hours on December 17 put an end to further operations by either side.

A Critical Analysis of the Operations

Strategy

India chose an aggressive defence strategy in order to dissuade Pakistan from conducting any large-scale offensive(s) against Indian territory. The activities of Indian 1 Corps were planned and carried out with this objective in mind. Without a doubt, 1 Corps accomplished this objective, and Pakistan was unable to conduct any offensive operations from the Shakargarh Bulge.

However, Pakistan's strategic reserves remained intact and were not drawn into battle. As a result, a threat persisted throughout the war. This can be attributed to the fact that Indian 1 Corps' plan was neither bold enough nor executed with determination at the Corps level. This may be attributed to both defensive and offensive responsibilities being assigned to 1 Corps. There would have been a perpetual tug of war over how much would be sufficient for defence at the expense of offence. Obviously, these factors influenced the speed and momentum of operations.

A bulge offers multiple choices for offensive operations and presents most difficult tactical choices for the defender. This ought to have been exploited. Pakistan 1 Corps had developed its defences in the shape of an inverted 'L' starting from Supwal ditch cum bandh from Degh to Basantar and continuing with the strong points of Jafarwal-Dhamtal-Narowal. Any early incursion into the area West of the above line would have unbalanced him and drawn the enemy reserves; thus, creating opportunities for further operations. In the event, Indian 1 Corps spent all its effort trying to capture areas east of the above line, which in Pakistan's scheme of things was not of much importance and could be traded for time.

Importance of Intelligence

Intelligence about the enemy's dispositions is of vital importance in formulation of offensive plans. It can be said, 1 Corps lacked sufficient knowledge regarding the enemy's defences, particularly the minefield belts. Similarly, it was also not known that Pakistan had planned to fight covering troops action ahead of the line mentioned above. Indeed, information on the enemy was extremely scarce throughout the operations, which contributed significantly to extremely slow pace of advance.

The Corps had two independent reconnaissance squadrons equipped with AMX-13 light tanks at its disposal. They were most suited for reconnaissance tasks. It would have been ideal to allot a squadron each to the Armoured Brigades but instead they were deployed to boost the defences.

Lack of Manoeuvre

The Indian 1 Corps offensive was a slow grinding advance that cleared all the opposition on the way. It was more in the nature of occupying ground from where the enemy's Covering Troops had withdrawn. There was noticeable absence of manoeuvres like isolation/investment of important objectives, break-in, break-out and setting up for battle at division and corps levels.

The two attacks by 36 Infantry Division to capture Shakargarh were reminiscent of the numerous unsuccessful attempts to capture Chawinda during the 1965 war, almost in the same area. The main reason for the same appeared to be lack of information about the enemy, inadequate fire support and poor coordination between the attacking forces. No effort was made to isolate/invest Shakargarh before launching the attacks.

Operational Control

There appeared to be lack of operational control by the Corps HQ. They allowed the divisions to continue at whatever pace they chose to advance. The regrouping carried out on December 12 was too late. The operations had been going on for seven days and by now the enemy had got a good idea of our intentions. The initial advantage of surprise by the attacker had been lost. The regrouping only split the Corps effort further between the attacks on Shakargarh and the bridge head across Basantar.

The 39 Infantry Division and a regiment of armour were not used to reinforce the offensive. The Corps HQ made no attempt to create and recreate the reserves which could have imparted the necessary momentum to the offensive. To further highlight the lack of operational control, I could do no better than quote Lt Gen Hanut Singh:[10]

> *"On the evening of 16 December, 4 HORSE was also inducted into the bridge head. There were now six major units in the bridge head; the three infantry battalions of 47 Infantry Brigade and, two armoured regiments and the mechanised battalion of 16 Independent Armoured Brigade, but surprisingly no senior officer of the rank of brigadier and above had ventured to come forward into the bridge head to either issue orders, or to coordinate the deployment and actions of these six major units. So, it was left to the Commanding Officers of these units to mutually sort out these matters."*

In the overall context, Indian 1 Corps performed fairly well in carrying out the operational duties given to them. The battle of Basantar was the crowning success of the campaign. However, Pakistan's strategic reserve of 6 Armoured Division and 17 infantry Division were neither drawn into battle nor was it degraded. This might be attributed to the slow and cautious pace of operations of the Indian 1 Corps as also a failure to achieve a breakthrough early on, in order to destabilise the defence and force Pakistan to commit its strategic reserves.

Notes

1. Major (Retd) Agha Humayun Amin, Defence Notes, Battle of Barapind – Jarpal, December 16, 1971, *Defence Journal*, October 1999, Vol 3, No. 8, Karachi.
2. Based on a personal discussion by the Author with Lieutenant General KK Singh, MVC on December 14/15, 2000 (eve of Operation Parakram) at Mathura.
3. Major Amin, n. 1.
4. Major General Sukhwant Singh, India's Wars Since Independence (New Delhi: Lancer Publishers, 2010), p. 97.
5. Ibid., p. 101.
6. Ibid., p. 100.
7. Ibid., p. 101.
8. Ibid., p. 105.
9. Major Hoshiar Singh and Second Lieutenant Arun Khetrapal (posthumous) were awarded the Param Vir Chakra.
10. Lieutenant General Hanut Singh, PVSM, MVC, The Story of the Poona Horse (Dehradun: Agrim Publishers, First Edition) p. 277.

24

Battle of Chhamb

AJS Sandhu

The Battle of Chhamb was perhaps the toughest, bloodiest and most intensely fought battle of the 1971 India-Pakistan War. After the 1971 war was over, Prime Minister, Mrs Indira Gandhi undertook visits to the front line in both the theatres to meet the troops. She visited Jammu Sector on December 29, 1971. The General Officer Commanding (GOC) 15 Corps and his five Divisional Commanders were also invited to a dinner organised in her honour at Raj Bhawan, Jammu. Prior to the dinner, while introducing his GOsC, Lt Gen Sartaj Singh mentioned their divisions and the areas where they had fought. When he came to GOC 10 Division, he said: "*This is Maj Gen Jaswant Singh, GOC 10 Infantry Division, who fought a tough battle in Chhamb,"* – to which Mrs Gandhi added – "*Not tough General, the toughest."*[1]

Strategic Significance of the Chhamb Sector

The Chhamb Sector has been attacked by Pakistan in all India-Pakistan Wars since Independence, and its geo-strategic location and terrain configuration make it significant. This territory gave Pakistan the best avenue for a major offensive in Jammu and Kashmir. In 1971, Akhnur had only one 'Class 18' Girder Bridge, which carried the only route serving both the 10 Infantry Division and the 25 Infantry Division in the north, making it a critical strategic goal.

Operational Plans

Major General Jaswant Singh took over as the GOC of 10 Infantry Division on September 11, 1970. The first thing he noticed was its weak defensive layout, in which the main defences were sited far in depth from the Ceasefire Line (CFL), along the Kalit-Troti-Dhon Chak ridgeline. The only forces forward of this ridgeline was a covering force of one infantry battalion and a squadron of armour (called the *Papa Force*) in the Chhamb Salient, and an armoured regiment (less two squadrons) with two infantry companies (*Quebec Force*) opposite the Nadala Enclave. This was tantamount to giving away Chhamb without a fight. To address this weakness in his division's defence potential, he briefed the Corps Commander in October 1970 on the forward movement of the 191 Infantry Brigade (from the Kalit-Dhon Chak ridgeline) into a deliberate defence in the salient, to provide a strong defensive posture in this vulnerable area.

Meanwhile, having assessed the vulnerability to a potential Indian strike in this area, Jaswant devised an offensive plan. The GOC felt that such an offensive (especially in conjunction with 26 Infantry Division to its south) would pre-empt any Pakistani plans in this sector, threaten the vital areas of Gujrat and Marala Headworks in their Punjab province and facilitate the operations of our 1 Corps in Shakargarh Bulge.[2]

This strategy called for seizing Marala Headworks and closing the GT Road near Alexander Bridge (near Gujrat). If this strategy had been carried out, the Battle of Chhamb would have taken a very different course; instead of India, it would be Pakistan that would be reacting to this offensive. Although the Army Commander gave no decision then, the green signal for this offensive came on July 10, 1971.[3] 68 Infantry Brigade, 3 (Independent) Armoured Brigade and 216 Medium Regiment were allocated to the division for the offensive.

General Sam Manekshaw visited 10 Infantry Division on November 1 and was briefed by the GOC. While he was fully satisfied with the offensive plan, the Army Chief queried the rationale of having 191 Infantry Brigade so far behind. Sartaj Singh, who was also present, admitted that Jaswant Singh also wanted to move this brigade forward, but he explained the rationale for this deployment, which he and the Army Commander (Lieutenant General K.P. Candeth) agreed upon, i.e. the indefensibility of the area forward vis-à-vis the excellent defence potential of this ridgeline. After much discussion, the Chief agreed with the GOC and advised the move forward into the Chhamb Salient albeit in the shape of a 'Forward Poise', for its role as a Firm Base for the planned offensive. When Candeth learnt of this, he rang up the Chief and requested a reconsideration of this move forward. The Chief, however, did not agree.[4] On December 1, the GOC was suddenly ordered to put the offensive on hold and adopt a defensive posture by the morning of December 4. This sudden change of plans was caused due to political compulsions rather than military considerations. Thus, to some extent the issue for which Jaswant Singh had fought was resolved; even if it was in the form of a firm base, it meant 'boots on ground' inside the Chhamb Salient.

This was the fourth change in operational plans for the 10 Infantry Division – from purely covering troops deployment, to an offensive plan, to a 'Forward Poise' approved by the Chief on November 1, to putting the offensive on hold and getting into the defensive mode on December 1! To make matters worse, Pakistan launched its attack while the division was still in the process of readjusting its defences. The Battle of Chhamb began from this initial unbalanced position.

Pakistan's Strategy

Pakistan's plans in this sector were focused on a clear objective – Akhnur. She wanted to replicate the spectacular advance of its forces in *Operation Grand Slam* during the 1965 War. They mustered a much larger force this time. The following additional forces were assigned to the 23 Infantry Division (which consisted of 4 AK, 7 AK and 20 Infantry Brigades and 26 Cavalry):[5]

- 2 Armoured Brigade and 14 Independent Armoured Squadron.
- 66 and 111 Infantry Brigade.
- 17 Infantry Division Artillery Brigade and additional Artillery Regiments.

A lesser-known fact is that the artillery allotted to support this attack was more than Bangladesh's entire defence force! It placed such a high value on this offensive. And, to command this formidable force, Yahya Khan posted one of his favourite generals – Major General Iftikhar Khan Janjua, who, having commanded 106 Infantry Brigade in the Chhamb Sector in the 1965 War, knew this area well.

The Pakistani plan was to strike along the full front of 10 Infantry Division's plains sector, while also initiating operations in the Hill Sector to conquer the Chhamb Salient earliest feasible. The division was then to advance and seize the intermediate target of Palanwala before moving on to Akhnur, leaving adequate forces to ensure security of the salient. By November 30, both 10 and 23 Infantry Divisions were ready and poised to launch their respective offensives. The question was, who would attack first and seize the initiative. And in a curious twist of fate, it was the Pakistanis who attacked.

Conduct of the Battle

In the first three days of the battle, the Chhamb Salient saw the highest 'per square kilometer' concentration of troops, tanks and guns compared to any other divisional sector during the war. From the Pakistani side, there were four infantry brigades, and an armoured brigade, ranged against one Indian infantry brigade and four squadrons. Add to this the artillery fire of 10 Pakistani and six Indian artillery regiments, coupled with air strikes, and you have a picture of the boiling cauldron of Chhamb Salient. The smell of cordite filled the air!

Early on the morning of December 3, Major General Jaswant Singh had left for 191 Infantry Brigade Sector to see the ongoing readjustments and tie up any loose ends. He was still there when the shelling started. He rushed with the Brigade Commander Brigadier RK Jasbir Singh to the 191 Infantry Brigade command post, where reports had already started coming in. He was there till midnight and then went to other locations to see what was happening in the rest of the sector.[6] While the main defences held firm, the enemy 66 Infantry Brigade had made a 3,000 yard penetration by 0200 hours, while the 111 Infantry Brigade (to its south) was stalled at the IB. A Combat Group broke out around 0500 hours and headed for Manawar Tawi near Mandiala. They were engaged by the HQ troop of Deccan Horse, who knocked out seven enemy tanks.[7] On contacting the Mandiala ridges around mid-day, a battalion launched an attack on Mandiala North platoon and captured it after a very tough fight. Brigadier Morlin was ordered to counter-attack, but his 7 KUMAON got delayed initially, and later shelled, resulting in loss of command and control. It was then ordered to occupy defences opposite the Mandiala Crossing in the Sukh Tao Nala area, but went off to Kachreal ridge instead, leaving the Mandiala crossing lightly guarded. The 4/1 GR, which was assigned the task to capture Mandiala North, failed to do so.

The Pakistani 4 AK Brigade less a battalion attacked through the Sukh Tao Nala (Mandiala Crossing) in the early hours of December 5 to capture the Kachreal ridge. The two attacking battalions were followed by a tank squadron to secure the bridgehead, through which an armoured regiment was to breakout towards Palanwala. The third battalion got lost and could not go in for this assault. Due to darkness, the leading waves of 13 AK Battalion lost direction. The northern column slammed into the medium gun area of 216 Medium Regiment near Chapreal, with some reaching the *Wagon Lines area* of 39 Medium Regiment. The enemy infantry and the gunners of the 216 Medium Regiment's forward two batteries engaged in a furious hand-to-hand combat. Simultaneously, its depth battery as well as 39 Medium Regiment engaged the enemy by direct fire. The area was littered with the dead and wounded from both sides, showing the intensity of this bloody combat. This needless engagement with gunners delayed their onward movement, and by the time the enemy reached Kachreal, 7 KUMAON was waiting for them; this attack was repulsed and they were sent down the hill. In hindsight, it was this skirmish with 216 Medium Regiment that blunted their offensive. The Mandiala Bridge which had meanwhile been captured by the enemy 47 PUNJAB, was retaken by a swift counter action by 5 SIKH and 5/8 GR supported by armour. Meanwhile enemy armour coming through the Sukh Tao Nala were engaged by 130 mm guns of 216 Medium Regiment and tanks of 72 Armoured Regiment, and three were knocked out. This Pakistani offensive ended in total failure, and by evening their forces were back across the river.[8] The Pakistani brigade suffered a total of 163 casualties, many wounded and taken in as POWs. The CO of 13 AK Battalion, Lieutenant Colonel Basharrat Raja, who was captured as PoW along with his 2IC, was the highest ranking Pakistani officer to be captured in the entire Western Theatre.

To achieve a breakthrough, Major General Janjua planned a two-brigade attack in the area of Darh Crossing on the night of December 7/8; however, the units of 2 Armoured Brigade failed to reach their assembly area, and so the attack went in only with 42 PUNJAB. The enemy captured a few forward posts of 9 JAT and 12 GARH Rif, but determined Indian counter-attacks soon threw them back.

Later the same day, a Pakistani F-86 Sabre was shot in full view of the GOC and Corps Commander who were driving towards the Darh Crossing area. Havildar Uttam Jawalge who had shot it down was awarded an 'on the spot' Vir Chakra.[9]

Meanwhile, Major General Janjua was getting increasingly frustrated at not being able to make a successful crossing after one week's fighting.[10] On the night of December 9, he ordered the 111 Infantry Brigade to launch another assault across the river between the Darh and Raipur Crossings, but was not destined to see it through. The next evening when he flew to 111 Infantry Brigade HQ to coordinate the attack plan, his helicopter crashed while trying to land when the pilot hit a tree in an attempt to dodge the Indian fire.[11] *Major General Iftikhar Khan Janjua is the senior most officer from either country to have died in any India-Pakistani conflict.*

On the night of 9/10 December around 0200 hours, the 111 Infantry Brigade attacked with two battalions. An intense fighting ensued between the forward companies of 9 JAT and 12 GARH Rif, but they eventually yielded. Major General Jaswant Singh ordered 52 Infantry Brigade to launch immediate counter-attacks to evict the enemy, but these were unsuccessful.

Jaswant Singh also requested HQ 15 Corps for maximum air strikes on the enemy bridgehead, and to send additional armour from the neighbouring 26 Infantry Division Sector. Based on this request, CIH and one company of 7 GRENADIERS (APCs) were ordered by the Corps Commander to move into the 10 Infantry Division sector. By the early hours of the morning, the enemy had made a bridgehead east of Manawar Tawi, and tanks of 28 Cavalry had started coming into it. The GOC then visited HQ 52 and 68 Infantry Brigades to inspect the situation first-hand and authorised the use of counter-penetration positions to prevent any break-out. Meanwhile, the Army Chief had ordered the Corps Commander to fly in to get a first-hand assessment of the situation. From the north and south, the 52 and 68 Infantry Brigades were ordered to launch counter-attacks against the enemy bridgehead. These attacks were carried out at night and by the morning the enemy had been thrown back across the river, leaving six tanks behind. According to Pakistani sources both battalions suffered identical losses – 26 killed and 60 wounded, i.e. a total of 172.

Lieutenant General Candeth, the Army Commander, paid a visit to the 10 Infantry Division the next day and praised Major General Jaswant Singh on holding the Pakistanis west of the river. Jaswant Singh took this opportunity to brief Lieutenant General Candeth on his counter-attack plan, and requested that the units that had been moved in, be allotted to him for this task along with HQ 3 (I) Armoured Brigade; this was agreed to. However, strangely even as the counter-attack plans were being coordinated and recces being done, the Corps ordered the move back of all additional armour and infantry. Later, even the division's integral 39 Medium Regiment was moved out to 25 Infantry Division.[12] Thus, we missed a great opportunity to recapture the lost territory.

Even as the counter-attack plans were being coordinated, Jaswant Singh decided to conduct raids on the enemy to keep him engaged, cause attrition and display moral ascendancy. Mrs. Indira Gandhi declared a unilateral ceasefire on the 16th of December with effect from 2000 hours of the next day, effectively putting an end to the 10 Infantry Division's plans to launch a major counter attack across the Manawar Tawi. However, with the imminence of the ceasefire, GOC 10 Infantry Division decided to improve the defensive posture by launching small-scale attacks on selected enemy posts. Thus 7 GARH Rif captured Post 15 ALFA and Sangam, 10 GARH Rif occupied Nathu Kulian, while 7 KUMAON went across the Manawar Tawi and captured Chakla West, Point 935 and Ban, which are still our enclaves across the river.

Major General Jaswant Singh recalled in his interview to Melville de Mellow that 'on the last day of the war, one of his stations cut into our own wireless net and acknowledged that he was an enemy station, but said for God's sake stop your guns.'[13] Though the Pakistanis were able to make initial gains due the sheer weight of their attack against an initially unbalanced defence, they were unable to capture their strategic objective of Akhnur. The stoic defence put up by 10 Infantry Division restricted them to the west bank of the Manawar Tawi.

To summarise, Lieutenant General K.P. Candeth, the then Army Commander, wrote the following letter to the GOC 10 Infantry Division:

> *"The main weight of Pakistan's pre-emptive attack on land was against your division, and although you had to give ground, you inflicted such attrition on him that his advance grounded to a halt without achieving a major success."*[14]

Map 1: The Chhamb Terrain

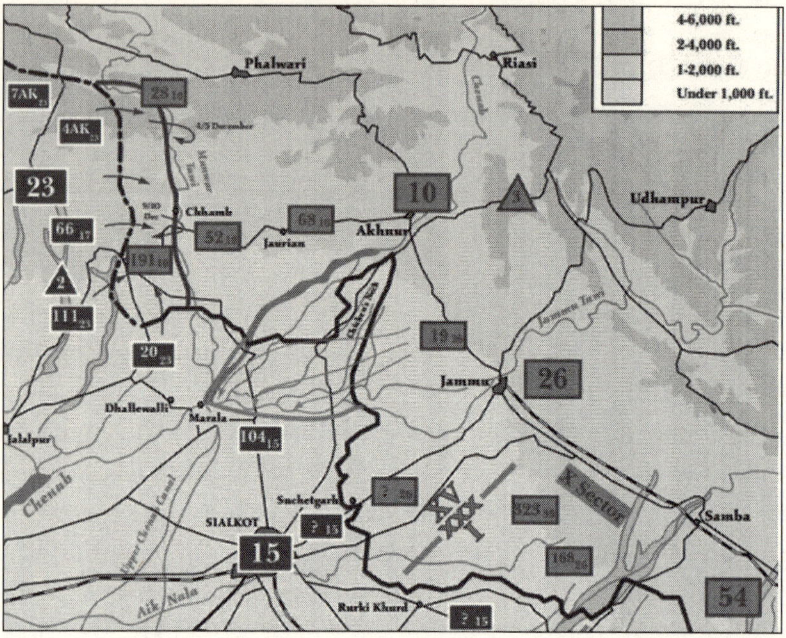

Notes

1. Maj. Gen. AJS Sandhu, *BATTLEGROUND CHHAMB: The Indo-Pakistan war of 1971*, p. 264.
2. Sandhu, n. 1, pp. 87-88.
3. Ibid., pp. 88-89; Col. Mahesh Chadha (then ADC to GOC 10 Infantry Division), in a telephonic conversation with the author on March 12, 2015.
4. Ibid., pp. 91-92; Maj. Gen. Jaswant Singh, entry dated November 1, 1971, in his personal diary.
5. Maj Gen Shaukat Riza, *The Pakistan Army 1966–71*, pp. 177–80.
6. Maj. Gen. Jaswant Singh, Personal Diary entry dated December 3, 1971.
7. Brig. Surinder Kaushik in an interview with Melville de Mellow of All India Radio, broadcast in January 1972.
8. Sandhu, n. 1, pp. 144-53, gives a detailed account of this failed attack.
9. Sandhu, n. 1,, p. 260, gives a detailed account of this incident.
10. Ibid., p. 200, quoting Lt. Col. (later Brig.) Shamjm Yasin Manto, the C.O. of 23 Cavalry
11. Ibid., p. 173-74; also Lt. Col. Ahmad Saeed, *Battle of Chhamb (1971)*, pp. 74-75.
12. Col. Mahesh in an interview with the author on March 25, 2015.
13. Maj. Gen. Jaswant Singh in an interview with Melville de Mellow, broadcast by All India Radio in January 1972.
14. Lt. Gen. K.P. Candeth, D.O. Letter dated 17 June 1972.

25

Capture of Lipa Valley (POK)

RS Sujlana

Pre-War Deployment

Prior to the outbreak of the 1971 War, 9 SIKH – a part of the Tangdhar Brigade – was specially earmarked to take up a defensive role in sub-sector Naugam, aimed to negate any offensive or infiltration attempt by Pakistan through this area. The Battalion, which was less a company, was deployed on Forward Defensive Localities (FDLs) along the ceasefire line (CFL) on a 10-km frontage, with Tutmari Gali (TMG) central to the defences. Along the steep Shamsha Bari Ridge, the posts were positioned at elevations ranging from 9,000 to 12,000 feet.

The fourth Coy was deployed at the Nastachun Pass, to guard the only vital road communication leading to Tangdhar Valley, where the Brigade HQ and other battalions were located. The lateral separation of 100 km plus was over very steep, rough mountains, and it took a day to travel by road and foot. The signal communications were most unreliable. Artillery in direct support was restricted to a battery of the 4.2 inch Mortars, an antique and erratic weapon with no infantry as reserve.

Due to the dangerous terrain and inadequate communication network, enemy operations in Lipa Valley was restricted to surveillance. They may have expected no action from the Indian Army. During the India-Pakistan War 1971, the Valley became famous for the activities of just one Battalion – 9 SIKH.

Planning for War

The Battalion was kept on high alert since mid-October 1971 – the Commanding Officer (CO) was directed to be prepared for a limited offensive into Lipa Valley at short notice. The CO, Lt Col (later Major General) Sam Chengappa, meticulously planned and worked out the attack plans. The CO had a battalion minus to plan, one coy was required to hold the firm base on Shamsha Bari. Thus, only two companies were available for the offensive. As such, the essence of operations had to be on speed and surprise using unconventional tactics. Thus, in conjunction with an attack, it necessitated plans to simultaneously reach forward to obtain enemy information in the rear and maintain the momentum of operations.

The CO's plan was three-fold – firstly, initial objective should fulfil two aims: provide depth to the FDLs and also a launch pad for further operations. The second phase entails consolidating the gains made and, eventually, assisting the Brigade with the overall strategy. Plans were brainstormed with the Company (Coy) Commanders and the officers. Early and speedy actions enabled one infantry battalion to repeatedly get the better of the enemy, in an area held with a Battalion plus (16 POK and Tochi Scouts) supported by artillery. The operations were launched with absolute gusto and an all-pervading spirit of 9 SIKH, true to their motto, "*Sir Qaim Jang Daim*" (Head Intact, Battle Continues)!

Establishing the Launchpad – Capture of Thanda Pani

The capture of Thanda Pani, about 2 km beyond the CFL, was the first target. On the night of December 4 and 5, a reconnaissance expedition led by Lt AS Sen established the existence of enemy presence there. On December 5, Lt Pushpinder and a section engineer cleared their own defensive minefield ahead of the FDLs. On December 5, by 1930 hours, Bravo Coy, commanded by Major KC Bali with Lt Sen crossed the CFL to launch the attack. The commando platoon under Captain Karam Singh was tasked to drop straight into the valley – to trap the withdrawing enemy from Thanda Pani, block reinforcements and carry out further reconnaissance. Charlie Coy was assigned to FDL *Shalimar* as a reserve under Major Jai Narain and Lt Pushpinder. Fire support was planned with battalion mortars (under Captain JN Maji) and Medium Machine Guns (MMGs), and the 4.2 inch Artillery battery under Captain Jagdish Chander. Strong winds across the TMG negated the fire support plans but undeterred, the Coy drove home the attack. The air shattering '*Jaikaras*' were enough; the enemy fled in a haste after firing a few shots, leaving behind clothing and rations. Thanda Pani was secured on December 6, by 0430 hours; a platoon exploited forward and occupied Point 3,101 metres (10,175 feet). Meanwhile, the commandos had found the next enemy position at Kaiyan, and their defences had been shifted southwards to cover the Valley.

Consolidating the Hold – Capture of Kaiyan Post

Without losing time, the CO directed Charlie Coy to capture *Kaiyan* Post the next night, on December 6/7, with a platoon of Bravo Coy in reserve. Due to a lack of reserves, the CO chose to strike first, denying the adversary any respite or opportunity to reinforce Kaiyan. By 2100 hours on December 6, Charlie Coy and the Commandos came together at the rendezvous, near Palani Baikh, north of *Kaiyan*. To minimise casualties and achieve surprise, the Coy and the Commandos silently rolled down from the heights to the north. Lt Puspinder positioned a cut-off towards the valley to attack the fleeing enemy and block reinforcement. The unexpected direction of attack was launched in two prongs – allowing the forces to close in on the enemy within 20 metres before being detected.

The confused enemy, in executing their 'illumination' plan, lit up their own position much to the advantage of the assaulting troops. The enemy fought resolutely; one of the .30 mm Browning MMG housed in a strongly built bunker turned to be a major impediment. In an extremely valiant act Naib Subedar Sarwan Singh, leading one of the prongs along with Sepoy Sowaran Singh crawled from a flank, lobbed grenades next to the hot barrel of the MMG and neutralised it. The entire position was captured by December 7, 0230 hours. Besides the MMG, five .30 rifles were seized, along with a substantial quantity of ammunition, equipment, stocks, and rations. Pakistan lost one JCO and eleven men, three of whom were taken prisoners.

The enemy made two counterattacks early in the morning in an attempt to recapture Kaiyan, but the platoon stubbornly repulsed both charges. Having failed, the enemy positioned themselves on the higher ground and continuously sniped at our troops. To neutralise this threat, Bravo Coy less a platoon reinforced *Kaiyan* by 2330 hours on December 7. The first aim had been achieved; the process of consolidation was soon underway.

Starting with first light on December 8, Bravo Coy started clearing the heights above *Kaiyan*, but progress was slow, due to persistent enemy artillery fire and well positioned snipers. By December 10, *Kaiyan* heights had been cleared. Alpha Coy under Major Hardul Singh on relief from *Padam-Gore* rolled down on December 9 to clear the left flank of Lipa Valley comprising *Karan, Nerian* and *Jabra*. A platoon of Bravo Coy had been projected to Point 3,062 metres (10,046 feet) above Mandakuli.

The Final Leg: Striking Deep on Road Muzaffarabad-Brithawari Gali-Lipa Valley (Road MBL)

Delta Coy, commanded by Major Balu Ram, reported to the Battalion on December 6, 1971 after receiving reinforcements from Nastachun Pass. The Coy Commander was immediately briefed on the task to establish a road block on the MBL Road, planned in conjunction with 6 RAJ RIF operations in Tangdhar Bowl. The task involved infiltration through enemy-held area over approximately 20 km, the establishment of a road block before first light on December 8 and continued surveillance until December 10, 1971. The Coy was self-contained with one 57 mm Recoilless Gun, cooked food, dry and survival rations. The boys were not weighed down by the 32 kg load of each individual; their morale was sky high after being chosen for the special expedition! True to the spirit of a soldier!

The Coy left *Kaiyan* on December 8, at 0100 hours; with forest fires all over, the area got illuminated thereby increasing the chances of detection. However, the infiltration was successful, but a little delayed as a halt became necessary to avoid detection. By first light on December 9, a block on Road MBL was established between Khudri-Dandkari – the road mined and covered by fire including recoilless guns. The enemy was clearly aware of our position in the area, as all vehicular movement ceased on the Road, but they failed to detect the Coy. Seeing the efficacy of the Block, it was ordered to be extended, but soon rations ran low. An attempt to replenish the Block did not succeed due to heavy enemy activity. On December, while exfiltrating, the Coy was ambushed at 1300 hours; however, the Coy took advantage of its strength to fight through and also pick up one enemy as POW. By first light of December 14, 1971, the Coy returned safely – the feat accomplished by them was an outstanding example of grit, physical and mental endurance.

Attempt to Re-establish a Block on Road MBL

With plans afoot to enhance operations in Lipa Valley, it was decided to disrupt communications on MBL Road again. On December 14, 1971, the job was assigned to the Commando platoon, along with a second platoon under Captain Karam Singh and Captain Amrik Sambyal. Taking a route along the higher reaches of the Mandakuli feature, they spotted an enemy barrack with troops mingling around in Chananian Village, possibly an administrative base. The Battalion mortars homed on and caused much damage. Had our artillery been available the damage would have been massive. Further ahead, they surprised four Razakars carrying a casualty, all were apprehended and sent back to *Kaiyan*. But soon thereafter, whilst crossing a Nala, the column was ambushed, two of our boys were hit – an NCO was martyred, the second Sepoy Baldev injured and was given first aid and rations, before being evacuated to a safe location for recovery. The column had to move on for mission accomplishment, thinking that they will recover the casualty on return. However, this evacuation did not fructify due to heavy enemy presence.

Of Human Will Power and Desire to Live

Sepoy Baldev, despite sustaining a terrible injury to his right arm, was determined to endure the physical and environmental hardship. He quenched his thirst with the snow and hunger with the limited rations, passing four agonising days. On the fifth day, Baldev woke up with a dog sniffing him and he shooed it away with superhuman effort. When the remains of the two boys were requested following the ceasefire, the enemy discovered Baldev alive and held him prisoner. Baldev's toes were frostbitten by this point, and during his evacuation to Rawalpindi, his right arm was amputated. On repatriation, both his legs, below lower shin, had to be amputated due to gangrene. Baldev had proved his resilience, grit and will power to overcome an ordeal of immense pain amidst extreme environmental challenges. Baldev continues to live in his Village with his well-earned honourable pension despite his artificial limbs!

Infiltration, Recce in Force and Capture of Three Pimples

On December 14, Alpha Coy was tasked to capture *Three Pimples*, along with Charlie Coy in reserve. Infiltrating by night, Charlie Coy established a Firm Base at Point 2,962 metres (9,718 feet) to the north of *Three Pimple* by first light of December 15, 1971. To encash on their undetected movement, Major Hardul moved forward by 1200 hours with a strong recce in force to exploit the area. Being day, they manoeuvred discreetly and quickly got within 50 metres of the enemy's location at *Three Pimples*. Oblivious of any danger in this depth location, the enemy were totally at ease. This opportunity could not be missed. The balance of the Coy and a platoon from Charlie Coy was whistled forward and the attack was sprung at 1400 hours by day.

The enemy was in complete panic, creating a *sauve-qui-peut* situation, and as their resistance collapsed, the Sikhs were unstoppable, and by 1600 hours the entire feature was captured. The success signal surprised the CO, as much as it surprised the enemy, as this attack was planned the following night! This was an outstanding example of initiative, boldness, surprise and presence of mind. On December 16 at 0900 hours, the enemy launched a two-pronged attack; our troops fought from behind trees and logs as the existing enemy defences faced the other way. The attacks were unsuccessful and the enemy lost heavily. Casualties on our part were less than that of the enemy. We captured some weapons, which included four 3-inch Mortars (with 280 High Explosive Mortar shells), one 83 mm RL, two LMGs, Six rifles, One Pistol Signal, other miscellaneous stores and ammunition.

Epilogue

With indications of an early ceasefire, effort was made to capture maximum area. The *Bali* spur leading to the Valley was cleared by Delta Coy, by last light on December 16, 1971 and linked up with a platoon under 2/Lt RS Sujlana. This enabled replenishment of ammunition, rations and evacuation of the wounded. At the final count, 9 SIKH had single-handedly captured 46 Square km of enemy-held POK, imposed heavy physical and weapon casualties, with few own casualties. The crux of the laudable success and minimal casualties was due to meticulous pre-planning, directions of the CO, unconventional tactics, speedy execution by perseverant and highly motivated sub-unit leaders at all levels, which ensured repeated surprises. Unfortunately, numerous acts of bravery went unrecognised. Finally, it was three Sena Medals (Lt Pushpinder, Naik Purshotum and Sepoy Joginder) and one Mention-in Despatches to Nb Sub Sarwan Singh. 9 SIKH, led by the versatile Sam Chengappa, proved their professionalism, high morale, gallantry and bravado true to its Regimental Motto – ***"Nischay Kar Apni Jeet Karon!"***

26

Battle of Dera Baba Nanak

JKV Singh

December 1971 – Operation AKAL

I was one of the fortunate young officers who had the opportunity to participate in the Operation AKAL during the 1971 War on the Western Front as an Intelligence Officer (IO) of 1/9 Gorkha Rifles (GR). Some of my observations of the Dera Baba Nanak (DBN) battle may sound contrary to what one has known till today. However, I will attempt to present the facts, specific challenges encountered and how we overcome them.

Pre-Operation AKAL (Defensive Role)

1/9 GR moved from Ambala as part of 86 Infantry Brigade under 15 Infantry Division in Sep/Oct 1971. I joined the Battalion (Bn) at Rampura Bridge on road DBN – Fateh Garh Churian, after completing a training course at the Intelligence School Pune.

Detachments were deployed on Basantar and Ghania Kee Bet Border Out Posts (BOPs) along with Border Security Force (BSF) in Kasowal Bulge, for carrying out observation of the territory across the International Boundary. Continuous reconnaissance of the border was conducted by officer led patrols every night. Late 2nd Lt SS Rawat was the Observation Post (OP) Officer at Basantar Tower BOP, while Lt Jagdish Ram (later posted to 13 Jammu and Kashmir Rifles) was at Ghania Kee Bet BOP.

On December 3, 1971, a patrol for Kasowal Bulge led by Capt AA Athale and Naib Subedar Mukta Bahadur left at about 1630 hours as per schedule. I, as IO of the *Paltan*, was with Commanding Officer (CO) Lt Col SK Kapoor at Forward Bundh, observing as to how the features across (our attack objective) would look as they merged into darkness. Suddenly two low flying planes came from Pakistan and zoomed past us into Indian territory. We ran back to Bn HQ to report this Air Violation because the nearest BSF Post's telephone was out of operation. It was then that I was given the news of Pakistan air attacks on Amritsar, Srinagar and Pathankot. The '*Balloon*' had gone up!

Radio Telephony messages giving directions of tank noises started coming from Basantar and Ghania Ke Bet BOPs. Capt Athale was not in communication! 'A' Coy at Dharam ferry also confirmed these activities. Thus, it was known that Kasowal Bulge was under attack by enemy armour and infantry. Around midnight on December 3/4, orders were issued for the withdrawal of BSF BOPs. After their withdrawal, Dharam Ferry, being 'Reserve Demolition', was blown off by pioneers of 1/9 GR, on orders.

By that time, Lt Jagdish and 2nd Lt Rawat had safely crossed across the river Ravi. There was no word on Capt Athale's whereabouts. Later on, it was confirmed during the flag meeting on December 6, that had been requested by Pakistan to pick up bodies of their soldiers from the Ravi riverbed following our conquest of the DBN Enclave on the night of 5/6th, that Capt Athale and his patrol had been taken prisoner at night on December 3.

There was another unfortunate incident. On December 3, at approximately 2300 hours, our Pioneer Platoon got caught in an ambush by a Pakistani raid party that had infiltrated. Pioneer platoon was moving in a 3 Ton from DBN to Kalanaur to clear a mine field lane. Two Junior Commissioned Officers (JCOs) and four Other Ranks (ORs) were killed, two ORs were wounded, and two ORs went missing (later on confirmed prisoners).

Operation Akal (Attack)

The long-awaited Warning Order for Operation AKAL was received on December 4, 1971, at about 1200 hours. The same evening, Bn HQ and 'D' Coy moved up to join 'B' Coy location and hid in the communication trenches in Forward Assembly Area (FAA) to avoid ongoing heavy shelling. 'A' Coy had moved to build up their platoon at Dharam Ferry. It stayed at Dharam itself to face the onslaught of enemy's shelling right till the end of war.

Extensive patrolling of *Forward Bundh* was carried out on 4th night. Two patrols under JCOs were sent to fire Light Machine Guns (LMGs) from both sides of *Kink* and also to carry out some movement in *Sarkanda*. Pakistanis fell for this trap and obliged us by opening most of their weapons. For a constant 30 to 40 minutes, star shells, artillery, Medium Machine Gun's (MMGs) and Recoilless (RCL) Guns fired at us until they realised it was pointless.

On 5th, around 2100 hours, Battalion less 'A' Coy advanced in a single file line along the Dhussi Bundh. We passed 15 Division General Officer Commanding, Maj Gen Bhattacharya and Brigade Commander Brig Gowri Shankar standing near a *Topaz* command post next to *Forward Bundh*. I overheard the Commander talking to our CO saying, "I don't know what the hell is happening and where my boys are?". He was referring to 10 DOGRA mounted on 71 Armoured Regiment, which was meant to cross Ravi from Gujartur side as Phase I of Brigade Operations.

Our MMGs, LMGs, Tanks and RCLs had been placed in covering fire role on *Forward Bundh* and were being replied by enemy shelling, automatics and RCL's aimlessly. We were waiting for success signal of Phase 1 of attack at our Forming Up Place and entry point of Pakistani mine field for Phase 2 of the attack. Even in the midst of combat noise, firing, and the chilly December weather, several '*Kanchas*' could take a short nap on rear slopes of *Forward Bundh*.

At 2300 hours, when there was no news about Phase 1, we were asked to push in before the planned H Hour of December 6 0100 hours. On receiving the confirmation from CO, I said my prayers and cut the wire concertina of Pak minefield and led the Bn in single file through an 800-metre-deep enemy mine field along with my Intelligence Havaldar Til Bahadur and my navigation party. In the minefield, six Pakistani weapon detachments known as Ring Bundhs had sprung up by that time, firing on their fixed lines. My assistant, Sepoy Chandra Bahadur, was struck on the chest by one of these bursts and he had to be carried across the minefield.

On reaching across the minefield, I saw Lt Col Chimni, CO 71 Armoured Regiment, standing and giving directions to his tanks struggling at full throttle. These were the leading tanks carrying Dogra's column, which had bogged down in the river Ravi. The Dogras had already dismounted and were moving along the water line.

We started our attack in small echelons along the Dhussi Bundh. The first phase of the attack created nervousness, as none knew the design and way of tackling those live pillboxes. We only discovered where the first pillbox was when one Rifleman began yelling and was shot in the chest by an automatic discharge. We were moving north of the Dhussi Bundh, on Pakistani territory.

There was utter confusion. A party went on top of the pill box. They lied down and tossed hand grenades into the building. Everything fell silent. Boys tried to break through the entryway that was being guarded. A burst of fire from inside stopped them again, and another soldier got hurt. Some more grenades were thrown in, along with 77 Grenade. One Pakistani soldier came out with clothes burning and was shot dead.

Someone found a Pakistani Toyota RCL jeep standing in *Sarkanda (Reeds - tall plants that grow in shallow water)* nearby. A Jerrycan full of petrol was brought and thrown into the pill box along with 77 hand grenades. Three Pakistanis came out with their clothes on fire. One managed to vanish in *Sarkanda.* The other two were bayoneted badly. Another tall injured Baluch soldier began pleading for compassion. I used my newly learned interrogation technique, inquiring about the Ring Bundhs, the distance between each pill box, and the particular design of pill boxes. He told us that there were weapons on the *Ring Bundhs*, and they were hidden inside mine fields to attract us on to the fixed lines of weapons sited on Dhussi Bundh. He also told us that we were attacking defences held by 'D' Coy of 38 PUNJAB with a Platoon from recce and support Bn of 21 BALAUCH Regiment. I gave him some water and put him aside, away from track, in Sarkanda, as he was unable to move. This information was passed on to all concerned and here onwards we became more alert. The pill boxes on Dhussi Bundh were cleared one by one as the attack pushed on.

Many Pakistani prisoners were being caught and it was becoming difficult to manage them, as that meant less manpower for the main attack. We had to look after our own casualties as well. As a result, enemy telephone wire was the solution. Khukris came in handy for cutting that, and we used it for tying the prisoners. Enemy's pill boxes were heavily stocked with arm/ammunition and winter clothing. We all used their grenades, as by then everyone had realised that in this Close Quarter Battle the HE/77 Grenades, *Khukris*, Molotov cocktails, bayonets and Sten guns were best for use.

When 'D' Coy was clearing the *Colonels Hut*, we came under intense enemy shelling. We suffered casualties also. It was about 0100 hours when we heard tank noises following us. Movement of tanks, which had not been able to go across, invited lot of enemy arty shelling which we had to suffer. A Pakistani OP on a 90-foot tower across the river was watching their fire of MMG tracers and Main Guns.

As fleeing enemy from D Coy's objective had demoralised the surviving enemy on their target, B Coy's task became slightly simpler. However, clearing of *T Junction* by 'C' Coy was tough, as enemy had stuck to it. Our success signal was given when it was captured. Dograi's battle cry could be heard from the bridge side after half an hour.

It was around that time we noticed a tank standing next to us firing towards *Kink Bundh* (place where Brigade Tactical HQ was established). Three tanks were on fire opposite us. My CO took me along to congratulate the Troop Commander who was firing at these tanks. It was only at first light, they realized that this was Lt Tiwatia's troop, ex their own squadron in fire support role under Maj Sangha at *Kink*, which had been pushed across Dhussi Bundh in the Pakistani mine field to take on so called Pakistani armour!

Our Bn HQ was established at *T Junction*. There were a number of Pakistani prisoners. Companies had started bringing their casualties also, but no doctor was available with us, because the doctor who had been attached with the Bn had been moved on December 5, 1971 for the establishment of an additional Advance Dressing Station!

As the first light set in, heavy shelling of *T Junction* started, lasting almost one hour. Their OP, at 90 feet steel tower, was wreaking havoc on us. We all took shelters in concrete pill boxes and RCL emplacements of Pakistani defences. Minor readjustments were possible during day time on December 6, 1971. Many prisoners who had been hiding in *Sarkanda,* were also rounded up.

Seeing the casualties, I was ordered to take all serious casualties, including my helper, to 10 DOGRA Regimental Medical Officer (RMO), Capt Sood. I took them all through heavy shelling. When I arrived, their RMO informed me that all casualties needed to be evacuated immediately and that there was very little he could do. I was told to leave them all in Pakistani RCL emplacement on the bridge, under his care and return to my Bn HQ.

The road to DBN bridge was blocked with the three tanks of Capt Tewatia's troop standing and burning in the mine field. Tanks loaded with main gun ammunition were exploding at irregular intervals. We held on to these positions, till we were told to pull out and fall back to DBN town on December 17, on declaration of cease fire by India. All Pakistani defences were blasted and destroyed, using tons of explosives before we moved out.

In general, things do not go as planned in war, but the mere presence of mind and calm head in a fluid scenario always results in a positive solution. To my mind, the important role of the 1/9 GR had turned the tables of battle of DBN for the whole brigade. The Unit earned two Vir Chakras and many Sena Medals. In addition, the Bn was also awarded the only post-Independence **Battle Honour of "DERA BABA NANAK."**

Map 1: Map of DBN

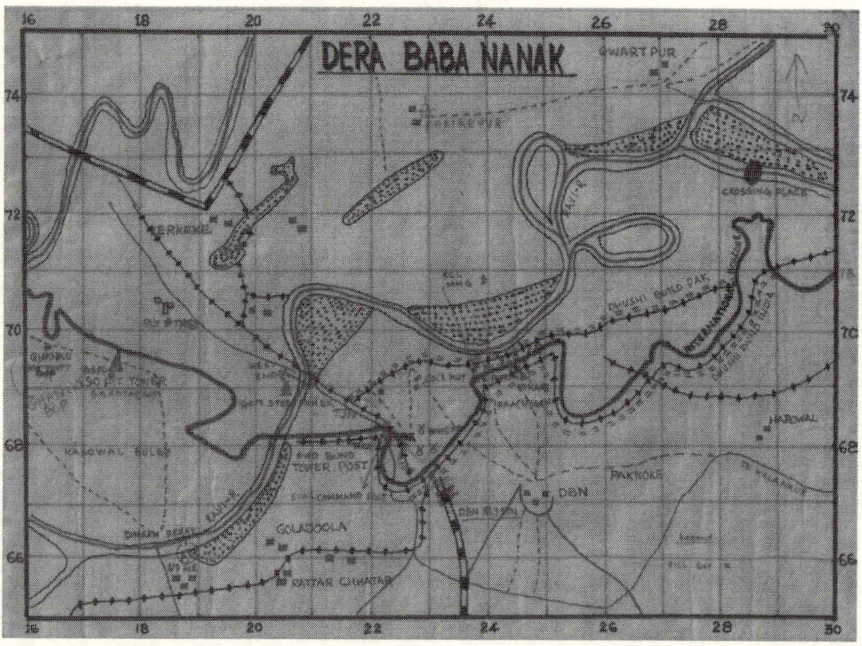

27

Saga of Capture of Parbat Ali (Nayachor)

DC Berry

Under the command of Lt Col P K Dasgupta, 2 MAHAR moved from Nagaland to Pune in September 1970. The Battalion (Bn) was part of 85 Infantry Brigade and the operational task of the Bn was in Barmer sector of Thar Desert in Rajasthan. By mid-1971 the Bn was ordered to get ready to move at short notice to our operational area. By this time Lt Col Dasgupta was posted to the East to take part in covert operations in East Pakistan. Lt Col SD Mehta of 10 MAHAR was posted to take over command.

Finally, on Diwali night, in October 1971, the Bn moved close to Munabao near International Border. Then came the long wait for the 'balloon' to rise. We kept ourselves busy in training and keeping the morale of the troops high. During this time, we were visited by our Chief, General SHFJ Manekshaw, MC, who minced no words in declaring that war was inevitable and we should be prepared. We were given two hours' notice to move in by the end of November 1971, but were asked to stand down on December 3 around 5 pm. While the *shakarparas* and *poories* were being consumed, the news came around 7 pm the same day, that the Pakistan Air Force had struck at various airfields. We were immediately asked to move to the Concentration Area near the International Border. We spent the whole day of December 4 in Concentration Area.

At night around midnight, we got orders to cross International Border. Our objective was Naya Chor. As the Support Company (Coy) Commander, I was entrusted to take combat elements ('F' echelon) and other vehicles by a roundabout route and 'marry up' with the rest of the Bn at 'Bhitala'. After an eventful journey through loose sand and trackless terrain, where vehicles got stuck and were brought back on track by innovative means, we touched Bhitala at daybreak. The village was deserted and Bn had already moved towards Khokhropar station having overcome the opposition.

We too moved ahead and 'married up' with the Bn. We were asked to await further orders. Our Brigade Commander Brig K S Kataria met us there and told us that Rahim Yaar Khan will be the objective and not Naya Chor. Unfortunately, while the Brigade was moving towards Parche Ji Veri, Brig Kataria's jeep overran a mine, and he was injured and had to be evacuated. The Bn reached Parche ji Veri on December 7 and were subjected to an Air Attack in which we suffered our first two fatalities. I may mention here that we were moving towards Naya Chor astride the Metre Gauge Railway track, which earlier used to link Munabao to Naya Chor and further to Hyderabad Sind. While moving towards Parche ji Veri, I met Maj Sharma, Adjutant, and while exchanging notes Capt SS Azrot, Mechanical Transport Officer (MTO) also joined us. He was very hungry and suddenly saw a rooster moving around. It was entertaining to watch him chase it down and finally catch it. He killed it with his bare hands and threw it in the fire. The chicken tasted great, sans salt and spices!

From Parche ji Veri, we made a slight detour and moved out on December 8. We encountered some artillery and small arms fire from a large sand dune, which we christened as 'Apex'. Through extensive patrolling, we discovered that the enemy held 'Apex'. On December 10/11, an offensive was launched. I was part of the attack. The enemy fired at us and after a brief resistance we captured 'Apex'. From there we saw that the enemy had withdrawn to an imposing sand dune. Patrols later confirmed that they were the main defences and the feature was 200r or Parbat Ali. Two Companies of the 39 Frontier Force Rifles held the feature with a deep minefield around it, with a frontage of nearly 2,500 metres. They were supported by the Mortar Platoon and four Medium Machine Guns.

Based on the Patrol reports and discussions with new Brigade Commander, Brig Vankunga, it was decided to launch a Brigade attack on the night of December 12/13. 2 MAHAR's task was to capture Right Bump and finger, and 10 SIKH the left Bump. H Hour was 0350 hours. Col SD Mehta called all Coy Commanders for a briefing. 'A' Coy under Maj Bhimrao Patil and 'C' Coy under Maj MMS Battu were to attack Right Bump in the first phase, and 'D' Coy under Maj SK Sarda was to attack finger in the 2nd phase. 'B' Coy under Maj Jagdish Pal was assigned to secure firm base. Maj NS Singha, second-in-command, was deputed as the overall leader and yours truly was assigned to him to 'run around' during the attack. Much before the attack could be launched, Col Mehta magnanimously invited us all to a drink at the objective, but with a stipulation 'Whisky is mine, Water is yours.'

The attack began at exactly 0315 hours. The entire frontline came to a halt after moving a short distance, with jawan's whispering '*Sahib, Taar.*' It was the edge of the minefield. We urged them to continue, and with a deep breath and a prayer on our lips, we did just that. By this time, their Medium Machine Guns had commenced fire on us, and their small weapons fire had become effective after a few yards. Fortunately, there were more Anti-Tank mines than Anti-Personnel, so casualties were minimal. By now our attack had gained momentum and we reached the base of Parbat Ali. With our thundering Battle Cry "Hindustan Ki Jai" we charged up the sand dune. Sand was soft and for every two steps forward we slid a step back. Anyhow, we reached the top and a furious hand-to-hand combat ensued, in which quite a few Pakistani soldiers were killed. The ferocity of our attack unnerved the enemy and they started running away towards the finger and rear base of Parbat Ali. We quickly regrouped and took defensive positions to ward off any counter attack. It must have been around 0415 hours. Maj Singha and I, as well as our signaller, buried ourselves into the right bump. Then all hell broke loose. The Pakis opened up with all artillery guns and mortars and we were subjected to heavy bombardment. Shells were whistling overhead, and their sound gave us solace; as a shell that hits you will not make a sound. This continued for over an hour. Finally, it stopped when our artillery neutralised their fire. It was around 0500 hours and we realised that we had made our trench next to their 'Survey Point'. Thank God for them missing us.

'HELEN', the success signal, was sent to Commanding Officer (CO) who launched the second phase immediately. Maj Sarda with 'D' Coy launched the attack on Finger, around 0600 hours. They quickly mopped up the remaining enemy and entrenched themselves. They repulsed two counter attacks, but in the bargain, Maj Sarda was wounded and had to be evacuated. Col Mehta asked me to takeover 'D' Coy, which I did. My first task was to send a strong patrol under Lt Dalal and Sub Vishwanath Bhosle to capture some Pakistani soldiers hiding at the base of Parbat Ali. They turned out to be their Mortar Platoon. Our Patrol did a commendable job and captured several soldiers with lots of arms and ammunition.

By 0900 hours, we had captured both the high ridge and the finger, and our National and Regimental flags were hoisted. The Pakistanis kept on using artillery fire with sporadic shelling on us until the ceasefire on December 17 at 2000 hours. The enemy deployed star shells at night, which made it impossible to go outside for ablutions for fear of being caught with your pants down. After taking over 'D' Coy, I was summoned to Col Mehta's bunker by Intelligence Officer Lt G R Ford, who had moved up with Bn HQ by that time. He was profoundly serious when he told me that I had been chosen to go for a task behind enemy lines along with 10 Para Commando and that I had to move out immediately. I saluted and turned to go when he said that there was a problem; they only want a Field Officer to go with them, so he was making me a Major. Thus, on that fateful day I got back my Major's rank, which I had to relinquish subsequently, due to low medical category and the addition of senior officers to the Bn. The Bn was running short of water and provisions, which was overcome when the Railway line between Munabao and Khokhropar was restored, and we got a train full of water.

When the guns were being removed on December 17 at 2000 hours, one of the shells hit on our listening station, and I lost Hav Sonawane of my Coy. On our side Lt HKL Sahni, Mortar Platoon Commander complained that he had not got a chance to fire even a single round during entire operations, so CO permitted him to fire a round. To everyone's chagrin it landed near CO's bunker, with no casualties! The saga of Parbat Ali's capture by 2 MAHAR in the land of "SAND, SNAKES, and SCORPIONS" comes to a close here. We will never forget our daily encounters with deadly Viper snakes and scorpions. We had to check our bunkers/tents for these slithering snakes and scorpions several times a day and sleep with our boots on.

Even after the declaration of the cease fire, we, like the enemy, continued with our routine patrolling. Unfortunately, we lost Maj Jagdish Pal, 'B' Coy Commander, when his recce patrol was captured by the Pakistanis on January 2, 1972, and he was tortured to death!

The Bn was conferred with four Vir Chakras, four Sena Medals, one Vishisht Seva Medal and three Mentioned-in-Despatches. The Bn was bestowed with Battle Honour 'Parbat Ali' and Theatre Honour 'Rajasthan and Sindh 1971' for their outstanding achievement.

Photo 1 : Officers of the Battalion and The COs of the Bde with Captured Arms and Ammunition belonging To 39 FF at Parbat Ali

28

Strange Gift for a Regimental Medical Officer

David Muthumani

Life with 10 SIKH LI

In October 1971, I was posted as a Medical Officer in 411 Medical Battalion, which was in Ahmedabad. Within one week, I was sent as Regimental Medical Officer (RMO) 10 SIKH LI to help them move from Bombay to Munabao. It was my first experience of moving with troops by train. Everything was new. We camped near Munabao amongst sand dunes. I shared a 180-pounder tent with Capt John Jacob. We had nothing to do except attend PT Parade and walk to the Mess tent thrice daily for our meals. The Officers used to huddle around a Sand Model and then brief their companies on what to do if war broke out. The mood seemed tense, as though war could break out at any moment. The 10 SIKH LI was part of 85 Brigade commanded by Brig Kataria, and the Commanding Officer (CO) was Col Basant Singh, who was well-liked by all troops. One day, during the CO's Durbar, one Other Rank (OR) Jaswant Singh stood up holding a letter from his mother, stating that his mother had asked him to die for the country and he was willing to do so. Later, I learned that he lost his life during the Parbat Ali battle.

Towards the end of November, we had a inter battalion football match. The other 2 battalions were 10 SIKH and 2 MAHAR. We managed to win it. The aftermath of this was, everyone who participated in the match was limping when the war started on the night of December 2. The battalion moved on foot into Pakistan. I was requested to start 2 hours later, along with other football players and my Regimental Aid Post (RAP) one tonner (Army truck). The medical platoon along with the nursing assistant moved with the main body. We were walking along with the 'one tonner' through the night. We were a group of 20. At sunrise we halted, ate our packed ration and tried to sleep inside the vehicle, under it or in its shade, after camouflaging the vehicle. The Pakistani Air force planes used to fly over us during the day. During the night, there was an eerie silence. We came across many abandoned vehicles as we moved forward. One of them was full of boiled eggs being carried to the forward troops. The truck had been abandoned after being hit by aircraft fire. This was on December 5. We feasted on the eggs to our hearts content. They were the tastiest boiled eggs I have had in my life. After devouring the eggs, we all fell asleep soundly for what seemed like an eternity. We resumed our night-time treks and rested throughout the day. We were about one hour behind the battalion on foot. On the morning of December 8, as we were settling down for the day, I got a call on the walkie talkie that the Battalion was under attack and there were casualties. I grabbed the one tonner and hurriedly asked the others to follow on foot. When I reached the Battalion, I saw that the Unit had been pinned down by heavy shelling and Medium Machine Gun (MMG) fire. I learned that the 'C' Company Commander Maj Sharma was injured along with some men. I took the CO's jeep and drove to within 100 metres from the front line. It was impossible to drive any further, due to heavy MMG fire. I crawled the last 100 metres to reach the injured, gave them first aid in the midst of firing and shelling. I managed to get them into the Jeep and return to the Battalion HQ, where I was able to arrange their evacuation. I stayed with the Battalion for only one more day. I was ordered to move to the Advance Dressing Station (ADS) attached to 85 Brigade by 10th morning, as the new RMO posted to 10 SIKH LI was scheduled to arrive the next morning. I left them late at night in the CO's jeep and reached my new unit early morning on December 10.

Tenure in the ADS

When I reached the ADS around 4 AM, I found a number of Ambulances standing and about 29 to 30 casualties on stretchers. The Officer Commanding ADS was in a trench refusing to come out because of Pakistani planes strafing occasionally. I quickly assumed command and began triaging the most seriously injured (mainly mine blast victims). They required pain relief, resuscitation and control of haemorrhage. For the first time in my life, I witnessed such injuries. In any case, after the bleeding was under control, we transferred them to ambulances and moved them to the Field Hospital at Munabao. I had no time to think of tea or food until late at night. I just collapsed and slept like a log. By 4 am, casualties started arriving again. We were more organised this time, and were able to handle them without making them wait.

Rough Experience

On December 12, 1971, we were attending to a new lot of wounded in the afternoon. We had not slept properly for nearly 72 hours and were living on rationed water and practically no food. Our Brigade Commander Brig Kataria was killed in a mine blast, and Brig Randhawa Commander 31 Brigade had taken additional charge of 85 Brigade. I was holding a soldier's shattered leg in my lap trying to locate the Posterior Tibial artery, which was pumping and if I didn't stop the bleeding immediately, he would die. Brig Randhawa arrived unexpectedly, and he was brought to me by one of the Ambulance drivers. We had no time to shave and wore crumpled uniforms. Brig Randhawa started berating me, saying that we were a shame to the Indian Army because of our appearance. I continued my effort to stop the bleeding. He was enraged and shouted that I was insubordinate. I pushed the leg at him and replied, "I joined the Army to save lives," and asked him if I should leave the casualty to die in order to shave? Moreover, there was practically no water even to drink. He went away fuming. That was the last I saw him. Even though I was subsequently ordered to move on 14th and was in charge of the ADS attached to his Brigade (31 Brigade), which was to attack Nayachor. However, before the battle for Nayachor could commence ceasefire was declared.

The Best Gift of My Life

On December 24, I got a call from Col Basant Singh, CO 10 SIKH LI, inviting me to join him for lunch on Christmas day.

Water and rations had to be transported by road from Barmer after the war, until the Army restored the Munabao-Kokrapar railway line. Water was rationed to 5 litres per person for meeting all their needs, both drinking and washing. None of us had a bath till the rail line was restored by end of December or early January. I drove to the unit on Christmas day and reached by 11 am. I found the whole unit lined up to welcome me. Col Basant Singh graciously welcomed me and led me to a canvas bucket full of hot water. The CO told me, *"The men had sacrificed one glass of water from their 5 litres ration, so that their 'Isai' (Christian) doctor can have a bath on Christmas Day."* My eyes were filled with tears of gratitude as I completed my bath with the whole unit cheering. The rest of the day is a haze in my memory.

29

Unheard Voices of the Indian Armed Forces

(Excerpts from Personal Interviews)

Jyoti M Pathania

Hussainiwala Bridge: Story Would Have Been Different

Col RK Sharma

15 PUNJAB (Patiala), under the command of Lt Col GBVL Sastri, was moved to Hussainiwala Enclave in February 1971 and tasked to defend it. It was about 7 km from Ferozpur on the western bank of River Sutlej with Headworks to control and release water. There were many flood control embankments called 'Bundhs', which provided raised grounds for deployment of troops and weapons. The Ferozpur-Kasur-Lahore Road was the only land route open between India and Pakistan, hence it had Joint Check Posts (JCP) to control the activities of custom clearance, transfer of goods, clearance of tourists, etc.

Due to open borders, the troops were not allowed to wear uniforms, and support weapons were not allowed to be deployed between down and dusk.

By 2300 hours on December 3, four spans of the bridge had been blown off, causing the dedicated Armour Squadron to be delayed and unable to reach the forward defences! Imagine the plight of the unit, with river obstacles at back, a bridge that had been blown off, and there was no chance of getting any support from the armour! Moreover, the information of the PAF air strike on advanced Indian airfields in the afternoon of December 3 was also not passed on to the unit, due to lack of communication. There was a reinforcement plan in place, but was never implemented! The outcome of the battle would have been different if the Armour Squadron had crossed the bridge.

Image 1: The Hussainiwala Barrage 1971

The Hussainiwala Barrage in 1971. On the home side are the Twin Canals irrigating the Indian Side. The far side bordering Pakistan, has limited tree cover and the area was covered with Sarkanda grass.

Source: 15 PUNJAB Unit

Around 1800 hours on December 3, the enemy Arty started shelling the company localities. It was immediately followed by a simultaneous attack with a battalion each on Perimeter company ('D' Company – commanded by Maj Kanwaljit Singh) and Samadhi ('C' Company – commanded by Maj SPS Waraich). The repeated attacks were repulsed by 'D' Company, inflicting heavy enemy casualties. However, 'C' Company strongly held on at Samadhi Tower, despite being surprised at first and suffering some fatalities and POWs. Major Kanwaljit was critically hurt when he rushed to lay Mine Necklace on the major route when he heard enemy tanks approaching. He directed our lone tank, which had crossed the bridge, to retrieve the balance of tanks immediately. The tank commander, however, put the tank in reverse gear due to the non-availability of the turning circuit. Little realising, the bridge by then was blown off due to 'sympathetic detonation'; the tank fell into the shallow end of the river shattering all hopes of tank support. Since the bridge was damaged, the CO also had to remain south of bridge and coordinate the battle from there.

Image 2: Deployment Plan

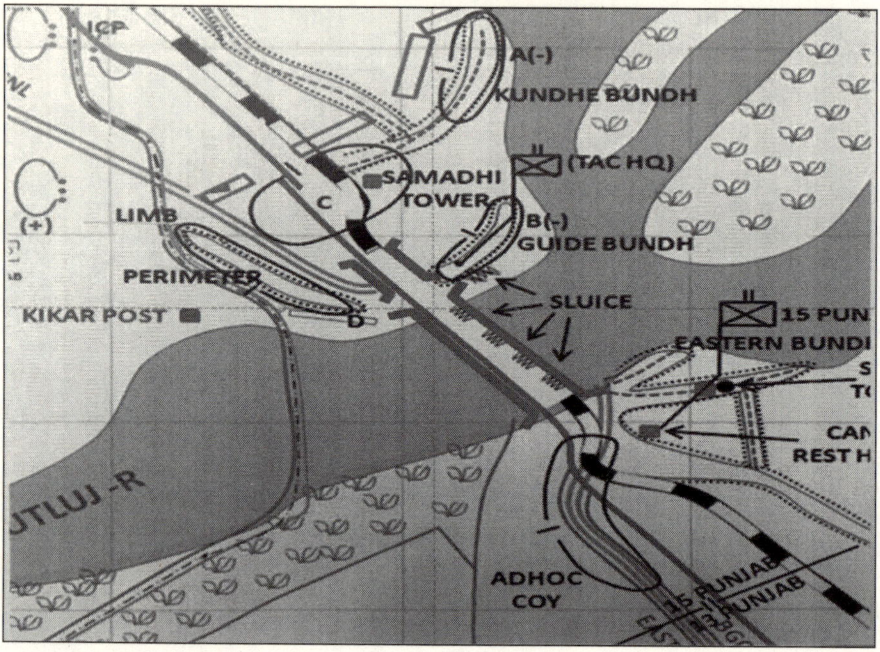

Source: 15 PUNJAB Unit

The sectors Perimeter and Samadhi were in enemy hands by 0900 hours on December 4, but the Companies at Guide and Kunde Bundh held on strongly and troops were in high spirits. Our Airpower played havoc with the enemy tanks. With a section at Samadhi Tower, Naik Surjit Singh demonstrated unrivalled heroism in repelling several attacks that resulted in numerous losses.However, despite the Battalion still holding on to the compact defences at Guide Bundh and Samadhi Tower, the orders of withdrawal were given. The withdrawal was carried out most systematically under the strong leadership of Maj AS Cheema, the second-in-command of the unit on the night December 4/5.

Post the War, the Battalion was honoured with the Theatre award of **'Punjab'**.

Pakistan Prisoner of War (POW): A Reality for Me

Brig Hamir Singh, VrC (Retired)

Brig Hamir Singh, VrC (Retired) is a third generation Army Officer who was commissioned in the Grenadiers Regiment in December 1962. He fought the 1971 war as a young captain, company commander with 14 GRENADIERS. He spent a year as POW in Pakistan and was repatriated to India in December 1972. Recipient of the **'Vijay Marshal'** – a symbolic torch meant to honour his role in the 1971 war to mark the fifty years of victory.

"I was captured on 14 December 1971 along with a few of my companions. We were first handed to the civilian police and then taken to a PoW camp after a thorough investigation. I was taken from the Poonch-Mendhar sector with bullet wounds on my right arm and a broken wrist bone. My abode was an isolation ward, about 10 feet by 10 foot room (later I came to know that this room was built to be used by Pakistani JCOs for treatment of any contagious disease). I was kept apart from the other PoWs, presumably because, I was apprehended in the Poonch-Mendhar sector and they mistook me for a 'commando'!"

I had no idea where I was for the first few months. I was the senior most PoW, but there were junior Pakistani officers who misbehaved with me. The medical care and food were adequate, but there was no newspaper, radio, or even someone to chat to, save for the Bengali *Farishtay* (medical assistant) who knew English and informed me of my location – MH Rawalpindi. However, soon my Bengali friend was repatriated to Bangladesh. My stay got even more secluded once my Bengali companion left, with only two sentries/guards remaining; one next to my bed and the other guarding outside my door. I underwent two to three surgeries on my arm, and I was given excellent medical care.

The arrival of the Red Cross offered me a glimmer of optimism, that I might be deported to India soon. In fact, a Red Cross European gentleman handed me a postcard-sized card and instructed me to write a few sentences so it could be sent to my home. Whenever the cleanliness campaign ramped up, I knew there would be a visit; shortly after, I began receiving newspapers and, perhaps, a radio set as a bonus. It was during the Red Cross's second visit, when I complained about my loneliness and depression. Thereafter, I was assigned to the Railpur POW Camp, where six officers and approximately 600 Indian POWs were stationed. At the very least, I was able to move around among my comrades now.

On Sundays, we alternated between a Mandir and a Gurudwara parade. The Muslim POWs were segregated. As the company commander of 'C' company (Muslim Company), I would lead my company's troops in a religious namaz on the first Friday of each month at 1 o'clock. To my surprise, the Pakistani officers and troops were completely taken aback! *"Aapke jaise humare yaha hota to kya baat hoti ..."* (If it would have been like this here, it would have been great) said one of them. My sentry guard would also tell me, shouting, *"Hum log pehle Peshawar se Kolkata or Bombay jate thei, Waise Wapas Kyo nahin ho sakta?"* (We used to go from Peshawar to Kolkata or Bombay, why can't it be the same as before?)

Around November 25, 1972, Prime Minister of Pakistan – Zulfikar Ali Bhutto paid us a visit (ironically, this was the same place where he had spent years in prison). We had been joined by ten air force officers by this time, and Mr Bhutto told us that, *"we would be sending you all back to your country soon,"* (I thought to myself, 'you had no choice but to send us back, because we had 90,000 Pakistani PoW with us'). I was finally released on December 1, 1972. We were sent by train to Lahore, and from there by bus to Wagha, where we were received by the Chief Minister of Punjab – Giani Zail Singh, my father, and the Commanding Officer (CO) of my unit.

Another episode I would like to share is that when the war started on December 3, some soldiers of the Mujahideen Battalion had come across and captured the Kalai Bridge in Poonch sector, only to be thrashed by 13 MAHAR and 9 PARA units. The Pak CO was killed in action and we buried him with proper rituals conducted by our unit's Maulvi. One day during my stay, I was told that a lady wanted to meet me. She was the COs wife who was killed in action in our sector. A young lady, with perhaps a 5-6 years old girl came along. She suddenly screamed, *"Arrey yeh to humare jaise hai, no choti and no Tilak!"* (He looks just like us, no ponytail, and no incense paste on the forehead). I realised that they had been taught to visualise an Indian soldier in that manner. Furthermore, I informed them that the Colonel and the Unit had fought well. When I told her mother about the unit's Maulvi (Muslim religious instructor) performing appropriate burial rights, tears streamed down her cheeks, combined with a sense of relief. She inquired about my family, and wished me well.

SECTION 5

Fire and Fury of the Sister Services

The Synergy

30

Geopolitics of Cold War: How it Impacted the India-Pakistan 1971 Maritime Operations

SCS Bangara

The often-repeated story of the Indian Navy's historic attack off the coast of Karachi in December 1971, has broadly focused on the strategic and tactical brilliance of its concept and execution. The severe blow to the Pakistan Navy, so early in the war, had devastating ramifications on the morale and subsequent deployment of their naval assets. More importantly, logistic support from West Pakistan to East Pakistan was choked by the actions taken by the Western and Eastern Fleets of the Indian Navy. A post-facto analysis befits the occasion of the Golden jubilee activities presently in progress.

The cold war between USA and the Soviet Union had reached a crescendo by 1960. Ironically Soviets and the Chinese had begun to escalate border skirmishes on the Sino-Soviet border, just when India was desperately seeking assistance for upgradation and modernisation of the Indian Armed forces in the wake of the Chinese invasion. The Americans had rushed some hardware in response to our appeal to stall the Chinese. In our effort to remain non-aligned during the cold war, we had soured our relationship with the West. Even before the Indo-Soviet Friendship treaty was signed, the perception that India was gravitating towards the USSR had unintended implications. One such event was the sudden decision of UK not to release the top-of-the-line submarine, the Oberon class to India. Despite the fact that the first few batches of selected Indian officers and sailors had completed their training.

Pakistan, on the other hand was benefitting from the status she enjoyed as an active member of the SEATO and CENTO from 1954. Not only did she receive financial aid and grants periodically, but was well supported by front line Military platforms, sensors and weapons from NATO allies too. The induction of the Daphne Class submarines from France was almost completed in the late 1960s, much before the Indian Navy acquired its first submarine from the Soviet Union.

In the mid-1960s, India negotiated a series of acquisition agreements with the Soviet Union, which continued for the next 40 years and even after the disintegration of the Soviet Union.

What is often glossed over is that Indian Navy, which was predominantly Western trained and equipped, had to grapple with tectonic changes related to manning, training, logistics, language, more importantly, operations and tactics of the Soviet Block. The challenges were unprecedented.

This narration aims to exemplify the obstacles that the Indian Navy encountered, as well as the ramifications that opened the door to a syncretic approach, much like eclecticism, that enriched the Navy in particular. As a result, what follows is the author's postulate necessarily drawn from a rear-view perspective. In the mid-1960s, the Soviet package for the Navy s consisted of a wide array of surface ships, submarines and aircraft. The upgrading programme included eight Osa class Missile boats, with four surface-to-surface missiles each. For purposes of brevity, communications and secrecy they were christened as AK Boats. AK were the initials of the then CNS, Admiral AK Chatterji. Given that the Navy was the smallest service and that it had just completed the induction of an aircraft carrier from the British, in 1961, it is axiomatic that the manpower needs multiplied dramatically. The Navy chose to use the short service commission route of induction with reduced training and flexible employment, based purely on performance appraisals.

The Artificer entry for mechanical and electrical personnel was beefed up in the below officer category to account for anticipated technology improvements.

The missile boat crew consisting of eight sets of personnel with a spare crew and the Squadron staff, and personnel of the missile preparation facility to be set up ashore, left for the Soviet Union in June 1969.

The author was the second-in-command of the boat, to be named INS Veer later. The entire crew was transferred from the Moscow international airport to Vladivostok via Khaborovsk, in a giant and noisy aircraft on a 14-hour sortie. Because of the confrontation on the Sino-Soviet border between the two communist republics and Vladivostok's proximity to the conflict zone, we had to shift to a smaller aircraft to reach our final destination.

At that point in history, we were unaware of the power struggle inextricably linked to the Cold war, and which resulted in the USA cozying up with China. Hence, events that unfolded between 1969 and 1972 and now available in the public domain, reveal a link that needs to be contextualised for the benefit of the reader.

After Pakistan played a facilitator's role, Kissinger, was able to make his first visit to China in July 1971. It would be reasonable to assume that the preparatory work kept under tight wraps commenced much earlier. The ground work for Nixon to make history in 1972 quite clearly overshadowed the developing events in South Asia. Pakistan as a facilitator, held a trump card that could be utilised to enlist the complete support of the US government in the event of an India-Pakistan conflict. No less than the Secretary of State was in constant dialogue with the Pak leadership.

Declassified documents from the Nixon-Indira Gandhi meeting, clearly prove the antagonism that existed between the two leaders. Kissinger duly supported the sentiments of his President, as India was seen to be firmly in the Soviet camp. In retrospect, the British Government's decision to deny us the top end submarine and the French resolve to equip Pakistan with Daphne Class submarines are but some connected examples of the geo-politics of the era.

Another fact that bears scrutiny is the deployment of Task Force 74, led by USS Enterprise, in the Bay of Bengal in support of Pakistan in December 1971. The Soviet Union reportedly neutralised the intent of the Task Force by deploying both surface ships and nuclear submarines in the vicinity. In our context these were remarkable events born out of the raging Cold War and its impact on Indian Maritime operations.

Going back to 1969, it appears that some of the calculus and imponderables associated with shifting to the Soviet philosophy of training from purely Western-oriented methodologies, were underestimated.

When the need to lean on the Soviet Union arose in the mid-1960s, the Military in India had the least knowledge of what lay behind the Iron curtain. Until then, the majority of countries that went to the Soviet Union for acquisition and training were either from the Warsaw pact or from autocratic/military governments opposed to the Western-NATO led alliance. Briefly none in our chain of Command could have foreseen the challenges and conflicts that could euphemistically be termed a "clash of civilisation".

A smaller version of the Osa class, the Komar, acquired by Egypt had sunk an Israeli Frigate in 1967. However, in a blue water environment the boat was meant to be a defensive asset, as its endurance had to be necessarily linked to its fuel carrying capacity. Equipped with high-speed diesel engines adapted from an aircraft engine, the boat could speedily ingress and egress in a limited theatre of war. They could be manufactured in large numbers to enable them to carry out divisional attacks from multiple directions, saturating the defences of the enemy Aircraft Carrier if it ventured closer to the coast. This was a quantum jump in technology for the Indian navy.

The Indian Submariners and Petya class crew were already being trained on an Island off Vladivostok when the Missile boat crew landed in the summer of 1969. On arrival, the first challenge was the language. There were no interpreters to assist in basic communication needs. Desperation and necessity for routine needs drove the crew to acquiring proficiency in record time. Most Indians spoke multiple languages. This, in particular, aided correct pronunciation and learning difficult syntax and phonetics/phonology. Within a few months, some officers were able to recite Russian poetry and dwell in serious literature. It takes years of study to reach this level of comfort. Clearly the Russians had not encountered professional competence and the ability to absorb technical content in comparison to others who had trained with them.

On the flip side, their routine activity of subtly introducing Communism as an ideology to our sailors, often without our officer's knowledge, met with little success. There were many factors that thwarted their subtle efforts. Due to the extraordinary circumstances, the Indian officers and sailors bonded as never before. Winter temperature hit –32 degree Celsius. We were both limited in our ability to communicate with the Soviets, the accommodation and food continued to be irritants, and we were all forbidden access to the city except on weekends since the boats from the island were monitored. Interaction with the locals was discouraged as Vladivostok being on the fringes of the East was always short of resources and was akin to a secret city where their nuclear submarines were based. Overall, these circumstances helped our ability to form bonds with our soldiers. In addition, the lack of freedom to travel provided the rare opportunity to focus on our training and master the subject of surface-to-surface missiles.

The training facilities were more than adequate and the instructors were experts on their subject. The crew as a whole was graded for combat efficiency after the post-training evaluation process and crew efficiency on all aspects of the boat. For the Squadron Commander this was an invaluable input.

The invisible dividends of being exposed to both Western and Eastern philosophies did result in some turbulence too, in structuring the training for Soviet-origin platforms and later the Indian built warships that began to populate our asset holding. It was not seamless, particularly when the Soviet Union collapsed. The long chain of training facilities along with the supply chain of logistics collapsed when the Union broke into smaller states. We maintained our connections with the West for courses and procurement of selected sensors and armament, despite our greater reliance on the USSR in all three dimensions. Furthermore, the integration of western systems with Indian platforms was secured by establishing organisations dedicated to marrying eastern and western systems on Indian platforms.

In summary, the Indian Military saga during and after the Cold war era is a captivating chapter with valuable lessons for the future. When India begins to export arms to friendly countries, our experience of the cold war would be of value if it is documented.

31

Commissioning with Five Medals

Mani Singh Mamik

We graduated from the training ships (Krishna and Tir) in early June 1971, after successfully towing a missile boat from Calcutta to Bombay and patrolling for a month off Ceylon, as part of the six ships sent in response to Ceylon Government's request after the uprisings in March 1971. I was fortunate to get the aircraft carrier, Vikrant during my training as a Midshipman (Mid).

Apart from the usual routine tasks of Officer of the Watch (OOW) and Officer of the Day (OOD), the training as Mids was further rounded with attachment to various departments and doing watches with the professional duty personnel on site. My first such attachment was with the Engineering Department for a month, which had all machinery under their charge. We had to do two four-hour watches in a day besides other duties including PT on the flight deck while not on duty elsewhere with the aircrew when embarked. The two duties exhausted us being subjected to temperatures greater than in Sahara, with only lime cordial as hydration.

These strenuous duties in the engine room and pressurised boiler room hardened us, where we were apprentices in watchkeeping for Turbo generators or for evaporator (making feed water for boilers from sea water). A highlight was operating main steam valves when challenged by the duty personnel, which was actually a "*tel nikalne wala*" (oil squeezing or strenuous) experience with super-heated steam leaking all over. One incident I will never forget is the vertical climb and descent of almost 3,500 feet between decks to record plummer block temperatures of the propeller shaft bearings as a consequence of being late for midnight duty in the engine room!

Getting Ready

The ship sailed to Madras rounding Ceylon at a very far off distance. Now all the technical staff and others got busy in getting all the armament and equipment operational. The steam to the catapult was tried out and aircraft were embarked and worked up using Meenambakam airport as diversion. The ship's operation was standardised, and operational drills were conducted for all departments.

It must go to the credit of the aircrew and engineers that they trained their attack skills with guns and rockets with accuracy on towed targets that were blasted off more frequently and became tough to replace for the Shipwright (fabrication specialist). Although restoring catapult to its full operation with limited steam during high speed posed a challenge, it was overcome by the engineers. Also, the entire clockwork drill, of at sea cyclical launch and recovery of aircraft within a few seconds of each other, went accident free, except for one oleo damaged of a Sea Hawk while landing, which was later safely recovered at Meenambakkam.

Morale

One of the most memorable moments at Madras was the visit of then Chief Minister of Tamil Nadu, Shri MG Ramachandran. He was kind enough to donate a few Tamil movies, mostly with the well-known heroine J Jayalalitha. Besides the ship broadcast playing "Monica Oh my Darling", the only other form of entertainment at sea on non-night flying days, was provided by hanging a screen to the Island superstructure and seating all keen watchers on the flight deck. The most looked forward announcement was 'Mailman Abreast ACR' (Aircraft Control Room) – which meant that the ships mailman will go by chopper and pick up the rerouted mail to the ship. Everyone hoped "Chitthi Aayegi" (of getting mail) but whoever was lucky found it a month old.

All this time the clouds of war were gathering. The ship received many high-ranking visitors, including the then Defence Minister, Mr Jagjivan Ram, who promised that "*Bangladesh ban ke rahega*" (Bangladesh will be a reality) and we hoped that this uncertainty would pass soon. However, Dussehra and then Diwali came and went and that no one could go home, which was certainly a damper; but the ship's morale remained high, keeping up the tempo of operations.

In mid-November, the Eastern Fleet was created with ships Vikrant, Brahmaputra, Kamorta, Beas and Kavaratti with RAdm SH Sarma as the Flag Officer Commanding Eastern Fleet (FOCEF) and they embarked Vikrant off the East Coast.

The Times moved fast, and INS Vikrant was now ready for battle, fully equipped with eighteen Sea Hawk fighters, half a dozen ELINT/ASW capable Alizes and three search and rescue (SAR) Alouette III helicopters now was battle ready. The carriers' guns crews of four twin-powered 40/60 mountings and five single mountings were led by enthusiastic Midshipmen who learnt to live in the gun sponsons with a high readiness level.

Preparing for Action

In the third week of November, on a dark moonless night, the IN ships Vikrant along with Beas and Kamorta entered a bay in North Andaman. With little navigation information available from an old survey chart, risk mitigation was done by placing a shallower draft ship to lead. A radar invisible island was on the centre of the channel. It was a very risky manoeuvre for the carrier in untreaded waters. Being on the bridge I cannot forget the cold sweat drops on Navigator Cdr MML Saxena's forehead, as he was locked on to the navigation radar scope – such was the risk for this manoeuvre and the high degree of professionalism required and displayed.

On the evening of December 3, the ships broadcasted the PM's message after the Pak air strike and of declaring hostilities against Pakistan. The atmosphere changed from one of uncertainty and anxiety to celebration with Mids performing Bhangra. Almost on the spur of the movement in the evening, the Mids invited all aircrew from INAS 300 and 310 to share a beer in the Gun room, to which they responded very warmly.

The War

On December 4, 1971, at around 10 am, INS Vikrant launched eight Sea Hawks for strike on Cox's Bazaar airfield and a few Alizes for recce role to gather the maritime picture from less than 100 nautical miles (say 180 km) from the target. The aircraft were recovered and rearmed for the next strike on Chittagong without incident. In the afternoon, eight Seahawks armed with bombs and rockets were launched for a strike on Chittagong airfield, from about

100 nautical miles. Also, three Alizes were also launched for offensive tasks against merchantmen and harbour installations and targets of opportunity. It so happened that my cruising duty station was Radar Detection Room Officer, which required me to report any intruder, estimating height and reporting the same to operations (ops) room.

When the strike returned, I took note of the number of blips on the radar and reported the matter to Ops room. It was estimated that their fighters may have confused themselves with ours and intended to attack. Immediately action stations were sounded, and I went to the bridge to be with the Captain. Within a minute or two of my arrival on the bridge, both escorts reported varying degrees of probability of submarine detection, with one or both intending to attack. At the same time, Lt Cdr Gupta, CO and leader of the Seahawk strike on Chittagong reported elevator failure of his aircraft. While Cdr (Air) was conveying this emergency, Aircraft Control Room in charge of aircraft movement on the deck and hangar informed that the aft lift (over which the landing arrester wire runs) was stuck in the down position, rendering the aircraft unrecoverable with only few minutes of fuel remaining. All these three reports came simultaneously within less than a minute. Anyone confronted with this unprecedented, never-before-gamed circumstance, would have been in shock; risk of losing one aircraft (elevator failure), risk of losing half the aircraft that were in the air (aft lift stuck in down position), and worst of all risk of losing ship due to a submarine attack!

This is the moment when leaders display their courage and composure. The unfazed Captain at the spur of the moment authoritatively issued three commands –

> "*Pilot while the escorts prosecute* (attack) *the submarine, you do evasive steering and torpedo countermeasures.*
>
> *Cdr (Air) to tell Seahawk with elevator failure to come abreast* (next to) *of the ship and eject and Jumbo* (SAR helicopter) *to pick him up and*
>
> *I am going to the aft lift and I will be back in five minutes.*"

Saying these words, he went down to the lift. There was total calm on the bridge, and everybody was in a state of as if nothing had ever happened, and the situation was gulped down like taking a pill without water and instantly feeling better.

Indeed, he returned after having encouraged the lift engineers by his presence, and as soon as the lift came up after some '*jugaad*' (local improvisation), he asked the Navigator to steer the flying course into wind to recover the aircraft.

In the meantime, the experienced Seahawk pilot had regained some control of the elevator situation and chose to attempt a landing. Captain told Cdr (Air) to let him land at the end and he did so safely. Both the Captain's choice, to accept the risk and enable him to land, as well as the Squadron Commanders' confidence in his ability to do so, sprang from what is at the heart of mutual faith and confidence in one another's talents; that is team work. As ordered, the escort ships were busy carrying out their strikes on the possible submarine and after a few hours rejoined Vikrant, which continued day and night operations against enemy targets.

Leadership in the Face of the Enemy

In those three sentences delivered in the heat of a crisis, I learnt the essence of leadership by example and required fewer lessons thereafter – clear concise decisions focused on the end state, delegating where required, willingness to take losses to save lives, and above all, keep your head cool and trust your crew – they will deliver regardless of the odds. My belief in him was reaffirmed the following day; I was on afternoon watch when an officer handed him the message regarding the successful missile attack on Karachi and the loss of PN ships listed. There was a smile on his face and he remarked "(Adm) Gorshkov told me that these boats are worth in gold." I then came to know that he was the Naval Attache in Moscow when the deal for these boats was signed and had met Admiral Gorshkov on that occasion. It taught me that while planning is critical, the difficult task of converting plans to operational reality, such as the speed handicap that has been in place for over five months, requires guts and determination – and only a leader with vision and foresight has the guts, determination and professionalism to implement, regardless of the odds.

Strike First Strike Hard

From December 4 to 15, Vikrant planes relentlessly attacked targets on land and sea. Many of the aircraft came back with bullet holes on their wings and one right between the pilot and the observer seats. A few landed at night with hydraulic fluid drained out from leaks caused by bullets, as they were flying low and attracted heavy enemy fire. Towards the latter part, the winds dropped to almost nil and aircraft had to carry less load due to the limitations of ship speed while giving steam to the catapult. To give an example of the morale among the marine engineers working in the hot and humid boiler and engine rooms, they made garlands of one-rupee notes and chilies and presented them to the returning pilots of the strike on December 4.

Targets all along East Pakistan's coastline, including Chittagong, Cox's Bazar, Chalna, Khulna, Pusur River, etc., and ships on the high seas were attacked and many were boarded in order to search for contraband, before being transported to Calcutta. As mentioned earlier, the submarine threat being real was globally known when PNS Ghazi perished off Visakhapatnam on the night of December 9. The Eastern Fleet's blockade of East Pakistan was completed with constant day and night raids, as Vikrant surveillance and strike capacity thwarted any movement throughout the whole seaward evacuation routes. The reported arrival of the US Seventh Fleet only enhanced the resolve and never affected the morale.

On December 12, an aircraft was detected about 130 nm (235 km) away, and an interceptor ready on deck was launched. Soon after launch, a message was received that it was a UN aircraft and should not be harmed. Accordingly, the interceptor pilot was asked to return. By the 14th there seemed to be no targets left to destroy but vigil was maintained 24×7. In less than 12 days, its over 150 day and night sorties, resulted in the sinking of more than a dozen gunboats, damaging airfields, coastal installations, harbours, and targeting over a score of merchant ships besides boarding ships for contraband. It accomplished all of this despite engineering limitations and performed better than expectations without a single life or aircraft or equipment being lost.

Five Medals

On the 16th, as soon as the surrender was announced, there was a celebratory mood all around.

Being Captain Swaraj Prakash's Midshipman intern (called Doggie in the Navy) I always accompanied him during action station and while entering and leaving harbours. I got two campaign stars, a Videsh Seva medal, and the

Service Medal for participating in these operations in the three ships in different geographical locations, and service during hostilities during my commissioning in INS Valsura on July 1, 1972, while pursuing a Sub Lt Electrical Engineering course. A bonus came on August 15, 1972, when a fifth was added celebrating the 25th year of India's Independence. Thus, we became the proudest Acting Sub Lts with five medals. Such a history is rare – our naval course got a bloodied head start and a tough salt seasoning to their career.

Lessons

The strategic decision to deploy a speed limited carrier to the east, taken early in the year, was a game changer. It was no easy task thereafter to execute this strategy meticulously, headed by the patient, courageous, cool professional Captain who lead from the front, and motivated the crew to perform flawlessly. No further lesson in leadership by example was required, as it got deeply embedded in our memory.

32

Indian Navy's Biggest Bonfire in the Arabian Sea

Soumya Nair

Among the array of operations executed by the Indian Navy in the eastern and western theatres during the 1971 India-Pakistan war, the most celebrated are Operation Trident and Operation Python that saw the daredevil 'Killer Squadron' of the Indian Navy mount an audacious attack on Karachi – the citadel of Pakistan's naval force. The attacks, which Admiral SM Nanda, then Chief of Naval Staff, famously described as the "biggest bonfire" in the Arabian Sea,[1] dealt a severe blow to Pakistan's warfighting capabilities while establishing the nascent Indian Navy as a force to be reckoned with.

Owing to the continental focus, the Navy has been limited to defensive missions in all of India's prior wars since Independence. In 1971, however, as the war clouds loomed, the Navy was resolute to play a decisive role if hostilities broke out. "If war comes again, I assure you that we shall carry it right into the enemy's biggest ports like Karachi," Admiral Nanda had declared.[2]

The day was not far – on December 3, 1971, following pre-emptive strikes by Pakistan Air Force on Indian airfields in the western sector, Prime Minister Indira Gandhi declared in a midnight address that war had been "forced on us" and the "unprovoked aggression would be decisively and finally repelled."[3] With the war having begun formally, it was time for the Indian Navy to launch one of its most daring offensive operations for which it had been planning for long. The objective of the operation was to execute a complete naval blockade to choke supply routes and, thereafter, cut off sea lines of communication (SLOC) between East and West Pakistan. The Indian Navy's attack was to take place in two operations – Operation Trident and Operation Python.

Operation Trident

Admiral SN Kohli, then Flag Officer Commanding-in-Chief, Western Naval Command, writes in his book 'We Dared' that the intention was "to strike Karachi with a composite force on the very day that Pakistan carried out their first act of war." However, since that was not possible, it was decided to launch the operation the following evening.[4]

The first raid codenamed 'Operation Trident' involved three newly acquired sleek and stealthy Russian made OSA class missile boats – INS Nirghat, Nipat and Veer, of 25 Missile Boat Squadron led by Commodore Babru Bhan Yadav. They were escorted by two Petya class frigates – INS Katchall and INS Kiltan.[5] OSA, which translates to 'wasp' in Russian, are known for their lethality and high speeds. However, owing to their low range and endurance, the boats were first towed from Mumbai and positioned at Okha.[6] Rear Admiral SR Sampath Gopal who was Executive Officer on INS Nipat recalls – "At around sunset, we proceeded in an arrowhead formation at the best speed with Nipat in the lead. The aim was to arrive at off Karachi post 10 pm so that before midnight the attacks could be carried out."[7]

The first radar contact was made with PNS Khaibar, a Pakistani battle class destroyer. INS Nirghat, commanded by Commodore Inderjit Sharma, was detailed to engage the target nearly thrice its size. The missile boat broke off from the formation and fired the first missile, which hit Khaibar's starboard side. A second missile fired from a closer range ripped it apart into two pieces, recalls Commodore Sharma.[8] The next target was a Liberian merchant ship MV Venus Challenger carrying ammunition for Pakistan, which was hit by a missile fired by INS Nipat.[9] The ship's debris was seen "burning fiercely for over 70 minutes before it finally sank in that position, about 19 miles to the south of Karachi," writes Vice Admiral GM Hiranandani in his book 'Transition to Triumph'.[10] Thereafter, about 25 nautical miles from Karachi, the radar picked contact with the Keamari oil installations, which were successfully hit and set ablaze.

Operation Python

A second attack, named Operation Python from a south-westerly direction, was carried out on December 8. The strike force was led by INS Vinash, supported by INS Trishul and INS Talwar. The first missile fired by Vinash was on shore targets; the second and third were on Pakistani merchant ships anchored outside – SS Gulf Star and SS Harmattan, and the fourth targeted Pakistan Navy's fleet tanker PNS Dacca.

The element of surprise and perfect timing were critical components of the operation, which required painstaking planning and months of intensive training. Vice Admiral SC Suresh Bangara, who was Executive Officer on INS Veer, says a number of attacks were planned, including those as diversionary tactics: "That was the beauty of the whole planning. Surprise element apart, there were obviously a number of attacks planned from other directions. Nobody knew the war was going to be over in 15-16 days."[11]

Strategic considerations such as the deployment of anti-ship missile boats – designed primarily for coastal defence – for offensive action, their towing to the Gujarat coast, use of Russian language by the Indian crew to prevent easy interception, etc., assured the mission's resounding success. The Navy had complete control over the western seaboard, which tipped the scale in India's favour.

During the operations, the Indian Navy suffered a significant loss when one of its anti-submarine-warfare frigates, INS Khukri, was torpedoed by a Pakistani submarine – Hangor while on a search and attack mission with INS Kirpan a few kilometres off the Diu coast. Over 18 officers and 176 sailors lost their lives in the incident. Reportedly, the Commanding Officer of the ship, Captain Mahendra Nath Mulla, refused to abandon the ship and opted to go down with it. He was posthumously awarded the Maha Vir Chakra (MVC).[12]

Speaking on the significance of the 1971 naval operations, Chief of Naval Staff Admiral Karambir Singh said, that although half a century had passed since the Indian Navy achieved the spectacular feat, "the core tenets of planning, decisive action, operational synchronisation and out-of-the-box thinking" held valuable lessons for the future.[13]

The 1971 war was a rare instance when all three services – Army, Navy and the Air Force – worked together in perfect synergy. The naval operations provided vital support to the sister services and proved to be one of the most crucial battle-winning factors. Marking the legendary feat of the 1971 operations, the Indian Navy has since celebrated December 4 as Navy Day commemorating its valiant 'Killer' warriors.

Notes

1. Admiral SM Nanda, *The Man Who Bombed Karachi: A Memoir* (HarperCollins, 2015), p. 1974, 221.
2. Ramananda Sengupta, 'Karachi Burned for Seven Days,' rediff.com, May 13, 2009, at https://www.rediff.com/news/interview/interview-with-admiral-s-m-nanda/20090513.htm, accessed on June 26, 2021.
3. Charles Mohr (1971), 'Mrs. Gandhi Vows to Repel the Foe,' *The New York Times*, December 4, 1971, at https://www.nytimes.com/1971/12/04/archives/mrs-gandhi-vows-to-repel-the-foe-indians-charge-pakistan-started.html, accessed on June 26, 2021.
4. Admiral SN Kohli, *We Dared: Maritime Operations in the 1971 Indo-Pakistan War* (Sangam Books, 1989), p. 45.
5. Arjun Subramaniam, *India's Wars: A Military History 1947-1971* (HarperCollins, 2016), pp. 401-402.
6. The Nehru Centre, London, May 31, 2021 at https://www.youtube.com/watch?v=IEQusRUlPAs.te Military History 1947-19711. Available at
7. Ibid.
8. Ibid.
9. Arjun Subramaniam, India's Wars: A Military History 1947-1971 (HarperCollins, 2016), p. 402.
10. '1971 War: The First Missile Attack on Karachi,' September 9, 2020, at http://www.indiandefencereview.com/interviews/1971-war-the-first-missile-attack-on-karachi/sne of the most crucial battle-roviding
11. The Nehru Centre, London, May 31, 2021, at https://www.youtube.com/watch?v=IEQusRUlPAs.te Military History 1947-19711.
12. Ajay Sura (2011), 'Sinking of INS Khukri: Have facts been sunk too?', *Times of India*, March 22, 2011, at https://timesofindia.indiatimes.com/blogs/contentions/sinking-of-ins-khukri-are-facts-been-sunk-too/, last accessed on June 26, 2021.
13. The Nehru Centre, London, May 31, 2021, at https://www.youtube.com/watch?v=IEQusRUlPAs.te Military History 1947-1971.

Operations by the Indian Air Force

33

Spectacular Joint Operations in the Eastern Theatre

Arjun Subramaniam

Sometime in late November or early December 1971, General Sam Manekshaw – the iconic Indian Army Chief – was coordinating the final operational briefings by all the three services, in front of a tri-service audience of senior leadership. Following the completion of the naval and air force briefings, he got up with his customary flourish and remarked, *"So that's it?"*. A hand shot up from the audience! It was Air Marshal YV Malse, the maintenance chief of the IAF during the run-up to the 1971 war. Malse had earlier served as the AOC-in-C, Eastern Air Command, around the same time when Manekshaw was commanding Eastern Army Command and had supported him well during the Mizo operations. "*Sir, what about the army briefing*?" queried the Maratha airman, as Air Chief Marshal PC Lal looked on phlegmatically. Manekshaw realised the glitch and recovered well, adding cheerfully, *"Ah! I almost forgot, but it is late and we will have it first thing in the morning."*[1] While the incident was a light moment, it demonstrated a renewed confidence inside the IAF, that it would be a force to reckon with in any future conflict with Pakistan.

Planning for Victory in the East

Was Dacca's submission that straightforward, or was it the product of combined coordination of troops across various operations, resulting in psychological breakdown rather than physical destruction of combat capability? Group Captain Manna Murdeshwar (Retd), one of the key members of the operational planning staff at the Eastern Air Command, had a ringside view of operations in the Eastern theatre and recollects vividly that it needed a little over six months of continuous effort by way of visits, discussions, conferences and persuasion to build a rapport with 2 Corps, 33 Corps, 4 Corps and 101 Communication Zone – the formations tasked with conducting the multi-pronged ground offensive into East Pakistan.

The first objective of the IAF was to neutralise the only Sabre squadron based at Tezgaon, outside Dacca, by drawing it into the air and shooting down as many fighters as possible in aerial battles. A second approach was by cratering the airfield and rendering it unusable by the fighters, thereby preventing the Sabres from interfering with the Indian Army's operations.

The second objective was to provide effective Close Air Support at some of the tough peripheral battles being fought at Hilli, Kamalpur, Akhaura and the Belonia bulge. The one significant difference this time, as compared to 1965, was that every Corps had a Tactical Air Centre (TAC) with several trained Forward Air Controllers (FACs), who orchestrated the Close Air Support in response to the requirements of field commanders.[2] The overwhelming superiority of numbers meant that the IAF could not only provide air support to the forward battles being fought, but also carried out interdiction of trains, ammo dumps and defences around the fortresses of Dacca, Narayanganj and Sylhet. This was done primarily by the rocket-firing Hunters and Sukhoi-7s as they blasted logistics reinforcements and defences around the beleaguered garrisons.

The third and most decisive objective was one that emerged as the ground battle progressed and involved the possibility of vertical envelopment using the IAF's helicopter and transport fleets. The idea of vertical envelopment emerged from the dynamic duo of Lieutenant General Sagat Singh and Group Captain Chandan Singh. While the former was the 'hard-charging' Corps Commander of 4 Corps, the latter was the Helicopter Task Force Commander tasked with providing Sagat with several opportunities to isolate Dacca by leapfrogging his troops across the Surma and Meghna Rivers at multiple points.

Heli-Landed Operations at Sylhet & Narayanganj

The first joint operation that had a major impact on the will of the Pakistan Army to continue fighting took place as early as December 6. A battalion of 4/5 Gorkha Rifles was heli-lifted across the Surma River and landed within sniffing distance of Sylhet Garrison, which was manned by over 5,000 Pakistani regular and irregular troops.[3] The operation was conducted in several waves over two days, by Mi-4 helicopters from 105 and 110 Helicopter Units (Hus), with Chetak helicopters chipping in with continuous reconnaissance missions. A very audacious operation, over 350 ferocious Khukri-wielding Gorkhas repulsed many half-hearted counterattacks from the garrison, which thought that a brigade had been heli-lifted.

The Gorkhas had not anticipated such fierce resistance at Sylhet and as Harolikar and his men fought the Sylhet brigade in a series of skirmishes, a young IAF FAC, Flt Lt Sharma was right there at the forefront of the battle with Harolikar as part of his 'Rover Group'. For days Sharma directed air strikes by Hunters and Gnats against targets in and around Sylhet and ensured a steady stream of dropped supplies and regular casualty evacuations by Mi-4 helicopters of 105 HU. Harolikar is effusive in his praise for Sharma as he repeatedly directed IAF fighters onto targets in the Sylhet garrison.[4] The young IAF officer was awarded a Vir Chakra for his courage and willingness to stay with forward elements of the battalion as they closed in on Sylhet.

If Sagat Singh's heliborne operation at Sylhet was a heavyweight boxer's right hook, then he followed up like any good boxer with a solid punch to Niazi's gut between December 9 and 11, when he heli-lifted almost a brigade worth of troops from Major General Ben Gonsalves' battle-hardened 57 Division across the mighty River Meghna to two landing zones at Raipura and Narsingdi, approximately 60 km from Dacca. Not satisfied with that, he pressed-on with a left hook on December 12 by heli-lifting a similar force to Narayanganj, around 40 km south-east of Dacca. Between December 6 and 12, a 14 helicopter task force from three units (105, 110 and 111 Helicopter Units of the IAF) had landed over 4,000 troops and most of their supporting equipment, including ammunition and light artillery guns in three locations, by flying around 350 sorties including over 100 by night.[5] Air Vice Marshal Chandan Singh, then a Group Captain and the Helicopter Task Force Commander, who developed an excellent professional rapport with the flamboyant Sagat, summarised the action as follows:

> *"The success of the heliborne operations was mainly due to the guts, determination, perseverance and courage of the pilots. However, it must be said that without the air supremacy achieved by our fighters and fighter-bombers, this colossal task could not have been carried out."*[6]

Joint Pressure on Dacca

Adding to Lt Gen Niazi's woes was the Tangail para drop operation by the Second Battalion of the Parachute Battalion (2 PARA) on December 11 in the area to the north of Dacca. This was in an area that was under the operational control of 101 Communication Zone, the division-sized force under Major General GC Nagra. Initially planned as a brigade-sized drop by 50 Para Brigade in three separate operations of a battalion each, with objectives that ranged from capture of a bridge, an airfield, and at Tangail to secure a bridge, it was reduced to a battalion drop. Suffice to say, it was a cautious decision that looked at leveraging the surprise of a small force and making it look like a large force, rather than risk a large force without much strategic pay-off. Even then, the successful operation involved over 50 transport aircraft of different types along with Gnat and MiG-21 fighter escorts, which got airborne from two airfields – Dum Dum and Kalaikunda. While the bulk of the heavy drop equipment and a small complement of troops emplaned at Dum Dum, primarily on Packet aircraft, the majority of the paratroopers got onboard Dakotas at Kalaikunda.

The psychological impact of innovative operations generally gets underplayed in any post-war analysis, as it seemingly takes away some sheen from the hardcore contact and aerial battles that occupy pride of place in conventional warfare. One operation that caused a disproportionate impact on the psyche of East Pakistan's leadership as they huddled in Dacca during the closing stages of the war, was the strike by IAF fighters on the Governor's House in Dacca on December 14. Analysing the impact of these attacks, Jagan and Samir Chopra write:

> *"The IAF's attack, an act of visible, spectacular intimidation, was the last psychological blow to a crumbling regime."*[7]

Joint Operations – The X-Factor in the East

The operations of the IV Corps operations provide an ideal case study for the conduct of aggressive joint operations driven by operational commanders.[8] Group Captain Chandan Singh, the Station Commander at Jorhat and an accomplished and aggressive transport pilot with extensive operational experience and a gallantry award under his belt for his exploits during the 1962 conflict with China, was the single point contact between Eastern Air

Command and Lt Gen Sagat Singh. They juggled a sizable complement of helicopter resources and a few support fighter units between them. Sagat and Chandan worked tirelessly to prepare various heliborne and heli-lift operations to outflank and surprise the enemy, almost two squadrons worth of Mi-4's put together from 105, 110 and 111 Helicopter Units, and a few IAF and Army Aviation Aloutte helicopters. Over 350 sorties were flown by the Mi-4 and Alouettes of the IAF and the 659 Army's Air Observation Post (AOP) unit in Sylhet and Ashuganj sectors, lifting almost three brigades with their logistics and artillery requirements – this came to be known as the 'Meghna Air Bridge Operation'.[9] This operation is also termed as the '*baptism by fire*' of the Indian Army's small helicopter arm, as pilots like Major Sihota flew risky communication and reconnaissance sorties under the command of the daring Sagat Singh and one of his equally enterprising divisional commanders, Major General Ben Gonsalves, as they put the pieces of their innovative heli-lift operation across the River Meghna together.[10] He was one of only a handful Army pilots to earn the Vir Chakra for his efforts in Bangladesh. Two fearless leaders, Sagat Singh and a much younger Chandan Singh, altered the course of the 'Race to Dacca'.

Even in the case of Close Air Support (CAS), IV Corps exploited the IAF's fighter assets to the maximum. Over 500 of the approximately 1,350 CAS operations flown in the Eastern theatre supported IV Corps.[11] Sagat Singh understood the importance of offensive air power and the psychological impact of CAS and pushed both his TACs to their limits as they struggled to cope with the pouring requests from Sagat's formation commanders for continuous air support.

To its credit, Eastern Air Command responded brilliantly and supported Sagat's rapid advance by even sending Gnats of 24 Squadron to operate in the ground attack role from Agartala runway on December 12. The runway was extended by a few thousand feet so that fighters could operate from there and strike targets at Sylhet, Maulvi Bazaar, Ashuganj, Bhairab Bazar and Brahmanbaria within minutes.[12]

Notes

1. Arjun Subramaniam, *India's Wars: A Military History 1947–1971* (New Delhi: HarperCollins, 2016), p. 363.

2. P.V.S. Jagan Mohan and Samir Chopra, *Eagles over Bangladesh* (New Delhi: HarperCollins, 2013), p. 159.
3. For a detailed account of the Sylhet heli-lift operation by the CO of 4/5 Gorkha Rifles, Lt Col A.B. Harolikar, see Brig A.B.Harolikar, 'The Battle for Sylhet Nov-Dec 1971 by Maj (Retd) Mumtaz Hussaini Shah, Pakistan Army – A Rejoinder by Brig A.B Harolikar, Indian Army, at http://bravestofthebrave.com/?p=66, accessed on October 25, 2014.
4. Brig Harolikar, 'Inside a Chakravyuh in Sylhet', at http://bravestofthebrave.com/?p=14, accessed on October 25, 2014.
5. For a personal narrative of the operation from the man who orchestrated it as the IAF commander alongside Sagat Singh, see, Air Vice Marshal Chandan Singh, The Meghna Crossing, In, Maj Gen Dhruv Katoch & Lt Col Quazi Sajjad Ali Zahir (eds), *Liberation: Bangladesh 1971* (New Delhi: Bloomsbury, 2015), pp. 218-222.
6. Ibid.
7. Jagan and Chopra, p. 336.
8. Email exchange between the author and Gp Capt Murdeshwar in Feb 2014 on his perceptions of what was right and what went wrong during the 1971 War.
9. For a detailed narrative of the Meghna Air Bridge Operation, see Jagan and Chopra , pp. 215. For a recent analysis of the heli-bridge and heliborne operations by an IAF helicopter pilot, see Air Commodore Rajesh Isser, *The Purple Legacy: Indian Air Force Helicopters in Service of the Nation* (New Delhi: KW Publishers, 2012), pp. 63-79.
10. Mandeep Singh Bajwa, 'Flying to Victory: An Air OP pilot's story,' *Hindustan Times*, Chandigarh, January 12, 2014, at http://www.hindustantimes.com/punjab/chandigarh/flying-to-victory-an-air-op-pilot-s-story/article1.aspx, accessed on October 18, 2014.
11. Jagan and Chopra, p. 383 (summary of Sector-wise CAS Missions)
12. P.C. Lal, *My Years with the Indian Air Force* (New Delhi: Lancer, 1986), p. 212.

34

Radar Orbat of Pakistan 1971: Reminiscences

AG Bewoor

The long preparatory period that India had before the India-Pakistan War of 1971 provided an opportunity for India to ascertain the radar ORBAT of Pakistan Air Force (PAF). This job was done by ELINT (Electronic Intelligence) operations I was fortunate to be a part of the process. On December 3, 1971, the PAF launched Operation Chengis Khan with a pre-emptive strike against Indian Air Force (IAF) airfields. I've composed some of my memoirs on various incidents that occurred prior to, during, and after the War.

The War Began Before the Shooting

Evacuation of Refugees. The intensity of the atrocities by the Pakistan Army in March 1971, forced the people of East Pakistan to vacate the state. As a result, there was a large influx of refugees into India including, Agartala, the capital of Tripura. I flew many flights out of Agartala ferrying refugees to Guwahati and Bagdogra, the first one being on April 3, 1971. I will never forget the intense fear in the eyes of these men, women and even children; they were carrying nothing more than just few bundles of their possessions (whatever was available) and their tales were heart wrenching. Our AN-12 is designed to accommodate 96 passengers, but we carried over 130 passengers on each journey; families could not be separated, and we had to take their word for it when they declared, "all 12 of us are one family". The AN-12 is a very robust aircraft and invariably got airborne very safely with 130 refugees on each flight. When they were safely landed, the expression of thankfulness on their faces was reassuring and justified every breach of the SOPs on which we had been trained.

Transportation of Members of the Bangladesh Government in Exile. The Bangladesh Government in Exile was established somewhere close to Calcutta. On August 1, I flew its members from Calcutta to Delhi in a C-46 aircraft late in the evening. The personalities included Syed Nazrul Islam (Acting President), Tajuddin Ahmad (Prime Minister) and Colonel Osmani. Readers will be surprised to know that Col Osmani was one of the architects of Operation Grand Slam – Ayub Khan's 1965 Pakistani offensive into J&K.

Meeting the Heroes of Boyra Air Battle. On November 22, I was flying from Kumbhigram in late afternoon and as we neared Calcutta from the North, we were made to orbit at 5,000 feet about 10 Nautical Miles. After 15 minutes, the controller asked us to land. Soon after, an Indian Oil tanker arrived to refuel us. That is when the Indian Oil Cooperation (IOC) operator told me that our Gnats had shot down a Pakistani aircraft – we knew the Gnats were on the eastern side of the airport. I requested the operator to lend me his jeep so I could go to meet the pilots, as I knew most of them; this is how I met the heroes of the Boyra air battle, just hours after their victory. My orbiting North of Calcutta was because the Gnats were 'beating up' the airport with Victory Rolls as befits an air warrior who has shot down enemy aircraft.

Electronic Sweep of Eastern and Western Fronts

First Passive Offensive Operation. On December 3, subsequent to the PAF strike, I was airborne in the ELINT aircraft at about 1900 hours to reconfirm the radar ORBAT that had been recorded in the preceding months. It was a full moon night with terrific visibility; we flew at about 28,000 feet charting a course from Kolkata northwards, turning East around East Pakistan keeping a good 20 km inside India, till we reached Guwahati. We had no idea if any fighter cover was available because we heard no other radio telephonic transmissions – it was quite unsettling knowing that hostilities had been declared and here we were carrying out the first passive offensive operations against the adversary. Almost certainly, all Indian radars were operational and scanning for enemy aircraft; we maintained constant radio communication with them and avoided contacting the airfield in order to escape detection. If anything, the ELINT platform is most precious and extremely expensive piece of airborne equipment, and critical for knowing what the enemy radars are doing, where they are and whether they are mobile or static. After three hours, I landed back, exhausted, tense, yet excited by the events that would follow the declaration of hostilities. I wondered how many would perish? Many people did, friends and course mates. That is war!

By nightfall on December 5, I was at an airfield in Western Uttar Pradesh. The next morning, I flew a lengthy ELINT sweep starting near Jammu and thereafter flew Southward just inside the border. During this time, multiple thoughts crossed my mind, and I talked it over with the crew. Losing the ELINT would be unacceptable and disastrous. We were at 30,000 feet by 0730 hours, everyone very quiet, knowing that many fierce land and air battles must be raging below us. The navigator in our aircraft was extremely busy logging his position every two minutes, while the ELINT operators were recording their findings; later the data would be correlated and enemy radar dispositions would be confirmed. We had flown this path many times during the last six months, adversary was almost certainly aware of our intent. It was a very good day to revalidate the enemy radar ORBAT. Were they not doing the same thing we asked each other?

Unarmed Across East Pakistan

It was confirmed that the PAF ceased to exist as a fighting force in East Pakistan on December, and that not a single PAF fighter got airborne after that date. True or false, I do not know, but I flew right across East Pakistan on December 8. I was on a routine flight in an AN-12 from Sarsawa to Guwahati. Those familiar with the airways will know that after Katihar, we turn North for Kishanganj and then onto Bagdogra. Over Kishanganj we got a call from one of our radars advising us to turn on an Easterly heading of 90 direct for Guwahati. At first, my co-pilot and I ignored it, assuming it was a Pakistani controller enticing us into his trap, and kept flying towards Bagdogra. Soon enough the same radar called up again giving the same instructions. We maintained silence, as we were convinced that though the call signs and frequency were correct, this had to be a devious trap – Why should the IAF make an unarmed AN-12 fly into East Pakistan at the height of armed hostilities? This was *gadbad (something wrong)*, and we remained Northbound.

Very soon a stern message came across, a different voice I clearly recollect, demanding why we were disobeying instructions. On the flight deck we decided to authenticate the credentials of the radar unit. We had an Authentication

Sheet which had alpha-numeric combinations. We decided to challenge the radar unit, and lo and behold, he answered correctly. We banked right and flew as instructed despite our reluctance. Thus, here we were in an unarmed AN-12 crossing East Pakistan at about 28,000 feet flying merrily above a hot shooting war – what a juicy target we must have been for the PAF! But we knew that our fighters had to be around, though we did not ask; in war you just fly.

War Booty from East Pakistan

On January 7, 1972, I flew to Chittagong to de-induct some special forces. I descended over the waters of the Bay of Bengal very confidently, but our efforts to raise Chittagong proved futile. Getting the troops out was critical and it had to be done that very day. I came over Chittagong and flew over the runway 'waggling' my wings, the International Standard Operating Procedure (SOP) saying "*No Radio Contact Request Clearance to Land*". Sure enough, I got a Green Flare – yes Chittagong was ready to accept me. I was sceptical, but the excitement of a victorious Air Force pushed me to land; after all, we would be the first Indian Air Force aircraft to land in Chittagong of Bangladesh. We were received by Major Bakshi and a young Captain as our liaison, who first took us to a Pakistan Navy shore unit called PNS Bakhtiar – it was in the Mess that I got my first War Booty. I saw a coffee cup and saucer with the unit's name in blue – PNS Bakhtiar. The base of the cup and saucer said 'Made in Pakistan'. I instantly took them (without being noticed). From there we drove to a hotel for lunch.

As I walked into the reception area following lunch and took a look around, I saw very large brass pieces attached to each room key – on the piece was written "Hotel Agrabad Chittagong, East Pakistan." I requested the man to remove the key and give me the brass piece as a memento – in any case they would be changing over to Bangladesh in place of East Pakistan. This was my second war booty.

My third war booty was a Step Ladder of Pakistan International Airways, used for their Dakotas and Fokker Friendships, which I saw as we returned to our landing point. I reached my room that evening and placed the ladder outside. Every evening the kids on the campus would push the ladder all over the Mess area, it became a tourist attraction and many of us would sit on it and have our evening drinks.

The 1971 War was indeed a memorable one!

35

The Attack on Governor's House: My Memories as a Flying Officer

Harish Masand

For us youngsters from Hasimara flying Hunters, the 1971 War for liberation of Bangladesh seemed to be coming to a close. We had achieved complete dominance in the air by the forenoon of December 6, 1971. After shooting down one on December 4, I did not see any Sabres, when we went Sabre-hunting the next day. Seeing our domination, they didn't pick up the gauntlet and challenge us in the air, which was perhaps wise. From then on, Command changed over to regular bombing of the runways at Tezgaon and Kurmitola by MiG-21s from Gauhati (later Guwahati).

I didn't realise the true effectiveness of the bombing campaign, till I later came to know of, the Flight Commander of the Pakistani 14 squadron at Tezgaon, Sqn Ldr Dilawar Hussein's remark, after a bombing raid on December 6, "With tears in my eyes, I almost said aloud that from this moment onwards, the fate of East Pakistan has been decided." Hereafter, all our effort was devoted to supporting the Army to aid in their rapid advance, reports of which kept coming to us from our friendly GLO (Ground Liaison Officer) – Major Tripathi.

General Sagat Singh of IV Corps had already hopped across the mighty Meghna and entered the West bank on December 9. The operation could be termed as a bold and innovative manoeuvre from the air, utilising the limited number of Mi-4 helicopters. He was rapidly building up almost a division-sized force for a pincer on Dacca from three different axes – from the East/South East. The para-drop of 2 PARA at Tangail had been successfully carried out on December 11. After linking up with units of 101 Communication Zone, 2 PARA was also making rapid progress towards Dacca from the North.

While all this was great news, most of us were sitting on the ground waiting for requests for support from the Army and, frankly, feeling that we were missing out on the war. There was a bit of frustration since we were all raring to go but not getting as many wartime missions as we wanted. On December 10, shortly after returning from a mission, my CO (Commanding Officer), 'Suppi' Kaul summoned me to the office and gently informed me of my younger brother's death. My brother – Lt Bharat serving in 7 PARA, had been shot on December 8 somewhere around Jessore. Suppi then advised me to get drunk that evening and take the next day off. I firmly rejected the suggestion, since losses in war were a part of life and one had to carry on with his duty, as my mother taught me from the Gita.

On the morning of December 14, Suppi escorted three of us to Base Operations, for a briefing on an unexpected mission. Last minute intelligence inputs, to which Command HQ had reacted with alacrity, indicated that Governor Malik of East Pakistan was going to hold a meeting with his senior officials in the Governor's House around noon and we had been tasked to attack that house to send a message, that further resistance was futile. Clearly, we all desired to know the precise location of that house in order to avoid collateral damage and avoidable human casualties. By an amazing stroke of luck, someone pulled out an old tourist street map of Dacca – 1940s vintage printed by Burmah Shell – and we all memorised the location – of the house by identifying the prominent features around. Remember, there were no photocopiers back then! Meanwhile, four aircraft had been readied and armed with 8xT-10 rockets and 4x135 30 mm guns.

Suppi and I took off first as the lead pair, with Squadron Leader AA Bose and Flt Lt KB Menon about 10 minutes later as the second pair. As per the RT conversation and the post-mission report, Bose did not carry out the attack due to some problems and orbited on top while KB went in alone. Having done some missions over Dacca by then, we knew the anti-aircraft fire was very heavy and effective till about 6,000 feet.

We cruised out at medium altitude and did an orbit over Dacca above 6,000 feet to spot the target and to align ourselves for the attack, all this while watching the balls of fire of the flak below us. We launched two attacks, the first with rockets and the second with weapons, swooping down from that height like eagles in a sharp dive. Our attacks were very accurate and I saw all the ordnance go right through the verandah around the conference hall without any collateral damage. After the second attack, when we exited hugging the deck at high speeds close to 500 knots to evade the flak, I noticed the Intercontinental Hotel towering above me right in front. We knew that this hotel housed most of the diplomatic community, foreign media and some local ministers and had avoided attacking it. However, just for the thrill of it, I headed straight towards it before pulling away at the last minute when I was close enough to glimpse the faces of the people in the balconies watching the whole attack. Somehow, this mission and the exit are still imprinted vividly in my mind.

As I learned later, Governor Malik resigned on the spot after this attack. Fortunately also, we came back without a scratch on our aircraft due to such steep and quick attacks. I was the regular wingman for Suppi and flew with him on all his missions including the many reconnaissance ones we did inside East Pakistan from October onwards – 'God was truly our co-pilot,' as always written on my helmet, because neither of us received a single bullet hole on our aircraft throughout the war.

We attacked the university area in Dacca the next day in a similar manner, where the troops tasked with defending Dacca were reportedly holed up, thus conveying the message that "you can run but you can't hide." By all accounts as I learned later, these attacks, which included MiGs from 28 Squadron in Gauhati, were great psychological blows on the Pakistani leadership that hastened the surrender of Pakistani Forces in the East, literally as the *coup de grace*. After the surrender ceremony on December 16, General Niazi, pointing to the wings on Group Captain Chandan Singh's chest, remarked that, "This had hastened the surrender. I and my people have had no rest during day or night, thanks to your Air Force. We have changed our quarters ever so often, trying to find a safe place for a little rest and sleep so that we could carry on the fight, but we have been unable to do that." In my opinion, these timely and accurate missions without collateral damage prevented street-by-street fighting in Dacca and should be examples of how air power could be effectively used for coercive effect and to prevent avoidable casualties and bloodshed.

36

Personal Accounts: The Untold Stories on the Eastern Sector

Ashminder Singh Bahal

"Victory smiles upon those who anticipate the changes in the character of war, not upon those who wait to adapt themselves after the changes occur."

– Giulio Douhet

On December 3, 1971, 'The Pakistan Air Force (PAF) conducted 'Operation Chengiz Khan,' which involved pre-emptive strikes on IAFs airbases and radar installations. They struck Amritsar, Ambala, Agra, Awantipur, Halwara, Jodhpur, Jaisalmer, Pathankot, Bhuj and Srinagar airfields as well as Amritsar and Faridkot radars. This marked the formal commencement of 1971 hostilities. IAF retaliated from both Western and Eastern theatres with Canberra bombers from five different squadrons at night, attacking 12 airbases including Chander, Murid, Sargodha, Shorkot Road (Rafiqui), Masroor, Chittagong, Jessore, Tezgaon and Kurmitola airfields. IAF rapidly increased its tempo of operations from the early morning of December 4, 1971.

Western Sector

Sukhoi-7s (Su-7s) from 32 Squadron carried out attacks on Shorkot Road and Sargodha. This mission on Shorkot was led by Squadron Leader VK Bhatia (aka Jimmy Bhatia). In his own words,[1] he says that not much was known of Shorkot airfield, as it was more of a secret airbase; in fact, its exact location was also not known. This airfield did not exist in 1965; information that was received from Bengali defectors, indicated that the airbase could be at two probable locations within 30-40 km area. This implied that the formation of Su-7s flying from the Initial Point (IP),[2] would need to plan for both locations – imagine the uncertainty while flying deep inside the enemy territory at high speeds and having only a few seconds to detect, identify and attack the target systems whose location was not clear.

Masroor, Sargodha and Shorkot Road were defended heavily with strong air defence elements. Jimmy Bhatia flew at extremely low altitudes and at high speeds, stepping up only to cross the High-Tension wires for a Time Over Target (TOT) at 1045 hours. The surprise of first raid was successfully achieved with no enemy opposition at all. After the formation was about 30 km from target and climbed up, the airfield identified, Sabres parked just outside the blast pens at each end of the runway; also two Canberras were parked for refuelling, co-ordinated attacks were carried out twice on either end of the runway. The formation was able to destroy three Sabres and one Canberra on ground in the first wave. On December 4 and 5, 1971, three sorties were undertaken for Shorkot, and five Sabres and two Canberras were destroyed.

PAF was well prepared for the second and third waves, and an intense umbrella of Ack-Ack fire from a large number of AD Guns resulted in the loss of two Su-7s, including a pilot, Flt Lt Tambe, who was killed in action. In the second mission, the formation was bounced by a pair of Sabres after finishing the attacks and whilst getting away towards the Indian territory, but the three Su-7 aircraft were able to disengage successfully despite being hit by two air-to-air missiles. An important aspect here is that the F-86 could carry air-to-air missiles, whilst the Su-7, Gnats and Hunters could not. Despite the disadvantage, the Indian pilots did amazingly well against the Sabre as they exploited the strengths of their aircraft.

A number of photo reconnaissance missions were flown from October 24, 1971, on targets including Muzzafarabad, Rahim Yar Khan and Fort Abbas. Numerous attacks were also carried out on trains, both on the plains and in the desert sector, also targeted ammunition and fuel dumps as well as providing extensive close air support to the Indian Army. Wing Commander Allen D'Costa, commanding the Squadron at Halwara, was awarded Maha Vir Chakra.

On December 5, Wing Commander Allen D'Costa led a strike mission over Chistian Mandi that scored a direct hit on the engine of a train and caused significant damage to the train despite intense anti-aircraft fire. The train was loaded with tanks, meant probably for operations near Lahore. Again, on December 6, he undertook another mission over Dera Baba Nanak (DBN) area and destroyed the vital DBN Bridge and attacked enemy concentrations. During this attack, while making a third pass over the target, his aircraft was hit by enemy fire and it crashed. He was subsequently taken as a PoW. An interesting aspect that he highlighted was that most Pakistani forward operations were led by JCOs rather than officers.

On December 12, two MiG-21s intercepted two F-104As and fired an R-3 missile, however the missile was redirected by flares thrown by the F-104. MiG-21s then approached to within 300 metres and fired weapons at the F-104. Two more F-104s were shot down later when they were escorting PAF bombers.[3] On December 14, 1971, Flying Officer Nirmaljit Sekhon took off from Srinagar airfield despite mortal danger to his life and when the airfield was under attack by four Sabres. He initially engaged the Sabres and damaged two of them. In this unequal fight, two more Sabres (who were escorts) joined in and he was eventually overcome by the sheer weight of numbers in air combat that was taking place at 'tree-top levels'. He was posthumously awarded Param Vir Chakra for exceptional bravery and supreme sacrifice.

Eastern Sector

PAF had based 18 F-86 Sabre jets as part of 14 Squadron in the Eastern sector at Tejgaon airfield, eight of which were Air-to-Air Missile capability. During November 1971, the Sabres repeatedly violated the Indian airspace to attack Mukti Bahini targets. Three Sabres were engaged by four Gnats in one such attack in Boyra Salient on 22nd November, and all Sabres were hit, with two pilots, Flight Lieutenant Mehdi Qureshi and Flying Officer Khalil Ahmed ejecting in the Indian territory. They were captured even before the war had officially started.

On December 3, the IAF responded with night strikes by 16 Squadron Canberra aircraft against a number of Pakistani airfields, including Jessore, Tezgaon, Chittagong and Kurmitola, while Otter & Allouette of Kilo Squadron attacked oil installations at Narayanganj and Chittagong. During the day, these strikes were significantly enhanced during day time by a large number of IAF fighters, including Su-7, Hunters, Gnats and MiG-21 aircraft.

On December 4, 1971, Kurmitola, Tezgaon, Chittagong, Jessore, Barisal and Rangpur were attacked by Hunters and Su-7s; some of them were escorted by MiG-21 aircraft. Several dogfights took place near Dhaka. According to then Flt Lt Vinod Kumar Nebb,[4] who was flying a Hunter as No. 3 in a 4 aircraft formation that was led by Sqn Ldr Lele, just before the formation reached the Initial Point(IP), he noticed three F-86 Sabres around 2000 yards behind two Hunter aircraft (presumably from 37 Squadron). Incidentally, Nebb was awarded VrC in both 1965 and 1971 wars for shooting down a Sabre aircraft each in aerial combat in both the wars, besides undertaking many successful missions. Almost simultaneously, the Hunters and Sabres turned into each other.

The Sabres in the Eastern Sector flew 30 sorties on December 4 and 22 sorties on December 5, 1971 before being grounded due to the repeated bombing of Tejgaon airstrip by the MiG- 21 aircraft in steep dive attacks. MiG-21s in steep dive mode were far superior against Su-7s or Hunters attacking airfields with Rockets, Guns, or Napalm, who proved extremely vulnerable to Ack-Ack guns. After Kurmitola and Tezgaon airfields were damaged, IAF achieved complete air superiority in this sector. This allowed rapid army operations to take place, as there was hardly any air interference. In the latter part of the war, PAF destroyed its own Sabre aircraft and flew out its pilots to Myanmar.

Two Squadrons operating MiG-21 fighters, based at Gauhati, took active part in the Eastern Sector. One of the Squadron flew 268 sorties during the war and they were the first IAF aircraft to enter Bangladesh airspace giving cover to Hunters. They were also instrumental in attacking Tezgaon and Kurmitola airfields. Flt Lt JS Raj was credited with shooting down an F-86 over Dacca, the only air-to-air kill claimed by a MiG-21 Squadron in the East. In these intense operations, only one MiG-21 fighter was lost to Ack-Ack fire.

Though limited airfield strikes continued till December 12, the focus shifted to undertaking interdiction, offensive air support and close air support missions to assist the army formations after December 6. Most close air support missions were controlled by Helicopter based Forward Air Controllers (FAC). MiG-21s undertook extensive strikes on Rajendraganj infantry battalion, providing a rapid ingress corridor for the army on Jaimalpur-Tangail-Mymensingh axis. They also undertook significant close air support missions in the Mainamati-Comilla Sector.[5]

A number of bunkers, ammunition dumps and gun positions were also destroyed. In one such attack, Nebb was tasked to strike Comilla Ammunition Dump. The intelligence was sketchy and the only information available was that there was a black top building about 600 yards from the Railway station. According to Nebb, they discovered one such structure and bombarded it mercilessly, but it refused to blow up even after they had exhausted all of their rockets. They used their common sense and sought out another black-top building on the other side of the railway station. Since the rockets had finished, he decided to use his 30 mm guns. This meant that he had to go in closer and ensure that some rounds went through the ventilator window onto the dump, and the rest of the work would then be done by the ammunition that was stored there. This also implied that if the dump exploded, the Hunter could still be in the debris zone. He continued, though, firing one long shot from a great distance, and the entire dump exploded in a mushroom of blazing red and black smoke.

Bangladesh is a riverine country characterised by a dense network of rivulets. Helicopters were used to create heli-bridges so as to speed up the movement of surface forces to enhance the tempo of ground operations. Troops of the IV Corps troops were heli-lifted from Ashuganj to Raipura and Narsingi. Under Operation Cactus Lily, a Heli-bridge was also created over the Meghna River. The helicopters ferried around 650 troops across the Meghna River at Sylhet under extremely difficult night conditions from the evening of December 10 to the morning of December 11.[6] This airlift is considered to be an important war winning factor.

Tangail airborne operations were carried out on December 11, 1971, using An-12s, C-119, Caribous and Dakotas, dropping 700 troops of 2nd PARA Battalion near Tangail, which is close to Dhaka. The main objective of the operation was to capture Poongli Bridge at Jamuna River, so cutting off access to Pakistan's 93rd Brigade, which was retreating from the north.[7] It is perhaps the best example of a successful co-ordinated action that created a significant psychological pressure on the East Pakistani Leadership. Added to this was Wing Commander Bishnoi's MiG-21 attack on the Governor's House in Dhaka on December 14, 1971, as well as other MiG-21 attacks on the Army Headquarters in the university campus.

Following the rocket attack, the East Pakistan Governor – Mr AH Malik resigned immediately. On being questioned as to why Pakistan surrendered with such a large force, Lt Gen Niazi clearly stated that the Indian Air Force made a huge difference.

The reasons for success in the Eastern Sector were many, including IAF's practical command of the air and the absence of impediments to surface operations. Second, considerable air effort was focused on Interdiction and Offensive Air support, which inflicted significant damage to the enemy's lines of communications and their movement was severely restricted. There was intimate co-ordination between the Army and the Air Force, hence the tempo of surface operations remained high. Further, severe psychological pressure was created due to relentless air and surface operations, which resulted in the enemy losing their will to fight. Lastly, Indian military operations were focused towards a just cause, supported extensively by Mukti Bahini and led gallantly by officers, whereas Pakistani operations were JCO led.

Notes

1. Air Marshal VK Bhatia was interviewed on June 26, 2021; these accounts are narrated by him personally to the author and hence there may be some differences with historical records.
2. Initial Point is the final navigational point before the target from where, when the aircraft sets course, then they get into attack formation and it is the final update point from where an accurate attack is carried out onto the target. It is usually 25-30 km from a target.
3. Guarding India, How Indian MiG-21 defeated Pakistani 104 Fighters in 1971 war, accessed from the site How Indian MiG-21 defeated Pakistani F-104 fighters in 1971 war – Guarding India on July 1, 2021.
4. Wing Commander Vinod Nebb was interviewed on June 27, 2021; these accounts are narrated by him personally to the author and hence there may be some differences with historical records.
5. Information obtained from historical records of No. 4 Squadron as enumerated in the Oorials Golden Jubilee Souvenir book 1942-92.
6. Sapra site "1971 India-Pakistan War: Air War in the East," p. 2. More information is available at http://www. indiandefencereview.com/spotlights/1971-air-war-battle-for-air-supremacy/0/
7. Information accessed from the site "The Tangail Airdrop: A landmark operation in 1971 Indo-Pak war (aviation-defence-universe.com)" on July 2, 2021.

37

My Husband: Squadron Leader Anil Bhalla

Sita Bhalla

A Warrior must constantly maintain a positive attitude. It is an honour to write about my late husband Squadron Leader Anil Bhalla who was a paragon of virtues and believed in 'bravery and discipline'. It is sad that having lived a vibrant life for 74 years, he passed away on May 11, 2021.This account is a tribute to the air warrior I knew. He was the first cadet from Sainik School, Satara, to join the Indian Air Force. He was commissioned as Pilot Officer in 1968 and won all the medals for Flying, Ground and All Round. He was the first Pilot Officer to fly the MiG- 21 with Elan, Pride and Military Precision. He was a flying ace who had a passion for flying fighters and serving the nation.

He proved his skills during the 1971 War. His attack missions were against targets in East Pakistan, later Bangladesh, which he adroitly tackled with accuracy and precision, rendering the PAF fighter jets unable of conducting operations.. He was involved in the mission of attacking the Governor's House in Dhaka which became instrumental in compelling Pakistan to surrender – "*All morning Governor Malik and his regional cabinet had been unable to decide to resign or hang on. The Indian air raids finally resolved the issue*," read a Reuters report on December 14, 1971. The report stated, "*Dr AM Malik wrote the draft of the resignation letter for his Cabinet with a shaking ball point pen on a scrap of paper as Indian MiG -21's destroyed his official residence, Governor House.*" Dhaka emerged as the free capital of independent Bangladesh on December 16, 1971. He was awarded 'Mentioned-in-Despatches' (MnD) – a coveted bravery award for his contribution during the 1971 War.

Squadron Leader Anil Bhalla was also the youngest Flying Officer to get the Master Green (instrument rating), which is awarded to pilots who demonstrate superior flying skills and airmanship. It recognises a higher level of experience and accomplishment in instrumental flying. He was also a Qualified Flying Instructor at the Fighter Training Wing at Hakimpet. He continued a colourful career in the Air Force till he decided to retire after 16 years in 1984.

Since then he worked in the construction business and was in Hyderabad. He was extremely successful. A natural leader who helped and guided people with whom he worked. He was an animal lover and was extremely loved by his family and friends. He believed in discipline and enjoyed taking up challenges. Possibly a fighter pilot has it in his psyche to venture into uncharted terrain. His unflinching optimism enabled him to conquer and execute daring operations throughout the 1971 War.

All in all, Squadron Leader Anil Bhalla was a great human being, who left an indelible mark and a void for his two daughters, son and me, which cannot be filled.

Image 1: Waiting to load a 500kg bomb

Source: Author's Own

SECTION 6

Subalterns

Baptised by Fire

38

"Write to my Parents, I fought Well"

Arun Patole

On commissioning, I arrived at my Unit's (19 MARATHA LI) rear location in Behrampur (West Bengal) on the night of November 24/25, 1971. The following morning, I was escorted to the Battalion (Bn) headquarter by a soldier, who instructed me to follow his footsteps to avoid stepping on mines! If I remember correctly, this village was Khurd Singhajauli.

I met the Commanding Officer (CO), Lt Col Shamsher Singh, who sent me to 'A' Company (Coy) at a place probably called Phulwara or Phulsara. Here I met Maj Madhu and as a habit saluted him. I got a full dressing down and warned not to salute in a war zone! At that time Maj Madhu along with few others were standing and discussing about the defences. On the far end of the open ground, there was dense growth and jungle where the enemy had taken up position.

While the briefing was taking place, the shelling began. There were deep booms followed by whistling sounds of approaching shells, and whirring of splinters as the shells burst on ground and air. All others were used to the shelling and could pinpoint exact location of where the shell would land. For me, this was my first battle exposure and my welcome to 19th MARATHA LI.

The Battalion was ordered to contact the enemy at Arpara. The advance commenced around 1,000 hours on November 30, 1971, amidst heavy enemy Arty shelling. The air was full of screaming shells and the flying splinters making the peculiar buzzing whirring sound of air bursts. I was learning fast. I remember Subedar Jadhav scolding me, "*Sahib Jhook ke chale, firing ho raha hai*" (Sir, bend down and walk. Firing is taking place). We were travelling over the narrow route with the JCO in front of me. Suddenly, the JCO fell; I hurried to assist him, believing he had slipped. Then I noticed blood oozing from his thigh. He was hit by a large razor-sharp splinter on the right thigh and large portion of flesh was missing. I tried to stop the bleeding with field dressing but the wound was deep and large. The bleeding could not be stopped. The JCO was in a state of shock and numb. Immediately, Naib Subedar Naik arrived and evacuated the injured JCO with the help of two sepoys.

The Greenhorn was getting hold of himself. At one point along the nallah/rivulet, the platoon was huddled in a ditch full of mud and slush. One young sepoy had dropped his rifle and was standing like a zombie. Totally shell shocked. His rifle was lying few feet away in open under fire. I shouted at him to pick up his rifle. He would not respond at all. Again, I shouted and ordered him to pick up his rifle and bring it. He stood still. The whole platoon was watching me, to see what course of action I would take. I took hold of the sepoy's arm and proceeded to pick up the rifle. Bullets and splinters were flying at all times. The platoon saw this and, I think, they approved of me.

On December 2/3, 1971, 2nd Lt Gambhir came to my location and informed me that I would be accompanying him on a Recce patrol as his 'Understudy'. Gambhir, myself and the Patrol party left 'B' Coy location and proceeded along the river bank. As we neared the suspected enemy location, we moved very cautiously, listening and observing. The silence was deafening. It was very dark and eerie. The ground was slushy, muddy and wet. Leeches were falling on us from the branches. At this time, I thought I heard a thudding sound and signaled others to be quiet, least realising that it was my own heart thumping loudly – my breathing sounded like a railway steam engine.

Gambhir acted with poise, composure, and deliberation. We moved forward and came up to some high ground near the bank. We crawled up and took our positions. Although it was very dark, but we could make out some structure. One looked like a bunker and a log/tree trunk on the ground. We observed and listened. We did hear some noises and what sounded like digging sounds, but there was no visible activity. We waited, but the darkness made it difficult to see well. We initially opted to proceed, but Gambhir chose to entice the enemy into open combat. Gambhir took the rifle from one of the boys and fired one single shot at the bunker-like structure and changed position. There was no return fire. There was lot of tension in the air and we waited apprehending some action. Gambhir fired another single shot, but there was no return fire. We were not sure whether the enemy had retreated/vacated the location or whether the enemy was luring us in a trap. Gambhir discussed with me on the best course of action and then he took the bold decision to enter and search the enemy location. We spread out and moved forward very cautiously in a crouch. But we found the location had been evacuated. We searched the huts and houses. It was terrifying.

Gambhir then informed the CO on ANPRC-25 of the location being vacant. The CO then ordered us to move ahead and join Capt Kurumbaiahs' patrol party and search the area along the track axis. Somehow, we managed to contact the Kurumbaiahs' patrol in total darkness without any mishap.

We organised ourselves and agreed that Gambhir's patrol would take the lead. We started moving along the track. One scout was ahead and the second person was me and the rest followed at a safe distance. After some time, the scout sat down and was looking down. The rest of us also sat down and waited. The scout did not move. I went up and joined him. I asked him to move, but he refused to stand up and move. I think the fear and uncertainty overwhelmed him. I talked to him and got hold of his elbow, forcing him to stand and we moved together. Gambhir told me to fall back, but I marched ahead along with the scout. This also helped me to overcome my own apprehension. After going ahead about 300-400 metres, we were fired upon and we could see flashes of rifle fire at close range. Gambhir and I dived towards the ground and returned fire. Gambhir shouted and told the patrol to break the ambush and disperse. We continued to return fire, firing at the flashes of gun fire all around.

Then I stopped firing and asked Gambhir to stop as well, as it was easy for the unseen enemy to throw a grenade at us. Gambhir and I started moving backwards in a half-crouched position, covering each other's move. The firing from both sides stopped. The silence was deafening, and both of us were on high alert and listening. To my right, there was a Bamboo clump and bushes, and I heard some rustling of twigs and leaves. I decided to lob a grenade, which was the first and only time I got to use a grenade in the battle. After crawling back to a safe distance, we both got up and started moving from tree to tree, covering each other. In complete darkness, there was a danger of shooting each other. We found our way to the track and reached the location of the 'D' Coy. The remainder of the patrol party had already returned safely.

I learned a great deal from Gambhir, including his composure in dangerous situations, his compassion for his men, and his capacity for swift decision-making. The former Greenhorn 'Understudy to Gambhir' had now become a battle-hardened soldier.

On December6, we got orders to advance to Arpara through the 2 SIKH LI position. We moved from Dakshinsagar early in the morning on December 7, 1971. We relieved 14 PUNJAB who were to provide a firm base for us to launch an attack on some Rail/ Rd junction.

From December 7 to 11, 1971, we were able to rest and recoup from the fatigue. We also carried out patrolling to prevent any riots and looting.

On December 12, our Battalion was tasked to secure Ferry point at Shyamganj. 'A' Coy under Maj Madhu moved out at about 2030 hours on December 12, 1971. The area was densely forested with undergrowth and trees. On December 13, 1971, at about 1200 hours, we reached Gilatala Ferry point. Our 'A' Coy was ordered to move further and secure the area around Shyamganj Ferry. We were moving along the river bank silently and listening to any tell-tale sounds. From the river banks to the edge of jungle was stretch of open ground/field. It was decided to cross the open field in an extended line and reach the edge of the jungle. The boys were huddling together; perhaps it was herd instinct or a sense of security in numbers. I had to physically push them apart to maintain an arm length distance. We crossed the open patch and reached the edge of jungle, luckily with no mine casualties (later on we came to know it was mined). We pushed through and saw some huts and shelters. The Coy Commander ordered us to dig trenches and secure the area. We could see the first light on the horizon and gradually the sky was lighting up. To our horror we noticed that on right edge of our trenches, the enemy position was just 30-40 metres away!

At approximately first light, Maj Madhu directed me to conduct a reconnaissance mission and check the region ahead for signs of hostile activity. I took out the patrol party along the bank of river. One of the boys was ahead of me as a Scout. I was about 20-30 feet behind him. It was early morning, and there was a light mist along the bank of the river. Visibility was about 20-30 metres. We had moved just about 200 metres, when I observed an enemy soldier about 30 metres on my right, sitting outside his trench and sipping tea. He waved at me and I waved back and suddenly both of us realised that we were enemies. I shot him with my carbine as he was getting into his trench. All hell broke loose at that moment. The enemy in the trench near the river bank, riddled the scout with bullets. At the same time, I was fired upon from the right-side trench of enemy. The bullet entered my right thigh (luckily it was only a flesh wound, and no bone was hit). The sensation of a bullet hitting is like a sting of Big bee. I looked down and saw blood flowing. All this in a fraction of seconds. I went into a crouch and fired back. The second bullet hit me on the left side of the chest rib cage, it was fired from the first trench on left side. The impact of the bullet was such that I was thrown into the air. The searing pain that cannot be described in words, is like a head exploding. Blood started gushing out of the gaping wound and out of my mouth. The third bullet hit me again near the ribs and it got lodged at the base of spine near tail bone.

My screaming with pain and tossing and turning stopped and I began pushing myself towards the slope of river bank. I was trying to crawl back when the fourth bullet hit me on the left shoulder joint. I was lying flat on the ground and the firing by the enemy continued. With my usable right hand, I drew my carbine and my helmet towards me. I started pushing myself with one arm towards the bank of the river. The movement attracted more firing but I kept on pushing myself. I loaded my carbine with a new magazine. Using the carbine butt, I managed to extricate myself from the muddy hole and started crawling towards 'A' Coy location.

My upper body was visible to the enemy. Some civilians (Razakars) were shouting, from across the river, and pointing at me, telling the Pakis to kill me. I was oblivious to all this; it did not matter. I kept moving step by step. After about 50 metres or so, I saw Nb/Sub Kashinath Naik in a ditch along the bank. He was shot in the legs. He requested me to write to his wife and parents. I also asked him to write to my parents, if he reached safely to our location. However, here the magic and power of War Cry takes over. The Pakis were shouting "*Allahu Akbar*" and the Marathas were roaring "*Bol Chattrapati Shivaji Maharaj ki Jai.*"

Our War Cry put a new life into me. I got up and stood straight. I gave my carbine to the JCO and told him "*Qaidee mat bano, dushman ko maro, ya khud ko maro*" (Don't be a prisoner, kill the enemy, or kill yourself).

I promised to send help to evacuate him. I started moving towards our defenses. After another 30 metres or so I saw one of our boys crawling. His feet were blown off by mines. This soldier (Veer Maratha) who was crawling, despite the loss of his feet said, "*Saheb tum aage mat jao, mai madat lekar ata hun*" (Sir, don't go any further, I will go get help).

[It is mind boggling experience. Consider a soldier who has been grievously wounded, both feet blown off, offering to help me. He was not worried about himself, but he worried about me]. These words of the soldier acted like a booster dose for me, and gave me more physical and moral strength. I replied to him, "*Agar mai pehle pahuncha toh main madat bhejunga, agar tum pahunche toh tum bhej dena*" (If I reach first then I will send help, and if you reach first, you send help). I crossed him and stumbled forward. I reached the abandoned boat/trawler. The bullets were hitting the wood work of the boat near my face. Where I fell, I saw Maj Madhu also laying and I thought he had taken position. I shook him and said, "*Sir, doh boys peeche hai*" (Sir, two boys are behind us). He did not move, and it was then that I noticed the bullet hole in his forehead. He was dead. A minute ago, he was alive. I could hear another JCO on the radio set. I think his name was Ambre. He sent some boys to evacuate me. But I refused to be lifted and asked them to first go and evacuate the JCO and the brave soldier with his feet blown off. Another 2-3 soldiers came and tore my shirt and tried to stop the bleeding. They made a makeshift stretcher, wrapped me in a blanket and started running. I was delirious with loss of blood and pain. They took me back through the shelling and firing.

It took me around 45 minutes to return from the location where I was shot. I was drifting in and out of consciousness and unconsciousness. At one point I saw CO Lt Col Shamsher Singh standing and briefing. He asked the stretcher bearers, "*Yeh kiska body hai?*" (Whose body is this?). They told him "*Naya saab joh abhi aaya tha*" (new officer, who had just joined). The CO saluted, thinking I was dead. I mustered some strength and in between gasps told him, "Sir! I am alive." I briefed him about the actual situation at 'A' location. My final words to him were, "Write to my parents, I fought well."

I remember the Subedar Major removing my dog tags and other things. He then sent me to Advance Dressing Station. I remember, one helicopter was there; they offloaded one less serious patient and loaded me in the helicopter. One AMC NCO was pumping my chest and putting an oxygen mask. The helicopter took off. This was my first ride in an aircraft of any type. I was very keen to see, how it looked down below. I signalled to the NCO with my head movements. He understood what I desired.

Below the pilot, there was glass bottom through which we could see the ground below. The pilot laughed and tilted the Helicopter on the right, so I could see. It was a moment of "*Marne ke pehle ichha puri*" (desire fulfilled before death). They had a good laugh. I struggled a smile. We landed at the playground of Military Hospital Behrampore and I was evacuated in an ambulance. The verandah was full of stretcher with battle casualties lined up waiting their turn to get an 'X' ray ...

I am very proud of my Fighting Nineteen and our brave Ganpats. May I be born again to be with my Paltan.

39

Probationer Paratrooper

LJS 'Lali' Gill

Fighter pilots can activate the ejection system in case of an unavoidable emergency, which automatically ejects the pilot from the aircraft and deploys the parachute. I found myself volunteering for such a first-time parachute jump!

Preparations for the Bangladesh War had commenced in earnest by mid-1971. Training courses were being truncated and establishments were closed to release personnel for frontline duties. My course, passed out from the Indian Military Academy, Dehra Dun – six weeks ahead of its schedule on November 14, 1971. I had opted for the Parachute Regiment and was commissioned into 2nd Battalion. I was not a trained paratrooper at this stage. When joining the Parachute Regiment, applicants undertake a four-week probationary period during which they are evaluated for their suitability to be a paratrooper. Every officer allotted to the Parachute Regiment is also assigned a parent, non-parachute, unit to revert to in case of an unsuccessful probation. Therefore, I was also assigned the 17th Battalion of the JAT Regiment.

Preparations to Win

My move instructions directed me to proceed to Calcutta. I was received by Subedar Govind Jadhav on arrival at the Howrah Railway Station, who informed me that the unit was out on training preparation for an airborne operation. We proceeded to the unit base at the Botanical Gardens, where we were informed that we should be ready to move at 4 AM next morning, i.e., November 30, 1971 for the exercise location. I spent the night in a 40 lb (called forty pounder in army parlance) tent on the banks of the Hooghly River and set out at 4 am, as was instructed. After a seven-hour drive, we reached Bashir Haat where the battalion was rehearsing for the planned operational task. I was received by Subedar Major Sita Ram Jadhav and we continued our journey for another 30 minutes until we arrived at the battalion. I was introduced to the other officers and learnt that the Commanding Officer (CO) – Lieutenant Colonel (later Major General) KS Pannu, was away at Headquarter 101 Communication Zone, Guwahati, for the final briefing. The same day the unit moved back to Botanical Gardens, Calcutta. On December 1, 1971, the Adjutant gave me my Probation Programme which was to start straightaway. Apart from that, I had no idea where the unit would be heading for the upcoming missions. However, my probation officer, Major (later Colonel) JS Mahalwar, commanding 'C' Company, gave me a vague idea of what was impending. Following successful completion of probation, a Basic Para Course is held at the Paratrooper Training School at Agra. The whole process takes about ten weeks. And here I was with the battalion ready to go on an airborne operation at any time.

On December 4, the CO returned and gave his final orders for the operation. There was nothing in it for me. On a query from the Adjutant and the Second-in-Command, I was told that as I was not a qualified paratrooper, I would not be able to take part in the operations with the unit. All my aspirations of para trooping in a war were dashed at that moment! But I made up my mind about not giving up on my dreams so easily.

The next day I met the CO and expressed my desire to go with the unit. To pre-empt my disqualification for lack of parachuting training, I volunteered to jump without such training. The CO appeared to be positive and said that he would speak to the Brigade Commander, who was scheduled to address the battalion the same evening. As planned, the address was followed by a basketball match between the brigade and unit officers, after which the CO introduced me to Brigadier (later Lieutenant General) Mathew Thomas, who had earlier been the CO of the battalion, and conveyed my willingness to jump with the battalion. The brigade commander thought about it for a while and said, *"What will I tell your father if something was to go wrong?"*

"Sir please convey to him the same you would for anyone else, I do not want to miss this," I replied. He gave his approval in an instant.

Now started the process to find a place for me. The companies had been grouped, equipped, trained and coordinated to the last man, load and aircraft for their assigned roles. The following three days were spent on probation and bouncing between the Adjutant, Second-in-Command and the Companies – no one was ready to accommodate me. The Probation Officer finally agreed to accommodate me in his company, which was tasked to secure the Forming Up Place (FUP) for the assault, post the drop. But there was a problem. The company was to jump from C- 47 Dakotas that needed a higher technical and skill level during the jump, which was not advisable and for an untrained paratrooper. C- 119 Packets, the other aircraft, were relatively easier and simpler to jump from. The Dakotas were to operate from Kalaikunda and the Packets from Dum Dum. My shift to Packets necessitated not only a change in company, but also in launch airfield. After various permutations and combinations in the Packet manifests, I was grouped with Path Finder (PF) Two on December 9, 1971. The PF is the first element to be dropped with the task of securing and marking the Drop Zone (DZ) and to receive the main force. In the event, Path Finder One failed due to the prevailing ground situation, PF Two takes up the same role at the alternate DZ. PF One and Two were to be dropped by one Packet – each taking off from Dum Dum.

The D-Day

Late in the evening of December 9, I finally got my battle kit and was briefed on my role in PF Two and later with the company in securing the FUP. On December 10/11, 1971, shortly after midnight, the unit slipped out from its bases in Botanical Garden and headed for the launch bases at Kalaikunda and Dum Dum.

We reached Dum Dum in the wee hours of December 11. Early morning, I was met by Sergeant Lakhan Pal, who took me to one of the hangers and introduced me to the procedure of jumping out of the aircraft as well as the emergency handling protocol once out of the aircraft. I was later taken to the aircraft and explained the layout and exit procedure. A couple of dummy drills were all that was required! I was put on the starboard exit as number 21 in the PF Two flight manifest. Normally each side has 20 persons jumping. I was an addition and an exception, and would be the last man to jump from the aircraft.

On December 11, 1971, at 1400 hours, we planned for the combat jump and took off at 1430 hours. I requested the Air Force dispatchers not to aid or assist me in exiting and assured them that I would do it on my own. After flying for about two hours and twenty minutes as we approached the DZ, the warning hooter sounded and the red light flashed, signalling that everyone should stand and attach their parachute static line facing the exit door. Each man checked the parachute of the man in front and tapped him to confirm correctness. Soon the doors opened and with the green light coming on it was *"Green On, Go"* and the men started jumping one after the other.

Number Nineteen on the Starboard side, was a Gunner who slipped near the exit door. However, he was helped to stand up and then jumped, delaying Number Twenty and me which would result in being separated from the others on the ground. I was out and the parachute was deployed. Looking down I saw a brown patch of flat ground and was assured of a hazard free place to land. It turned out to be a pond covered with algae and I was in the water but safe. Pulling myself out of the pond, I rolled up the wet parachute and carrying it on my back I ran towards the DZ. After sometime I met Major ML Tiwari, commander of PF Two who was heading in my direction to find and help me. When he saw me, he lost his cool and asked me as to why was I carrying the parachute. *"To deposit it,"* I replied, forgetting that the parachutes were to be abandoned in an operational drop! We were soon on the DZ and the main stream was being dropped as planned. Having regrouped, the battalion started moving towards the objective to capture the Poongli Bridge. Meanwhile the artillery battery had also grouped and deployed on the DZ, ready to support us.

The bridge was captured by 2000 hours, without much resistance. At this point, a convoy with headlights on was approaching from the direction of Jamalpur. The lead vehicle of the convoy was knocked off by Rocket Propelled Grenade and a firefight broke out. As 'B' Company was engaged in the battle, I was asked to take a platoon from 'C' Company to reinforce them. The withdrawing Pakistani column tried dislodging us from the bridge and the battle raged throughout the night. At dawn, our fighter aircraft appeared and began strafing the enemy who were hiding in the adjoining fields. When the aircraft reported enemy movement around the right flank of our defences, I was directed to send an ambush party to intercept them. I was assigned ten men to complete the task. As a result of my training at the Academy, I used my map to plan and brief the men. Captain Surjit Singh, the Medium Machine Gun (MMG) Platoon Commander, who was nearby, yelled at me to move. I sent two scouts ahead and requested the rest to follow. We were fired upon barely 500 metres out of our defences. Scout Number One was hit in the arm. I moved my party about 150 metres to one side and occupied a mount dominating the track along which the enemy was moving. We fired as the enemy approached, causing losses and scattering the attackers, but we had expended all our ammunition. With no ammunition left, I pulled out and got the party together when I found the Light Machine Gun (LMG) gunner missing. As I was contemplating the next move, Captain Surjit Singh came up with a small detachment and ordered my party back to the main defences and simultaneously asked for artillery fire from the Parachute Field Battery, dispersing the enemy.

At 1600 hours on December 12, the leading elements of the advancing 95 Brigade joined us at the Poongli Bridge. Thereafter, the advance towards Dacca commenced. After engaging the enemy and dislodging them from Mirpur Bridge on the outskirts of Dacca on the night of December 15/16, we entered the city at 11 am on December 16 – being the first unit to do so. The rest is history!

Image 1: Paras in Action

Source: *Airborne Operations in the 1971 War*

On December 12, 1971, after the successful operation, I was called to the battalion command post and the CO pinned a Para Wing on my sleeve and also promoted me to the field rank of captain. However, my status as a paratrooper remained a point of contention with the Air Force, which required me to complete the Para Basic Course and complete the obligatory training jumps in order to be eligible to jump from their aircraft!! In February 1972, I completed the course at PTS, Agra, and was given my Para Wing formally and officially. That made me a qualified paratrooper in both war and peacetime!

40

Battles of Nainakot and Bisso Buzurg

Rajiv Williams

I was commissioned on my birthday – November 14, and it was a rare endorsement on my officers' identity card, as my dates of birth and commissioning were exactly 20 years apart.

Move into War

After a short break of 10 days, I reached Lucknow Railway Station to embark upon my journey to Dhana in Madhya Pradesh, where I was informed that the unit had already moved to an operational location in Punjab. The next morning on November 24, we arrived at Pathankot the last railway station for any movement northwards.

Baptism in War

I vividly remember some interesting moments, both prior to the war as also during the 14-day ordeal. Mrs. Indira Gandhi's and Gen Sam Manekshaw's inspirational speeches at a forward location under a canopy of trees were the most motivating and outstanding addresses I have ever heard. The talk meant a great deal to all present, and precisely a week later, on December 3, the 14-day India-Pakistan war started.

That evening around 1700 hours, four aircraft from across the border flew past our defences towards Pathankot, and a minute later we heard the rat-a-tat anti-aircraft gun fire and saw red, white and green tracer bullets fill the sky as if it were a firework display. Approximately five minutes later the aircraft returned along the same path and flew back towards Pakistan as our fighters chased them close behind. This was not a drill and we understood that it was real war. That moonlit night as we dug our defences, Mrs. Indira Gandhi, the

Prime Minister of India, addressed the Nation over the radio and declared a state of emergency – she declared war on Pakistan.

Three days later we received orders to attack Pakistani positions across River Ravi on the night December 7/8. Lt Col Madan Mohan Wanchu spoke to me and said, "Rajiv, you are lucky to see war within a fortnight of your joining the Battalion, I waited 14 years for this moment." As I reflect back, I realise that many officers have served their entire careers without seeing a declared war.

One of the most daunting and daring tasks was to wade across the waist-deep river Ravi in the dead of the night, when temperatures dipped to minus 2 degrees Celsius, and then awaiting further orders to capture the first enemy positions across the village. The river crossing commenced around midnight and tanks from the home bank provided us the much-needed fire support, as the tracer bullets indicated our direction of move, making a beautiful pattern overhead. The cold water seeped into our bones, but the warm blood charged our bodies and negated the impact of the subzero conditions. However, the most discomforting and challenging three hours spent waiting to attack the abandoned enemy post after crossing the river in wet battle fatigues was a true test of real strength and endurance.

The narratives of enemy shelling, the villages on fire, tank fire drowning out the sound of planes flying low, were all great experiences as I think back on the moments lived during our approach towards Bien River, south of Shakargarh. The battles of Nainakot and Bisso Buzurg were tough and intense as we moved towards Shakargarh defences.

Nainakot and Beyond

We arrived in Nainakot in the early hours of December 9, having moved slowly for three days, covering only 14 km and capturing Nainakot with 14 HORSE leading. Soon after the capture, we moved to 'Malikpur' few kilometres ahead, where a major tank battle was fought and a dozen enemies Patton tanks were destroyed. The tank manoeuvres continued well into the night and our Recoilless guns supported the battle, taking pot shots at the Pak tanks with some alacrity. By late night, the guns fell silent and we took up defences on the frills of the village and slightly ahead.

Early next morning we were taken by surprise with a burst of MMG fire from behind. Was it a courageous enemy detachment that opened fire on us or was it a case of misidentification? It was certainly unnerving, but we did not retaliate immediately and instead sent a patrol party with a white flag to get a first-hand situation report. Sure enough the fire was a case of misidentification, as a freshly inducted troop of 14 HORSE moved into a cover and mistook us for Pakistani troops.

During the next one week we kept moving, though rather slowly cautiously, as the enemy aircraft were active during the day and so were the withdrawing enemy hard hitting mobile teams. We had to frequently move and were forced to keep our 'Pack 08' ready every few hours, as artillery fire remained active at regular intervals. Here were several significant lessons learned from this movement, such as the sequence of first observing the flash of a gun fire at great distance, then assessing the distance of the gun position by counting the number of shells fired until the shell landed, and finally assessing the point of burst. If the whistling sound of the missile continued to be heard as it flew past us, then we were safe; but if the sound of the projectile suddenly ceased, it was time for us to dive down as the shell would have landed close by. The deadliest type of shelling I experienced was the airburst, which had an impact proportional to the height of the burst above.

Battle of Bisso Buzurg

The other great happening was the 'Battle of Bisso Buzurg', when my Bravo Company was tasked to advance along with a squadron of tanks to village 'Bisso Buzurg', which was located on the flanks of 'Fatehpur Afghanan' the last village we captured along the Bien River. The enemy's hard-hitting teams kept firing at us from delay positions and retarded our speed, slowing our progress, which was seemingly faster than the tanks leading. To our surprise, we noticed the tanks rapidly withdrawing, their guns periodically firing at the attackers. Major Khanna, the Company Commander, was shocked by the unexpected shift in direction of the tanks and sensed something was wrong, as stiff resistance was encountered from the enemy. We were later informed that the leading tank had been hit by a Cobra anti-tank missile and Lt KJ Singh of 14 HORSE, who was standing tall in the tank with his hatchet open, was hit resulting in the tank's sudden rearward movement.

The Company Commander forced to make a hasty decision regarding the next step and chose to attack the position in the melee, despite the fact that there was considerable restraint and uncertainty. We attacked from three directions and the enemy panicked and decided to fight another day. The village was secured and the tanks came forward and occupied their hide, requesting close protection.

Detailed plans had been made for the capture of the enemy positions just across the Bien River, which were tactically occupied around the town of Shakargarh. The attack was planned for the night of December 13/14, and the CO gave detailed final orders from a vantage point. The objectives could be seen on ground and all commanders made rough notes and sketches in their diaries. Suddenly, four Pakistani Sabre jets flew rather low and strafed our positions continuously for over 15 minutes, which seemed like eternity and I think that deadly experience will remain etched in our minds forever. You could see the aircraft approach at an angle and releasing their ammunition in bursts, belching smoke and making very loud and scary sounds.

I soon realised the reason for their target practice was perhaps that when the aircraft made an initial pass above us, Lance Naik Darshan Singh of my platoon took his LMG out of the trench and started firing at the enemy aircraft. That was enough for the Pakistani aircraft in unison to disturb our peace. As I write about this incident after a span of 49 years, the events unfold with reasonable precision, and the name of Darshan Singh came to mind unexpectedly while writing this incident. After delivering ammunition, the enemy aircraft moved away, but not before releasing a 1000 pounder on our MMG detachment, killing Naik Ghisa Ram and his detachment of two and making a huge crater at the place where the MMG emplacement once stood.

After this episode, we hurriedly packed our 'Pack 08' and once again moved towards the firm base, which was not too far from the Forming Up Place for the attack on Shakargarh. The enemy was most active and kept shelling all through the night as 4 GRENADIERS, the other battalion of our formation, tried to cross the river. The shelling was very accurate and heavy, which forced the attack to be postponed by a day and then it was finally called off to a later date.

Early next morning, i.e., on December 16, the day the attack was to commence, we were informed about the capture of Dacca in East Pakistan and the cease fire on the Western front was to come into effect at sharp 1900 hours. There was absolute lull in battle till 1800 hours, when the enemy opened up their artillery might for half an hour with such intensity I had not witnessed in the previous 14 days. Interestingly, when the enemy suddenly ceased shooting, our artillery guns responded with similar, if not greater, ferocity for the following half hour. But precisely at 1900 hours on December 16, all guns fell silent and cease fire came into effect. That was the end of the 14-day war.

Post-War Reflections

The next day, i.e., on December 17, as I walked to a tubewell nearby for a bath after a long gap of 16 days, I found hoards of civilians from Gurdaspur, Dinanagar and other places in Punjab arriving in trucks, tractors and all kinds of transport, cheering us on. They took away buffaloes, horses, other cattle, foreign crockeries as well as furniture items from the Pak households. All food grain stored was put into their trucks and taken away. As a youngster, I was perplexed at their premonition and asked as to why such indulgence, to which their response was a supposed justification for their ordeal during partition.

The other post-war reflection was the repatriation of Pak civilian elders and children abandoned by their family members who left their homes in haste. Some households, even utensils on stoves/*chulhas*, were left behind as they must have fled at the last moment. I recall vividly, nearly forcing an elderly couple and their two grandchildren, aged probably seven and five, to leave their homes as I escorted them to the 'No man's land', which was delineated by a hastily strung barbed wire fence across the small route leading to Shakargarh. Such are the tragic consequences of war and the absence of peace. I was fortunate to have participated in 'The 14-day War,' and the experience was a great beginning in the long journey in uniform thereafter.

41

Battle along Akhaura-Ashuganj-Dhaka Axis

Balraj Kapur

My Unit 18 RAJPUT was located near the Tripura border. I joined them immediately after commissioning in the Assembly Area, where we camped in bivouacs and trenches. Two days later we marched to our Forward Assembly Area. Here, our Commanding Officer, Lt Col A K Verma held a very inspiring *Sainik Sammelan*. We were pumped up and ready to go.

First Assignment

Our Brigade, comprising 4 GUARDS, 18 RAJPUT and 10 BIHAR, had been tasked to capture Akhaura – a highly fortified border town. The plan was to surround the enemy, soften up his defensive positions with artillery and air strikes before launching an attack. 4 GUARDS was to cross the border first, followed by 18 RAJPUT. Major GS Sidhu, our Second-in-Command, accompanied by myself and two soldiers were tasked to familiarise ourselves with the 4 GUARDS deployment. This would help, in case a link up was required between the two units.

4 GUARDS started off after night had set in. Additionally, we were joined by a Commando Platoon from 10 BIHAR. They were to branch off and proceed on a separate mission. As we entered Pakistan, the enemy artillery shelling began. It was not very accurate, but for a first timer quite scary. Sometime later we came under small arms fire. We immediately hit ground and dug up fox holes. The earth was soft and we used our mini shovels. The opposition was tackled by the leading company, and we resumed our advance an hour later.

As 4 GUARDS reached their projected location around 2 am, we began walking towards the location where 18 RAJPUT were scheduled to arrive later. After some distance, we suddenly came under intense small arms fire. We took cover in the folds offered by the terrain, but were vulnerable in the open. The enemy position was just 200 metres away. We heard them shout *Niklo Kafiro*, accompanied by Punjabi expletives. It was probably a platoon-sized protective patrol. Towards one side, there was a small village about 100 metres away on a raised ground. Taking cover of the darkness we sprinted towards the village amongst a hail of bullets. We managed to reach the abandoned hamlet (8 to 10 houses). It offered us better safety and cover.

We waited in the village. The Pakistani soldiers were shouting at us. We decided, that we would shoot ourselves dead rather than be captured alive, if they came for us. My lifetime whizzed past me, I thought of my near and dear ones as we awaited likely death. It was extremely frightening. I could see the expression of fear on the faces of others as well.

Around 4 am we saw some soldiers coming towards our hamlet under enemy fire. We were relieved to see that they were from the 10 BIHAR Commando Platoon. They were about 12 to 15 men. Their Platoon Commander and some other soldiers had been killed and their mission had been aborted. Some of these soldiers were wounded as well. Having been reinforced, we took up positions all around the hamlet.

At first light, in the far distance we could see 18 RAJPUT marching in. It was a huge column of troops about 600 metres away. The Pakistanis got scared and started abandoning their positions. They ran in various directions on either side of our hamlet. Seven of them made the mistake of attempting to wade through a waist deep pond, 500 metres wide and close to the side where I was located.

A soldier of 10 BIHAR, who was bleeding from his head, started firing his Light Machine Gun (LMG) at them and verbally abusing them. His fire was inaccurate – probably due to his physical and mental state. I asked him to move aside and took up position behind the LMG. I started firing single shots. Seeing the fall of the bullets, I adjusted my aim. Aided by their slow movement, all seven of them went into their watery graves in the next 3 to 4 minutes.

It was a great relief for us to join back the Paltan, as it came marching sometime later. The relief though, was short lived as we came under an air attack, soon after. It was a most horrific experience, wherein our unit suffered casualties. Till the time the aircraft carried out their attack, it was not known who would be in their line of fire. From our positions, we observed the strafing by their cannons hoping that the alignment would not come over us. The deafening sound as they dived towards us added to the terror.

Capture of the Bridge on River Titas-Akhaura

In the battle of Akhaura, 'C' Company had captured their objective and exploited up to the Railway Station. Our ('B') Company had to pass through them to capture a railway bridge over river Titas, before the enemy could blow it off. Our objective was about a kilometre away. The time was around 7 am. We had to rush to capture the bridge intact.

The Company travelled along the railway line, which was perched on a 10 to 12 feet high embankment. All the low-lying areas around were filled with rain water, which had gathered and remained as ponds after the monsoon. Guided by the brave Mukti Bahini personnel, we had waded through these chest/waist deep waters on our way to the objective. The bridge was heavily guarded by the enemy. Our Company launched attack in a single file along the railway line. Enemy bunkers and trenches were facing the open fields. The direction and formation of attack was most unexpected. They were unable to engage us. We ran shouting our war cry '*BAJRANG BALI KI JAI,*' with the leading troops firing continuously. The enemy, who had been softened adequately by our artillery and air force for the past two days, started running across the bridge.

We captured own side of the bridge and my platoon was tasked to secure the far bank. We were rushing across the bridge when one brave (heavily built) Pakistani Havildar and another soldier took up positions about 200 metres away on the railway line itself and began firing with an LMG effectively. Our advance was held up due to casualties.

To evict them, I snuck up unnoticed across the bridge at the base of the elevated railway embankment. I got closer and closer till I was just 7 or 8 feet down and close to the two Pakistanis. I was carrying two primed hand grenades tucked inside my jersey. I took out one of them, removed the safety pin and gently lobbed it where they were positioned. I heard the spring action but the grenade did not explode; maybe because it had got wet as we waded through water.

I got scared that these two would now come after me. Fortunately, they were more terrified than I was, as they saw the grenade and concluded that we had closed in on them and that another one might arrive shortly, which could be lethal. They got up and ran for their lives. This was how the bridge was finally captured. It was fully prepared to be blown off and our Pioneer Section disconnected the charges.

As we had captured the Railway Bridge, the enemy wanted to inflict maximum casualties upon us and blow off the bridge. We came under intense artillery fire. We also came under a different type of fire where the explosion at our end occurred first and then we heard the bang at the 'gun position'. We later realised it was direct firing Recoilless (RCL) guns firing High Explosive ammunition. This one came with greater intensity and had a bigger shock effect.

We were digging fox holes, to avoid the use of Pakistani bunkers, which could have been booby trapped. During one such RCL shot, I felt something hot at my waist and could feel the trickle of blood. I had been hit by a splinter! Sepoy Naim Singh, who was with me, opened my web equipment, gave me a few sips of water and tied a bandage. But the bleeding did not stop. We remained like that for a few minutes till the shelling stopped.

The Commanding Officer approached the bridge to congratulate and encourage us. He advised me to return to the Regimental Aid Post (RAP), which was about a kilometre away near the Akhaura Railway Station. Our Company stretcher bearers had come, but I said I would walk as I was able to.

I resumed my trek along the railway line's steep embankment. Due to my exposed posture – and the fact that I was a lucrative target – one Medium Machine Gun started fire on me. I could make out, as the fire was from 400 to 500 metres away and the rate of fire was such. The bullets were falling all around me. I had the option of going down on the reverse slope of the embankment to evade the bullets, but that would have been cumbersome, as I was bleeding and in pain. Regardless, I decided to continue. The enemy fired at least one full belt of 250 rounds at me but was not able to hit me, such was my destiny. He gave up.

I reached the RAP, where our Doctor Captain Narula stitched and bandaged me, and gave some pain killers. He offered further evacuation, but I declined. The splinter remained inside me till it was removed in a Military Hospital a few months later. I realised its presence, as I trained for commando course and felt a piercing pain while carrying my back pack.

Onward to Ashuganj

After the capture of Akhaura on December 5, 1971, the enemy was evicted, demoralised and on the run. We got into hot pursuit. They blew off bridges over rivers and rivulets. We chased them regardless of the fact that our ammunition, artillery support and administration was getting out of reach. On December 9, around 5 am, we reached Ashuganj on the mighty Meghna River, whose far bank was barely visible due to its width. With its back to the wall and unable to cross this massive river, the Pakistan Army reorganised itself to give us a pitched battle, in a desperate do or die situation. We had been walking for the past three days and launched an attack straight from our line of march.

The 'B' and 'D' Companies got into assault formation against the enemy. My 'B' Company was commanded by Major Yudhvir Singh Sisodia. True to his name, he was one of the bravest persons. Setting aside all teachings, he insisted on being the leading man, as the Company marched. This had a positive impact on the men, as they followed him without hesitation. We were assaulting under very effective artillery/small arms fire and suffering casualties. Sepoy Jung Bahadur, a young soldier who was carrying my radio set, was killed by a burst of bullets on his chest. He died instantly. I picked up my set and continued. Major Sisodia too was hit by bullets in his leg and was unable to move forward. News also came that Major Pritam, Officer Commanding 'D' Company, was similarly wounded and incapacitated. In times of war, such news spreads like wildfire.

To our relief, we found a bund sort of raised ground (approximately 2 ½ feet high) ahead of us. Our Company took up positions on that and we tried to return fire. As we raised our heads above the bund, the enemy fired at us from dominating positions. Our artillery's 3-inch mortars were not there to support us. Around 7 am our Air Force Fighter aircraft came, but due to a bullet hit to our Forward Air Controller Flight Lieutenant Dhillon's radio handset, he was unable to contact them and direct them on to the enemy.

Meanwhile, Major TL Sharma, Officer Commanding 'A' Company, was sent forward to control the battle, as two Company Commanders were wounded. Another brave man, Major Sharma walked immediately behind us, encouraging us all to hold on and fight. In doing so, he was exposing himself to enemy fire. I felt very relieved and emboldened by his presence and I am sure the entire company felt the same. As he was standing behind me, I heard a sound as if he had been hit on his head by a hockey stick. I turned around and watched him fall, having been struck in the forehead by bullets. His helmet came off and he took one final long breath before passing away. It was a demoralising sight for the troops to experience so many deaths.

My Platoon Havildar Ram Das Singh then tied a bandage on Major Sharma's head as I held it in my lap. A thought struck me that I should take some item from his body to give it to his loved ones as a token of remembrance. My eyes fell on his wrist watch – a plain one with a small dial and a steel chain, as I recall. However, I changed my mind when I realised that troops viewing me might not understand my intention.

We had to withdraw from the location. I saw Major Pritam on a stretcher. He was sitting on it and telling his troops to leave him and head for safety. He was a charismatic leader loved by his men. He would rather be in a position to save someone else than be saved by others. Major Sisodia protested, but was carried out of danger zone by Lance Havildar Balbir, a middle aged, paunchy, superseded soldier who could never have passed the fireman's lift test. Yet he rose to the occasion and saved his Company Commander.

We regrouped and Ashuganj was captured the next day. We watched in awe as a massive heliborne operation took place and a build-up was carried out across Meghna River. This facilitated the surrender by Pakistani Army at Dhaka and other places. We also saw the huge railway bridge on River Meghna being blown off.

Our Unit was awarded the Battle Honour Akhaura and Theatre Honour East Pakistan. Our Unit also earned the title "Akhaura Tigers". 38 valiant soldiers laid down their lives while more than 100 were wounded.

42

When Time Stood Still

GG Dwivedi

It was really exciting to land straight into the War Zone on December 1, 1971, barely a fortnight after commissioning, at a young age of 20 years. My Unit (14 JAT) was operationally deployed in Dhanpora near Agartala, in close proximity to the East Pakistan Border.

A day after I joined the Battalion, the Unit got instructions to move for operations. Battalion 'Orders Group' soon assembled for Commanding Officers (CO's) 'Operation Orders'. As part of the 301 Infantry Brigade, 14 JAT was tasked to capture Lalgarh-Mian Bazar by 1300 hours D plus 1; D-Day being December 3, 1971. Salient details of plan were as follows (Map 1):

- 'A' Company to provide firm base in KK Nagar area by 1800 hours D-Day. Road blocks to be established by 'B' Company at Dharmatpur and Battalion less two companies at Dhanchakra by 1900 hours D-Day.
- 'D' Company to Capture Lalgarh by 0630 hours; 'C' Company to clear Bangalmuri by 0800 hours; 'A' & 'B' Companies to clear Mian Bazar by 1300 hours, by D plus 1.
- Battalion less 'A' & 'B' Companies to be prepared to move to Buschi on orders.

During the Company briefing, Maj KN Rai formally designated me Company Second-in-Command and assigned me to number 1 Platoon. Everyone was well armed and prepared for the following four days in terms of ammunition, rations and essential stores. We moved to Assembly Area on the night of December 2 and deployed as planned on December 3. Around 2300 hours on December 3, our protective patrol encountered an enemy in

Map 1: Action Plan: Lalgarh-Mian Bazar Operations

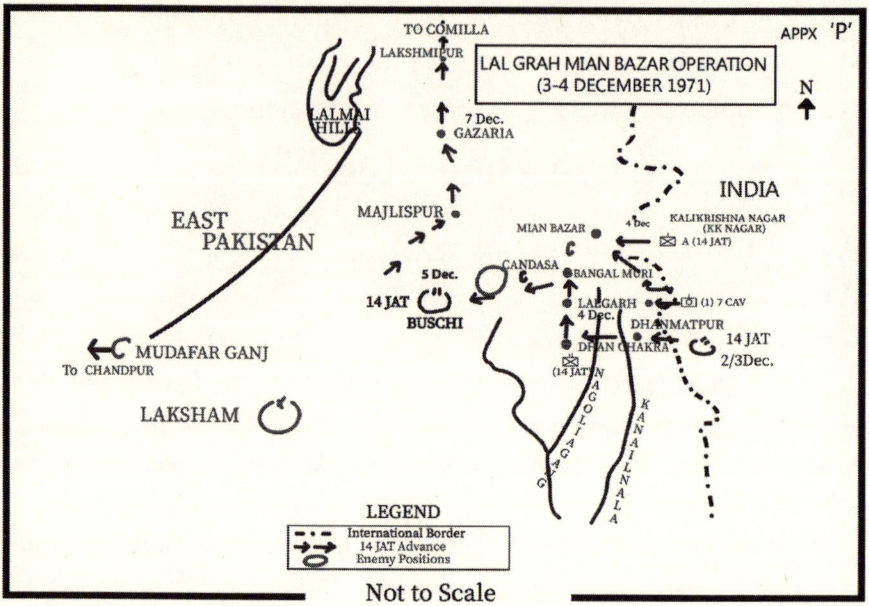

Source: Annotated by Author

Dhanchakra area. Prompt action forced the enemy to withdraw, suffering eight fatal casualties. The war bugle had been sounded on a high note.

Capture Lalgarh-Mian Bazar: Curtain Raiser

At the first light on December 4, 'D' Company under Maj SL Chadha commenced the assault on Lalgarh with Armoured Squadron of 7 Cavalry (PT 76-light amphibious tanks) providing support. Following the capture of four bunkers, the operation came to a halt due to strong enemy fire. The enemy position, which was anticipated to be a platoon locality was actually held by a company. The fire support from the tanks was not effective due to lack of coordination. Cancellation of 'infantry-tank training' on December 2, due to Battalion's operational move proved costly.

To isolate and put pressure on the enemy defences, Armoured Squadron and 'A' Company were ordered to move to Mian Bazar around 0930 hours. As tanks closed in on Mian Bazar and 'A' Company prepared for assault, the enemy withdrew, fearful of being cut off. Bold action by the Armoured Squadron proved decisive, although three tanks were lost with one fatal casualty.

To capture Lalgarh, Battalion attack was planned. 'A' & 'B' Companies joined the Battalion by 1230 hours. The attack commenced at 1530 hours, duly supported by the artillery. As the assault progressed, the enemy gradually pulled back. By 1630 hours the objectives had been secured at the cost of six casualties, three being fatal.

Buschi-Interlude (5-6 December)

From Lalgarh, the Battalion advanced to Buschi and secured it by late night. 'A' Company was deployed in the Grove area. I directed Sep Ramdin, my platoon runner, to dig up fire trench besides coconut trees in the vicinity of a small graveyard, as it provided good observation. It was past midnight when the enemy commenced intense artillery shelling. Suddenly, I heard a 'whizzing sound' right overhead – a shell fell barely 20 metres away. Few seconds later, there was an earth-shaking tremor, that buried Ramdin and myself under a heap of earth in our trench. This time the shell landed right next to our trench but its impact was considerably degraded as it first hit the coconut tree and after deflection got embedded into the mound atop the grave.

Alongside the artillery shelling, two enemy companies tried to close up with our defences, but their attempt was effectively foiled by our own coordinated response. The following night, I led a recce patrol, which was my first independent mission. Subedar Raghubir Singh, Company Senior JCO and CHM Kishen Singh were part of it. We returned by morning on completing the task.

Comilla-Zero (7-8 December)

On the morning of December 7, the Battalion was tasked to capture Comilla, a strategically important town and communication centre. It entailed a march of approximately 30 km with full battle loads. Advance for Comilla commenced at 1030 hours. The 'B' and 'C' Companies eliminated enemy positions en route at Gazariya and Lakshimpur. The 'A' Company resumed advance after last light and soon secured the airfield. Here on, as the navigation party's leader, I had to rely on captured Razakar (militia force) as guide in the absence of an updated map. Consequently, we missed the objective – Tomtom Bridge, envisaging it to be a prominent landmark, but actually it happened to be just a culvert. As a result, Company Headquarters along with leading platoon walked right into the enemy's defences, with CO's Party following on the heels.

By now it was almost midnight and we were hardly 50-60 metres ahead, when we noticed some Pakistani soldiers loading weapons into a vehicle. Due to radio silence and close proximity with the enemy, Maj Rai, Company Commander, asked me to personally confirm with the CO if we were to continue advance. I must have travelled no more than 30-40 metres down the road when two cars, a jeep and a 1 tonne truck with headlights on, approached unexpectedly at a distance. Assuming they could be our vehicles, I stepped back swiftly. Within few seconds, both the vehicles were under intense fire from our troops deployed around. The jeep came to a screeching halt right beside me.

I cocked my carbine instantly and fired a long burst on the persons inside the semi open jeep from almost handshake distance. As I was about to fire the second burst, someone jumped out from the jeep, right in front of me. Spontaneously, I swung around and fired at him. Ironically, after firing two rounds the carbine jammed and the individual managed to flee pleading, "Have Mercy on Allah's Name." (It was later found that the person who got away was Maj Shah Nawaz Khan, 2IC 30 PUNJAB, who was taken prisoner the next day at Comilla hospital in a wounded condition.)

Instantaneously, someone pulled me down as a volley of bullets from the jeep went whistling over my head. It was Chote Lal from Company Headquarters. Soon after, the jeep exploded, scattering the occupants' bodies. I quickly repaired the flaw in my carbine and looked around for Chote Lal, but he was nowhere to be seen. Keeping my cool, I began to inch my way to the Company Headquarters only to bump into men of 'B' Company, who momentarily took me to be a Pakistani Officer but timely intervention by Maj Bachan Singh, 'B' Company Commander, saved an awkward situation. Chote Lal also surfaced unexpectedly, as he too had got mingled up. As I passed by our 81 Mortar detachment, an enemy artillery shell landed right next to it, killing three of our men; again it was a very narrow escape for me.

Soon, I managed to link back with 'A' Company. Meanwhile, CHM Kishen single handedly destroyed two enemy machine guns by lobbing hand grenades into the bunkers – a technique he was obsessed with.

Tragically, in the process, he was mortally wounded. Major Rai also silenced an enemy automatic weapon. In the ensuing skirmish, Subedar Raghubir was also killed. It was tormenting to see the bodies of Raghubir and Kishen lying side by side. I had developed a close bond with both within a few days.

The operation lasted till sunrise and included house-to-house combat. By mid-day, massive crowds had gathered on the streets, extending heroic welcome and offering eatables and cigarette packets. They found it hard to believe as to how the Pakistani Army was defeated. Battalion Quarter Master Capt AS Bindra, who entered the town with a convoy of logistics vehicles, was profusely garlanded, taken to be a General, and declared "Liberator of Comilla".

The capture of Comilla was a spectacular success for the Battalion. The Army Commander Lt Gen JS Arora personally complimented CO Lt Col LN Sabharwal for the task well done. Mile Stone 'Comilla 0' was brought back as souvenir and occupies a place of pride in the Unit Quarter Guard. For the next few days, we were engaged in intense patrolling and assisting the East Bengal Rifles to take over the liberated areas. It was heart rendering to hear and see the signs of atrocities committed by the Pakistani Army, including mass graves.

Last Bastion: Capture of Bandar-Narayanganj (15-16 December)

The Battalion moved to Daudkandi on December 13 for capturing Narayanganj. We crossed the Meghna River on December 14 and concentrated in Baidya Bazar. The Battalion was entrusted with clearing the Eastern Bank of the Lakhya River on December 15 morning (Map 2).

Nabiganj, Bandar Railway Station and Madanganj were reported to be held with a platoon each. 'D' Company established a firm base by 1630 hours, while 'B' Company secured Nabiganj at 1830 hours. As the enemy had reinforced Bandar, hence it was planned to employ two companies for its capture: 'C' Company going in for Bandar and 'A' Company attacking position East of it. On closing up, it was realised that Bandar Railway Station was hemmed between deep water channels on its East and built up area to the West.

As a result of its limited deployment, 'C' Company was forced to attack in echelons. As a result 'hand to hand' fight ensued, and hand grenades

Map 2: Action Plan: Bandar-Lakhya River Operations

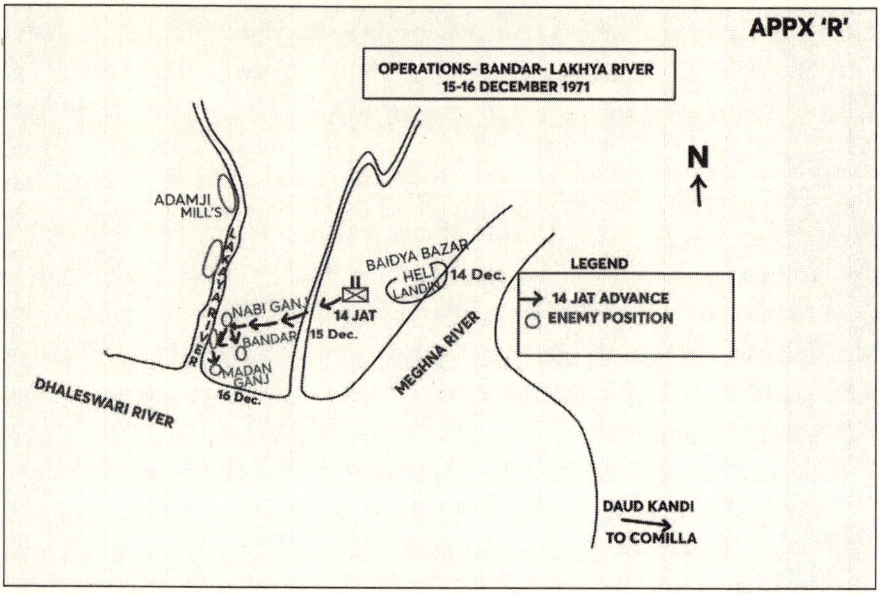

Source: Annotated by Author

were used extensively by both sides. Maj NP Singh, Company Commander, provided resolute leadership. Capt (Dr) SC Mohanty, Medical Officer, did a commendable job amidst thick of the battle, saving many lives.

'A' Company had to pass through 'C' Company to attack enemy positions, located less than 200 metres ahead. The situation was obviously nightmarish but the CO's presence indeed had a salutary effect. Maj Rai assigned me to the right bunkers with Number 1 Platoon, with Subedar Balbir Singh and himself taking on the left side. With bayonet fixed we charged with full fury. As we closed in, few enemy personnel came out of the bunkers to offer resistance, but the position was quickly overrun. It was around 2200 hours when orders were received to consolidate and resume the operations in the morning. At first light December 16, 'B' & 'D' Companies cleared enemy positions on the East Bank of Lakhya River. A captured Pakistani officer lauded the Battalion Mortar Platoon's fire assistance under the command of Capt Tanwar.

Meanwhile, 'A' Company resumed advance along the railway line to clear Madanganj – an attack duly supported by artillery fire. Soon Madanganj position was contacted and attack commenced. Mid-way during the assault, orders were received to hold the operations, but it was too late. As defender took to heels, heavy casualties were inflicted on the fleeing enemy. At 1400 hours the news came in that the Pakistani Army in Bangladesh had surrendered.

The Battalion was ordered to stop further operations and deploy around Narayanganj. The town which wore a desolate look soon came to life as small groups began to show up on the streets; many were holding a green piece of cloth with an orange colour patch, symbolising the Bangladesh flag and chanting slogans "*Joi Bangla.*" A frenzy of vengeance loomed big, with violent mobs rounding up accomplices to mete out 'on the spot justice' – it was an ugly sight. Time appeared to stand still, marking an end of the gory saga; awaiting the 'New Born nation' to announce its arrival.

Reflections

14 JAT fought valiantly, inflicting heavy losses on the enemy; over 100 killed and 60 wounded/POWs besides capturing large quantity of weapons and stores. The Battalion won two Vir Chakras, two Sena Medals and was awarded Theatre Honour of Comilla.

During the war, all commanders led from the front with an amazing team spirit that proved to be the cutting edge. Seeing a comrade right next to oneself was the greatest source of motivation. Maj Rai's help and guidance were quite reassuring to me personally.

Weapon handling, use of ground, battle drills and procedures were excellent. Standards of physical fitness and mental toughness were outstanding, as evident from sustained fighting, long moves on foot being self-contained. During critical junctures, artillery support was very effective. Bold employment of armour at Mian Bazar proved to be decisive. Importance of 'infantry-tank cooperation training' was adequately highlighted during the Lalgarh action.

Pakistani Army initially fought well, but later its officers lost heart. The men stood their ground till the end. The Pakistani Army role as an occupational force proved to be a major reason for its defeat. The conduct of the Indian Army was exemplary. The local citizens developed great admiration for us, both for our professionalism and our public behaviour.

The first fortnight turned out to be the most defining period of my service career. Amazing operational experience transformed me from 'Green Horn' to 'Battle Hardened' Junior Leader. I realised that the Battalion is the bedrock of the Army; its performance decides the outcome of battle and shapes the course of war. Its soul is defined by camaraderie and *'espirt de corps'*.

Down memory lane, it was a unique honour to be part of "Fighting Fourteenth" while history was in the making. Divine Blessings in the form of 'Fifty Bonus Years' and counting – the Greatest Reward for a Young Subaltern!

Image 1: Pakistani Bunker (Comilla)

SECTION 7

50 Years of Liberation War

We look Beyond

43

Major Takeaways: Liberation War

Ajinkya Jadhav and *Narjit Singh*

Three major wars have been fought between India and Pakistan. Pakistan has been the perpetrator on all three occasions. The 1971 war was the most significant victory for India, as it saw the liberation of Bangladesh and the humiliation of Pakistan. The lessons learnt were that victory could be achieved through a whole of nation approach, good leadership, employment of effective military strategies, jointness of the armed forces, effective logistical support and support from the people of the country.

Cohesive Employment of National Power

India employed all the elements of National power in cohesion thereby achieving synergy. Diplomatic efforts succeeded in isolating Pakistan and generating global support in India's favour. The political and the military leadership at the apex level along with the bureaucrats worked in unison to carefully formulate the national and the military aim which enabled the military leaders to evolve a well-articulated military strategy. The operational plans flowed out of it, leading to military success. The victory also defined India's much broader role in foreign politics, as many countries – including the United States – recognised that the balance of power in the region had shifted to India as a major player.

Aggression of the PM, Mrs. Indira Gandhi

An American Gallup poll in 1971 voted Indira Gandhi as the most admired person in the world. The PM was subjected to intense international pressure from President Nixon of the United States of America and President Mao of China. President

Nixon mobilised the seventh fleet of USA into the Bay of Bengal in support of its ally Pakistan. Mrs. Gandhi displayed sterling diplomatic acumen and signed a treaty with USSR, which countered the Americans and released the pressure. She showed astute leadership and controlled aggression to rise to the occasion and craft a new chapter in the history of the region. She repeatedly reiterated to the world about the annihilation of the citizens of Bangladesh by the barbaric Pakistan Army and the threat to the nation's security. On the night of December 3, 1971, she declared to the world, 'This war has been forced on us.' She bestowed immense faith in the Indian armed forces that delivered a swift and decisive victory in 13 days of war. Apart from the military success, it was a coup d'état in foreign policy, for which a large credit goes to the PM.

Pressure from the United Nations and Other Countries

India managed to withstand the influence of USA, despite the American show of military strength by positioning the nuclear-powered aircraft carrier – the USS Enterprise and US Task Force 74 comprising destroyers and amphibious ships from the Seventh Fleet into the Bay of Bengal. Suffice to say that any Chinese threat in any form was likewise successfully handled.

Despite India's early demands, the UN could not deter Pakistan, and so during the provocation of the war, India strictly prevented UN intervention and succeeded in an outright victory. India engaged the international community positively in such a manner that, despite seven ceasefire resolutions, the UN could not intervene in the war and obstruct India's war objectives.

Dubious Leadership – Pakistan

Yahya Khan was getting more frustrated by the inability of his troops to restore their authority over the Mukti Bahini in East Pakistan, and he was convinced that this failure was due to the active assistance of the Indian Army.

In an October 1971 interview with Newsweek, he exalted to "teach that woman a lesson." He also suffered from grandiose hallucinations and a legacy of past Muslim invaders coming from Central Asia vanquishing a divided India. He was convinced that the; 'superior fighting quality' of his army would easily make up the slight numerical superiority India had in Infantry. In Armour and Artillery, he had a slight advantage, and therefore felt confident to inflict a decisive defeat on the Indians in the west. In fact, such a victory would offset the loss of East Pakistan.

To function cohesively, Pakistan's diverse ethnic and linguistic groups required strong social and political institutions and prudent leadership. Suffice to say that the political and social structure necessary to integrate the nation never came into being, and the intellectual approach to deal with this was altogether missing. The glorious victory against Pakistan in 1971 was India's first decisive victory in a major war in centuries.

Availability of Intelligence

There was no shortage of general information, which came primarily from Mukti Bahini and East Bengalis – who had deserted and made their way into Punjab over the western border. In fact, East Bengalis had been segregated and so their information of operational plans, troop locations and movement was scant and hazy. They were, however, able to give information on the peace time locations of their formations and of neighbouring ones, as well as updates on terrain, which proved to be great help to the Indian Armed Forces. There was a void in electronic intelligence and a lack of coordination in acquisition and dissemination of real-time intelligence, which delayed decision making.

Timing of the War

The monsoon season was avoided owing to the water logging challenges posed by the riverine terrain in east Pakistan, and winters were chosen the period for the campaign due to China's inability to cross the snowbound Himalayas and achieve collusivity with Pakistan. The COAS, Field Marshal Sam Manekshaw, deserves praise for his strategic skill, since he kept his ground and convinced the Prime Minister that the campaign could be won if conducted in the winter.

Mukti Bahini and People's Support

The support of the Mukti Bahini and the population of East Pakistan, was also central to success in military operations. Mukti Bahini proved to be extremely committed and passionate to pursue their goal of achieving independence. They were adept at guerrilla warfare, which made the outstretched Pakistan Army vulnerable to several attacks against their lines of communications and installations. Additionally, they were instrumental in providing intelligence and guided the Indian Armed Forces through navigable routes. They complimented and synergised their actions with the Indian Army on the ground.

Clarity in Operational Aims

Following World War II, only three operations generated definitive outcomes: – the first was the six-day war (the Arab-Israel Conflict), the second was the Falklands conflict in 1982, and the third was the 1971 India-Pakistan war. In each of these three instances, air power was critical to achieving decisive outcomes. The myth of invincibility and pathological hostility towards India were among the most misread signals by Pakistan in commencing the war of 1971. In India a convergence of political, military, and diplomatic powers worked in tandem with each other, resulting in a full-scale preparation to win the war. As far as the objectives go, India was to assist the Mukti Bahini in creating a state in East Pakistan that would allow the refugees to return. The second objective was to prevent Pakistan from taking land on either side of the International Border (IB) or the Line of Control (LoC). Lastly, was to defend our integrity in case China intervened at any point during the conflict.

The 13-day war between India and Pakistan was a decisive victory that resulted in the birth of a great nation – Bangladesh – and the surrender of 93,000 prisoners. The Indian armed forces operations were fully supported by the Mukti Bahini and the people. In fact, the humiliating defeat resulted in greater animosity against India, which subsequently manifested in proxy war cum state-sponsored terrorism in the late 1980s. It continues till date. On the other hand, despite rapid changes in the geopolitics of the region, India's relations with Bangladesh have continued to improve progressively to the mutual benefit of both countries.

Selection and Maintenance of Aim

Selection and Maintenance of Aim is a fundamental principle of warfare. The political objective of going to war was accomplished by the establishment of Bangladesh and the repatriation of India's ten million refugees. Eastern command was successful in achieving the aim; however, Western Command, which aimed at maintaining a strategic defence that included offensive operations, was unable to defend its complete territory, which resulted in loss of Chhamb and some areas of Punjab. At the operational level, initial objectives for attack must be selected with greater deliberation, when the forces undertaking Offensive have the initiative and there are no constraints of time or resources. Capture of territory elsewhere, does not compensate for the loss. Maintaining the Morale of its forces is an important principle of war. The objectives must result in overwhelming success with negligible casualties; this will boost the morale of own forces.

Jointness

For the first time in the history of independent India, the three wings of the military participated in the war. Although the campaign was not designed in an integrated fashion, this led in a number of unanticipated and uncoordinated decisions being made. However, the operational momentum was synergised within the army and air force and was a key enabler for success during the war. While, the naval contribution was due to its indirect effect, since their operations were conducted from a standalone mode. One of the major lessons learnt was the delay and lack of proper coordination in close air support missions; the attack on Karachi Harbour by the Navy and Air Force was planned in isolation with neither knowing of the other Service's plan. The amphibious landing of a Brigade off Cox Bazar was done off a map and was unsuccessful. The successful conduct of the airborne operation at Tangail along with innovative deception measures, was a milestone in the history of joint operations, ultimately resulting in the surrender of Dacca. The need for jointness and integration very clearly emerged as a key battle-winning factor for the future. The positive step of creating theatre commands will perhaps achieve the desired results 50 years after 1971 war.

Military Victory

It was the first and only Indian war till date which culminated in Pakistan's surrender. All other wars have ended in a third-party-mediated ceasefire, following which both nations claimed victory. This war led to the birth of a new nation, and the strategic victory over Pakistan was unprecedented and historic. It was the result of the good leadership, sound decision making, good intelligence and operational plans, synergy among the three services and other elements of national power, overwhelming support from the people of East Pakistan and their leaders, commitment, and patriotic zeal on the part of the Mukti Bahini, who were adept at guerrilla warfare. Future wars would be brief and decisive, as the 1971 war demonstrated. Military preparedness and capability must be maintained at a high level in order to conduct such missions. All stakeholders should study the lessons learned in each field to ensure national security.

44

Regional Dynamics: Beyond the Liberation War

VK Ahluwalia

"The people stood by us in our darkest hour, and we will never forget it."
– Sheikh Mujibur Rahman, January 10, 1972, New Delhi[1]

The Bangladesh Liberation War of 1971 was a unique war in which the Indian armed forces, and the people of East Pakistan, the Bengali nationalists and their 'self-determination movement', duly supported by India, played an extremely significant role to achieve its political, humanitarian and military objectives. The war was one of its kind in that it lasted 13 days and ended in the birth of a new nation in the form of Bangladesh, and the surrender of 93,000 POWs. While the 1971 War elevated India's profile as a dominant power in the South Asian region, it did not help to solve India's problems with Pakistan – primarily its claim on Jammu and Kashmir since 1947, which later manifested into a persistent proxy war cum state-sponsored terrorism. In fact, much against the spirit of the Shimla Agreement of 1972, Pakistan continued to plan and take aggressive actions against India, including planned intrusion in the Kargil Sector in 1999. On balance, it proved to be a strategic miscalculation that led to another blunder for Islamabad.

It is significant to commemorate the War's 50th anniversary not only to rejoice and celebrate the triumph, but also to remember those who contributed to the making of history in 1971. That is, the contributions and sacrifices made primarily by the martyrs, the then political leadership of both India and East Pakistan (now Bangladesh), the Indian armed forces, the *Mukti Bahini*, and the local populace of both the countries. Given this historical context, the chapter's objective is to provide a concise analysis of the Indian subcontinent's current geopolitical situation, focusing on two factors: the rapidly changing geo-political-economic environment, and the regional security matrix from the vantage of South Asian and Indian Ocean Region (IOR). Thus, the Chapter tries to identify broad strategies to enhance the region's human security architecture while also addressing local socioeconomic concerns.

Security Landscape of South Asia

South Asia is one of the most unstable and volatile regions of the world. Of the nine regions, as per the Institute for Economics and Peace (IEP) rankings, South Asia is the second least peaceful region of the world.[2] Notably, while the majority of South Asia's regions have civilisational, historical, cultural, religious, linguistic, and ethnic linkages, it is also the least integrated region of the world.

The 'unresolved' boundary cum territorial issues of India with China and Pakistan, throughout the last seven decades, have made India vulnerable to various conflicts. The intensity of activities on the Line of Control (LoC) with Pakistan and on the Line of Actual Control (LAC) with China varies depending upon several factors, such as conditions on the borders, and the geopolitical and security environment in the region. Such conditions are ideal to trigger a conflict even due to misperception and misunderstanding, if not controlled at the earliest opportunity. With all three countries being nuclear-armed states, they should engage in urgent political, economic, and strategic dialogue to resolve outstanding issues.

After the Partition, Pakistan has always remained obsessed with annexing Jammu and Kashmir, maintaining an anti-India stance, and using religion (Islam) to promote its interest, both within and outside Pakistan. It chose to follow the Wahhabi Islamic practice of the Middle East, which has its own related challenges of sectarian intolerance, and extremist culture. The internal security remains fragile given the Shia-Sunni divide, which has resulted in the rise of sectarian violence. Pakistan is ranked 150th in the world's index of peaceful nations by the IEP 2021 Report, out of 163 countries analysed.[3] Thus, making it one of the least peaceful nations. Besides, it is also one of the epicentres of terrorism, having been placed in the grey list by the Financial Action Task Force (FATF) since June 2018.[4]

On the other hand, Bangladesh chose to be a pluralist democracy. Despite this, during the early years of the formation of Bangladesh, it too had its share of military coups, abortive coups and military rulers at the helm of affairs. However, it has remained focused on economic growth, addressing socio-economic challenges, and sharing its linguistic and cultural legacy with Indian counterparts of similar ethnicity.

Threats and Challenges

As of 2021, while South Asia has 1.958 billion population, which accounts for 24.8 per cent of the total world population, it has only 3.5 per cent of the world's land surface area. The population density in South Asia is 303 per square km.[5] Being poverty ridden, South Asia has one of the lowest human development indices in the world.[6] While the population is increasing, the land surface area and availability of fresh water are shrinking due to the growing economies, industrialisation, urbanisation and infrastructure development. In the future, this very equation between population and land surface (24.8 : 3.5 for South Asia), along with other factors such as socio-economic inequality, largest number of poor people in the world, vulnerability to natural disasters, environment degradation and climate change, and high rate of unemployment, is likely to result in instability and conflict situation.

The region is beset with myriad traditional and non-traditional threats and challenges: boundary-cum-territorial disputes with active borders; sub conventional conflicts like low-intensity conflicts, insurgencies, terrorism and militancy; intra-state conflicts based on sectarian, religious and ethnic differences; trans-national organised crimes like narcotics smuggling, human-trafficking, fake currencies and money laundering; religious radicalism; and other challenges like illegal migrations resulting in demographic inversion, piracy, poverty, health, unemployment, informational and cyber-attacks.

The region is also prone to natural disasters like earthquakes, tsunami, floods, draughts, and security threats due to environmental degradation. According to South Asian Disaster Report 2016, there were 481 natural disasters in South Asia between 2005 and 2015. Due to high density of population and inadequate health care systems in place, diseases with biological origins (viruses) make the population far more vulnerable to their consequences. A case in point is the successive waves of COVID-19 and its ill effects on health, economy, trade, investment, joblessness and psychological trauma and fear among the population at large.

Unfortunately, the geopolitics of the South Asian region is primarily shaped by boundary-cum-territorial disputes, and state-sponsored terrorism against neighbouring countries. These conditions also have an adverse impact on economic integration and ties among the countries in the region. Resultantly, most of the South Asian countries are least interconnected among themselves by way of surface connectivity, economy, trade, investment, people-to-people contacts, and more importantly trust and confidence. According to the World Bank report of March 2021, economic growth of the region is expected to increase by 7.2 per cent in 2021 and 4.4 per cent in 2022, climbing from a historic GDP decline of 5.4 per cent in 2020.

The China Factor in the Indian Subcontinent

The defining moment of the 21st century has been the undisputed rise of China as a regional-cum-global power. China's economic strength, military muscle, and technological prowess have all grown exponentially. There is a great power competition in the region, wherein Russia and China have been challenging the pre-eminence of the US, and influencing smaller countries of the region. China aims to progressively dominate the Western Pacific region, expand into the IOR and continue to exert increasing influence over geopolitics spanning the South China Sea, the Indian Ocean and South Asian countries, as well as West Asia and the Central Asian Republics (CAR).

It has already begun pursuing its Belt and Road Initiative (BRI) to achieve political, economic and strategic advantages. What is noteworthy is the strengthening of ties between China and Pakistan, as characterised to be 'stronger than steel' and 'sweeter than honey'.

China now has vital access to the Indian Ocean and India's near periphery, thanks to infrastructure investments in Pakistan and Sri Lanka. With China's investment in China-Pakistan Economic Corridor (CPEC) and creation of strategic assets since 2015, as part of Belt and Road Initiative (BRI), China now holds greater stakes in Pakistan, especially in Gilgit-Baltistan region (GBR). In view of this, the enhanced presence of PLA security personnel in the GBR, in the hinterland, and in areas around Gwadar port would certainly have immense security implications for India. In the future, it appears that China is likely to be more assertive in all its activities in the region. As a result, India should focus on the region's long-term political-economic-strategic implications. Geopolitical realities have shifted, as has the regional security matrix, and their impact on our security should be a critical component of India's comprehensive national security strategy. Since February 2021, India and Pakistan have moved towards a rapprochement by way of reimplementing the ceasefire agreement on the LoC of November 2003. However, going by the encounters of the Indian Army with the infiltrating terrorists on LoC since mid-2021, it appears that they (terrorists) would continue to make efforts to destabilise India, and Jammu and Kashmir in particular.

Notwithstanding these ground realities, it is now time to look ahead as a region – South Asia in general, with special reference to India, Bangladesh and Pakistan who were involved in the Bangladesh Liberation War of 1971. India's foreign policy has developed strategic partnerships, steered an alliance-free course, and placed a stronger emphasis on multi-polar engagements and neighbourhood-first policy.

Integrated Regional Approach

> *"For India, our vision for the region rests on five pillars – trade, investment, assistance, cooperation in every area, contacts between our people – and all through seamless connectivity [...]."*
>
> – Prime Minister Narendra Modi, SAARC Summit, 2014

South Asian countries are demographically young, with a median age of 27.4 years in 2020 (Sri Lanka 34, Maldives 29.9, India 28.4, Bhutan 28.1, Bangladesh 27.6, Nepal 24.6, Pakistan 22.8, and Afghanistan 18.4).[7] Due to the ongoing pandemic, COVID-19, most of the South Asian countries have seen high unemployment and underemployment rates, low productivity and low-income capacities. South Asia is rich in natural resources, and has a huge potential for solar and renewable sources of energy. Although it is one of the fastest growing economies, 'it is the world's least integrated sub region, with the value of intraregional trade being less than one third of its potential'.[8] The low level of intra-regional trade is explained by factors such as the poor infrastructure and trade facilitation at the borders, and the prevalence of a variety of non-tariff barriers. As a result, the area as a whole must address the following concerns holistically, and 'not just through the prism of security and strategic calculations alone'.

Multiple Connectivity Domains: Connectivity is the mother of 'development, prosperity and economic integration' to improve relations between the neighbouring countries. Here, connectivity can be understood from a varied perspective, such as: regional, Information, Communication and Technology (ICT), energy, economic, and enhanced people-to-people connectivity. While the essential recommendations have been covered briefly, their implementation would require the political will of all leaders.

- *Regional connectivity:* It requires extra focus on land, air, sea, inland waterways and border infrastructure, to serve economic, trade, investment, transportation, tourism, etc. South Asia is located at the cross roads to connect with South East Asia, Central Asia, West Asia and Europe. To establish an efficient road and rail transit corridor connecting various sub-regions, gaps in physical infrastructure must be filled and transit and transportation services refined. This could also give significant advantage to the landlocked countries, especially to have an easy access to the sea ports. Hence, it requires a comprehensive action plan to connect the region from within and with the extended neighbourhood.
- *IT and Energy:* As a hub for IT services, the region's expansion of IT and digital connections, as well as capacity building, should be a priority for the region's overall benefit. Apart from being cost effective, 'digital connectivity' in rural areas facilitates bridging the urban-rural gap, and address socio-economic challenges, such as education, health care, raising awareness, reaching out to the markets, skill development, e-governance, and employment opportunities. Energy security can be provided by optimising exploration, production distribution and transmission by 'regional power grids', as well as through the construction of petroleum and gas pipelines. Especially for electricity, regional grids should be effectively utilised through trade, cross-border investments and technical cooperation, thus minimising the inefficiencies in the energy production-transmission-consumption cycle.
- *People-to-People Connectivity:* This should be achieved at all available levels – educational, cultural, economic, trade, investment, tourism, military,

religious-cum-medical tourism, with relaxations in protocols and visa restrictions. While addressing the related security concerns, the countries must make concerted efforts to facilitate ease of travel in the region, which will enhance better understanding among the people. Besides high-level visits by decision makers, and the opinion makers must work towards cultural reconciliation by raising awareness of shared values. There is a need to promote cross pollination of ideas, students exchange programmes, and scholarships opportunities to build better understanding among the youth. Simultaneously, exchanges between think tanks, policy makers and higher education programmes serve as a tool of public diplomacy, to usher in the establishment of an open and multicultural society.

Regional Economic Integration: According to the World Bank, the intra-regional trade accounts for roughly 5 per cent of South Asia's total trade, compared to the ASEAN region where intra-regional trade makes up 25 per cent. Currently, trade between South Asian countries totals just $23 billion, significantly less than the expected worth of at least $67 billion. According to Brookings India, South Asia's intra-regional commerce is among the lowest in the world at 5.6 per cent (2017). There are several challenges: border infrastructure and transportation systems, protective tariffs, real and perceived non-tariff barriers, restrictions on investments in infrastructure and industries, and a broad trust deficit throughout the region. These merit urgent attention. These actions will also reduce the high cost of intra-regional trade. Given the geo-strategic location of South Asia, it facilitates most of the countries to position themselves as entry/exit hubs with other regions, which must be explored. As part of India's outreach, the chief ministers of certain states have already taken steps to strengthen ties with neighbouring countries. For instance, the Assam Government has launched its own 'Act East Division,' and established a new Bhutan consulate in Guwahati, Assam. Afghanistan had opened its new Consulate in Hyderabad in January 2020. Besides, there is a need to upgrade the existing trade and investment cooperation initiatives into a South Asia Comprehensive Economic Partnership (SACEP) and implement the recommendations progressively.[9] Despite several challenges posed by erstwhile mindsets, financial capacity, coordination and implementation of the projects on the ground, India's "Neighbourhood First" policy has given highest importance to regional connectivity. In bilateral trade, the aim of both countries should be to minimise the trade imbalance. It is time to 'boost business with digital connectivity' across the region.

Disaster Management: South Asia accounts for almost one-third of deaths globally and ranks second highest in terms of economic losses.[10] Given the region's vulnerability to tsunamis, floods, cyclones, earthquakes, draughts, glacier bursts, among other hazards, it is necessary to establish a network of multi-hazard early warning systems, as well as a system for sharing information towards building resilient cities in high seismic risk areas. Regional cooperative disaster risk mitigation centres with mutually accepted action plans could be established to address the natural disasters in the region.

Security Architecture: There is a need for a common platform to fight against terrorism and trans-national organised crimes, such as human trafficking, narcotics smuggling, money laundering, and fake currency racketeering. This common structure should include intelligence sharing, an effective communication system, joint training, and monitoring of new technologies used by terrorist and trans-national criminals, such as drones to transport weapons, dark nets, AI, social media and others. Simultaneously, smart management of borders between neighbours is important to minimise clashes and casualties – the neighbouring countries must institutionalise mutually acceptable monitoring and communication arrangements, with periodic cum emergency meetings in incident prone sectors or hot line communication arrangements.

Environment Security: On a broader perspective, there is a need to address non-traditional threats and challenges that affect human security. According to the Intergovernmental Panel on Climate Change (IPCC), '... the Indian Ocean is witnessing the fastest rate of warming and sea level rise globally with grave consequences for coastal flooding and the added threat of stronger tropical cyclones.'[11] Therefore, one of the most critical issues facing South Asian region is the 'climate change' and environment degradation, the effects manifest as increasing sea levels and the resulting displacement of people and pollution; adverse effects on flora, fauna, and habitat; species extinction; and extreme weather conditions. These have a long-term ramification on the health of all living beings, and the biodiversity. To minimise the impact of global warming and greenhouse emissions, all South Asian countries must work to slow the pace of urbanisation and industrialisation and reduce fossil fuel consumption.

Cyber and Information Attacks: The most potent threats could be from cyber-attacks: cyberspace is used extensively by the terrorists and non-state actors to spread propaganda and incite violence. Therefore, digital disparities must be bridged by capacity building in each state. Information warfare is lethal as it leads to moulding the perception and opinion of the public at large. It requires regional collaboration in the form of transparency, intelligence sharing, accountable leadership comments, a balanced media role, and best practices to counter such attacks.

Water Security and Climate Change: Water is the fundamental resource for human activities, such as daily living, economic activity, agriculture, industry, transportation, fishing, tourism and recreation, and sustenance of biodiversity. Concurrently, climate change and global warming have a huge impact on sustainable availability of potable water, particularly in South Asia's densely populated areas. Besides agreements on water sharing of rivers, the government and water regulatory institutions must coordinate and work seriously to analyse, recommend and implement solutions to the key challenge of water security.

Due to the geopolitical constraints in the region and alignments with different countries, economic interests, and strategic priorities, it may be appropriate to take initiatives on bilateral or trilateral type of arrangements in order to build cooperation in the economy, trade, investment, energy security, terrorism, organised crime, and socio-cultural fields. In this regard, India's 'neighbourhood first' policy should aim at building confidence and trust among the neighbours to bring about economic integration, improve connectivity and also meet the challenge of regional strategic encirclement by China's BRI.

Strengthening Multilateral Bodies

South Asia, as a region, has the potential to play a significant part in the global supply and value chains due to its unique geostrategic placement, on both the continental and maritime domains, its size, young demographic profile, history, culture, natural resources, and potential for growth. Geopolitically, it can be central to tilting the global balance of power in the future. However, at the foremost, this would require each country to respect the other's sovereignty and aspirations. India, by virtue of its geostrategic location, vibrant economy, strong military and security mechanism, has the potential to become a net security provider in the IOR.

South Asian countries must also work together to provide a safe and secure maritime environment to give impetus to economic growth. Prime Minister Narendra Modi's stated vision of SAGAR – Security and Growth for All in the Region – could be the guideline to move ahead. Geographically, Bangladesh's location makes it a strategic gateway to India, Nepal, Bhutan and other southeast Asian countries. South Asian countries have the potential to become economic powerhouses, but this will require bolstering regional commerce, facilitating transit, and establishing a dedicated logistics network. Additionally, if strengthened, regional cooperation frameworks can play a critical role.

SAARC: The fundamental framework and the primary principles of SAARC were 'respect for the principles of sovereign equality, territorial integrity, political independence, non-interference in the internal affairs of other States [...].' It was expected to develop as a Regional Integrated Action Programme and work towards a common goal of achieving social, cultural, and economic growth, human resource development, regional connectivity and environment security for the people of the region. SAARC has faced several problems since its inception, predominantly attributed to India-Pakistan hostilities primarily over Jammu and Kashmir, proxy war involving state-sponsored terrorism, water sharing and nuclear issues. The policy makers must play their full part to strengthen SAARC to fulfil its laid down motto 'Deeper Integration for Peace and Prosperity'.

Bay of Bengal Initiative for Multi-sectoral Technical and Economic Cooperation (BIMSTEC): The aim was to give impetus to economic, trade, technological and security initiatives among members. Geographically, it connects three important sub-regions: India, Nepal and Bhutan in the Himalayan sub-region; Sri Lanka and Bangladesh in the Bay of Bengal sub-region; and Myanmar and Thailand in the Mekong sub-region.

The political leaders can work together to make regional bodies like SAARC, BIMSTEC, Bangladesh, Bhutan, India, and Nepal (BBIN) and other regional organisations fully functional, only if the region drops the historical legacies and resolve their bilateral disputes. A few vital areas where all South Asian countries must work together and take collective actions are: terrorism, radicalism, violent extremism, cyber threats, illegal migrations, drugs trade, prevent environment degradation and global warming.

What India Can Do: Integrate South Asia through Soft Power

> *"South Asian countries should also consider creating a special visa scheme for doctors and nurses, so that they could travel quickly within the region during health emergencies, on the request of the receiving country."*[12]
>
> – Prime Minister Narendra Modi, 2021

Due to the geographical proximity, it would be possible to promote soft power – connectivity, culture, commerce – by way of a meaningful action plan. These include political and diplomatic engagements; medical diplomacy especially during the outbreak of pandemics; defence diplomacy to build relations; education and social exchanges and cross pollination of ideas; economic interdependence, trade, and investments; environmental security; travel and tourism; interaction with and affiliation with think tanks; connectivity and exchange of ideas by way of electronic and print media, and social media; providing ease of travelling through simplified visa procedures and facilitating tourism; and participation in multilateral platforms with common agendas to uplift the region and the society as a whole.

India can develop an 'education and IT hub' with world class facilities, for students from its neighbourhood. This will help to form closer political ties and spread the regional cultural influence and values to the surrounding regions. A regional network for promoting technology assisted epidemiology for preventing future pandemics, a regional air ambulance for medical contingencies, and a system to share successful public health policies and schemes could be put in place. With the revolution in ICT, social media and the growing digital interconnectivity in recent years, the media too has a vital role in shaping and moulding public perception and opinion. Since the societal values, customs and culture get reflected by the media of films, theatre, TV serials, art, and print and electronic media, these must aim to bring harmony among the people. On balance, some of these actions of 'soft power' will help to build a positive image, trust and genuine concern about each other's well-being.

Regional trade and investments, facilitated by connection across numerous domains especially people to people, are the fundamental drivers of regional integration and sustainable development, as previously noted. It would also help to address the socioeconomic-security-environmental challenges of the region. However, at the foremost it would require the 'political will and combined efforts of the leaders' to build a positive image among the population, enhance connectivity, and bring peace and harmony among South Asia's neighbours. The earlier the better!

Notes

1. SN Prasad and UP Thapliyal, *The India Pakistan War of 1971: A Story* (Dehradun: Natraj Publisher), p. 424.
2. Global Peace Index 2021, Institute for Economics and Peace, Sydney. Afghanistan ranks 163rd and remains the least peaceful country in the region and the world on the 2021 GPI. Available at https://www.economicsandpeace.org/wp-content/uploads/2021/06/GPI-2021-web.pdf
3. Ibid.
4. Amit Chaturvedi, "Financial Action Task Force (FATF) since June 2018", *The Hindustan Times*, February 25, 2021.
5. See World meter at https://www.worldometers.info/world-population/southern-asia-population/#:~:text=Southern%20Asia%20population%20is%20equivalent, accessed on April 14, 2021.
6. United Nations Development Programme's Human Development Report 2020.
7. Median age of the population in South Asia in 2020, by country, https://www.statista.com/statistics/591066/median-age-of-the-population-in-south-asia.
8. Unlocking the Potential of Regional Economic Cooperation and Integration in South Asia Potential, Challenges and the Way Forward, September 2018, p. v.
9. Ibid., p. v, SACEP could cover seven key policy priorities: (a) advancing the liberalisation of trade in goods, (b) strengthening facilitation of transport and trade at the land borders, (c) effective liberalisation of regional trade in services, (d) investment promotion to foster regional value chains, (e) harmonising product standards and conformity assessment procedures, (f) cumulative rules of origin and industrial cooperation, (g) coordination of international payment arrangements and banking cooperation.
10. Ibid., p. vii.
11. Intergovernmental Panel on Climate Change (IPCC) released the first part of its Sixth Assessment Report (AR6) titled Climate Change 2021: The Physical Science Basis. https://www.ipcc.ch/report/ar6/wg1/
12. PM Modi address to workshop on Covid-19 Management: Experience, Good Practices and Way Forward, February 18, 2021.

45

India-Bangladesh Relations: Expectations for the Next 50 Years

ANM Muniruzzaman

The year 2021 marks the golden jubilee of the Bangladesh Liberation War (1971). Bangladesh has risen on the map of global politics and the international economy as a remarkably formidable state, after 50 years of independence, from a war-torn secessionist state feebly regaining its footing to start a democracy in 1971. And throughout these 50 years, India has stood by as an ally. While Bangladesh and India share a common history, their ties go beyond the adjoining borders. India's support and recognition of a struggling East Pakistan gave the state a strong sense of emotional connection, a fraternity for sovereignty. Bangladesh and India are an example of bilateral relations on the subcontinent, an alliance that spans a wide spectrum of shared interests – trade and commerce, security, diplomacy and foreign policy, and politics, to name a few. In the last half-century, the connection has progressed significantly, and the people of the two countries have traversed a great distance together. Hence, time has arrived to look 'beyond the horizon' into the next 50 years. It is past time for us to reflect on our accomplishments, accept our faults and concerns, and think creatively to take our partnership to the next level.

India was one of the first countries along with Bhutan to recognise Bangladesh as a sovereign state on December 6, 1971. It is also worth mentioning that India shares its longest border of 4,096.7 kilometres with Bangladesh, which happens to be the fifth longest border in the contemporary world.[1] Furthermore, India and Bangladesh have exceptionally strong sociocultural, linguistic, and economic linkages as a result of their shared historical heritage and physical proximity. Despite these similarities, India-Bangladesh bilateral relations have seen numerous ups and downs over the last 50 years, as they have navigated the ebb and flow of politics in eastern South Asia.

While the bilateral ties of India and Bangladesh are going strong, a lion's share of the sentiment lies in the proximity of the states and their mutual amity. The sentiments rooted in the common colonial history, the liberation war and the respect and recognition since then may have been enough so far. Nonetheless, it may not translate well to the next generation, who has not witnessed or experienced the unity with which both East Pakistan (now Bangladesh) and India fought together. To further enhance the relations, the next 50 years must be built on the principle of 'mutual benefits and trust' and not merely on the principles of 'mutual love and respect' between the two governments.

Balance of Trade

Bangladesh has a trade imbalance due to the nature of India-Bangladesh relations. Bangladesh's massive trade deficit is a major source of worry in bilateral trade. The annual deficit continues to rise. With some notable swings throughout the second half of the 1990s, it rose from $166.69 million to $2.48 billion in 2009.[2] However, it did reach a high of $3.18 million in 2008. Bilateral trade between Bangladesh and India had run into a quagmire during the year 2020, following the novel coronavirus outbreak. According to the Bangladesh Bank, the bilateral trade volume between the two nations dropped to $421 million during April-May in 2020 as compared to $2 billion during the same time in 2019.[3] The data indicates a decrease in imports and exports over the first five months of 2020. While the trade volume is equivalent to a remarkable $6.5 billion, Bangladesh's exports to India account for only $500 million of the sum.[4]

The divide between India and the rest of the world must be bridged. India's intentions to increase its investment in Bangladesh must be expedited. There is a growing perception in Bangladesh that increased commerce benefits primarily India. Bangladesh is crucial in case of implementing India's sub-regional connectivity plans, which include Nepal and Bhutan. Trade can benefit Bangladesh under SAFTA if trade creation surpasses trade diversion.[5]

It is possible to establish new trade only when both countries' trade policies are conciliatory. Because of the ongoing trade deficit, Bangladesh requires a more sympathetic attitude from India. Despite the fact that India has been Bangladesh's main commercial partner since independence, experts are of the view that to further improve the trade and commerce between the two countries, India should be sensitive to Bangladesh's desires to bridge the trade imbalance through a variety of initiatives at various levels.

Preventing Violent Extremism

In the Post-COVID state of emergency, the unprecedented economic downturn has given an added advantage to extremist outfits, and is expected to offer a fertile ground for youth radicalisation by terror/militant groups operating in the region. Formulation of counter-terrorism and de-radicalisation strategies is thereby an urgent requirement. There is a chance to consider cooperation in the fight against radicalisation, particularly among young, which is quickly becoming a major concern. There is a need for collaborative anti-violent extremism policies, as well as perhaps creating a unified net evaluation on the changing threat of violent extremism and terrorism in the coming decades. Improved cooperation is equally crucial to the fight against terrorism financing. There is potential for bilateral collaboration in combatting terror and militant group activity in cyberspace that must be explored. Such cooperation should be increased and modernised as mutual dangers evolve and become more serious. Law enforcement and other security agencies must collaborate on a synergised training program (in addition to existing training cooperation). Furthermore, real-time intelligence exchange and adaptation should be recognised and addressed as a pressing requirement. Military collaboration in the area of counter-terrorism training could be improved much more. Furthermore, because both countries are important Troop Contributing Countries (TCCs) in UN Peacekeeping Operations, cooperative training programs could certainly be improved.

Collaboration in Agricultural Advancement

As two agrarian states, India and Bangladesh, collaboration in agricultural science and technology might open up new avenues of mutual benefit and potential for the two countries' bilateral relations. Collaboration and joint research amongst our agricultural sectors can open new doors to shared prosperity. Greater synergy in smart border management can be a force multiplier in addressing some of the most vexing border management issues. As we embark on this collaborative exploration of cooperation in the next 50 years, it is critical to strengthen the existing channels of cooperation and coordination between the strategic and policy communities in Dhaka and New Delhi.

Resolving the Issues of Water Sharing

Several rivers run through Bangladesh and India. Rivers are considered sacred in these states, serving as a source of livelihood and a route for prosperity and advancement. However, some of the most contentious disputes between the two states concern water distribution. Water is essential in India-Bangladesh bilateral ties. Apart from the Teesta River issue, Bangladesh raised severe objections to India's possible river-linking project, particularly in relation to the Brahmaputra. It is in this environment, that the two countries must collaborate. By 2026, the Ganges Water Sharing Treaty will be completed, and now is the time to revisit and conduct a detailed assessment of the hydrological content. Rising sea levels are displacing people in Bangladesh's southern provinces and posing a threat to India's coastal towns. The formation of a Joint River Secretariat could be considered. Additionally, de-salination programs that deal with potable water should be supported. Climate change continues to be a big threat for both Bangladesh and India, and more collaboration on the issue is urgently needed.

Transit Issue

The issues of transit and transshipment are critical for India's North Eastern Region (NER) to maintain its socioeconomic and sociopolitical stability. Since 1947, NER has conducted commerce with the rest of India or the rest of the globe through East Pakistan (now Bangladesh).[6] Trade between NER and the rest of India mainly takes place through the 'Siliguri Land Corridor'.[7] For enhanced economic growth, the Indian Government has sought transit through Bangladesh for its NER. Some feel that it has a variety of repercussions for Bangladesh, including security, political, and economic dimensions. Many have claimed that it should not be agreed to until some key bilateral concerns are resolved, such as the trade deficit and the Farakka and Teesta Barrages water sharing disputes. Additionally, some argue that transit is a commercial problem that should not be politicised.

The distance between Agartala and Kolkata Sea Port is around 1,400 kilometres, whereas the distance between Agartala and Chittagong Sea Port (Bangladesh) is barely 100 kilometres.[8] This increases the travel cost between NER and the other parts of India. The shipment of Assam tea to Europe must travel 1,400 kilometres through the 'Chicken's Neck' to reach Kolkata Port.[9] Therefore, India needs transit via Bangladesh for the shipping of its commodities not just for cost reasons, but also for security reasons.

The transit facility must be considered and addressed in the context of other bilateral issues with India. Many analysts believe that Bangladesh should go ahead with the project, but both the countries should first work on developing the railway connectivity between them. According to the business community, transit significantly impacts the economic, political and sub-regional development strategies, which must be addressed holistically. In terms of negotiation, it was indicated that the tariff issue requires considerable thought and consensus. The conclusion was that transit and transshipment should be expanded beyond India to include China and Myanmar, in addition to connecting the sub-region. When it comes to addressing transit and connectivity, the security problem is crucial. Considering the benefits, it appears that the dangers, as mentioned earlier, are economically insignificant. The NER is plentiful in mineral reserves, natural resources and raw commodities. Transit facilities would make future utilisation of these resources simple, quick and reasonably inexpensive.

Conclusion

Bangladesh's relations with India, which aided the country morally, materially and physically during the Liberation War of 1971, is yet to mature due to certain perception disparities. The direction of relations between Bangladesh and India will be established by conducting a critical analysis of future interactions between the two countries, taking into account both challenges and opportunities. The Indian Prime Minister Narendra Modi has expressed his wish to preserve strong and stable relations with Bangladesh based on economic cooperation and shared interests. The visits of the Prime Ministers of Bangladesh and India to each other's states are significant because the leaders can build trust and confidence. While the expectation of a historic breakthrough did not materialise altogether, but Bangladesh is hopeful that India will reciprocate by signing the Teesta Treaty, demonstrating its vision and daring.

Dhaka features as one of the important allies in India's "Act East Policy". The first 50 years of India-Bangladesh relation have solidified the basis. The future will present a plethora of opportunities to assist the two countries in achieving a new high point in bilateral relations, provided that the two neighbours' leaders play their diplomatic cards with more maturity and pragmatism, keeping in mind the regional aspirations and nuances of both countries. On both sides of the border, a careful aggregation of regional expectations will aid in the achievement of their shared national goals. Bangladesh and India have strong incentives to maintain the forward progress they have made, regardless of which government coalition is in power.

Notes

1. As Bangladesh celebrates 50 years of independence, India resets focus to restore 'Golden Chapter.' (2021). Retrieved March 30, 2021. Available at https://react.etvbharat.com/english/national/bharat/as-bangladesh-celebrates-50-years-of-independence-india-resets-focus-to-restore-golden-chapter/na20210326103632695
2. Zahoor Ahmad Rather, D. D. G. (2014). "India-Bangladesh Bilateral Trade: Problems and Prospects." International Affairs and Global Strategy, 22, 02.
3. Noyon, A. U. (2020). Bangladesh-India trade relations under strain. Retrieved March 30, 2021. Available at https://www.tbsnews.net/economy/trade/bangladesh-india-trade-relations-under-strain-102277
4. *Hindustan Times* (2015). 5 things to know about India-Bangladesh ties: From trade to security by Jayanth Jacob, June 6.
5. Rahman, Mir Obaidur (2016). Dumping and other issues: Trade between Bangladesh and India, *Daily Sun*, February 18.
6. Ahmed, Shakil (2003). Brigadier General, Bangladesh Army. "Transit and Transhipment: Implications for Bangladesh." *National Defence College Journal*, Vol. 2, No. 1.
7. Hossain, AKM Sadat, Brigadier General, Bangladesh Army. "Re-examination of the Discourses on Transit to India": Individual Research Paper, National Defense College, Bangladesh (August 30, 2012), pp.1-2.
8. Rahmatuallah, Dr. (2010). "Regional Transport Connectivity": Opportunities for Bangladesh. BIISS, 30(1), January.
9. Murshid, KAS (2011). "Transit and Transhipment: "Strategic Considerations for Bangladesh and India." *Economic and Political Weakly*, Dhaka. Vol. 19, No. 17.

46

India-Bangladesh Relation and Way Forward

AN Jha

India-Bangladesh Relations

The first 5 decades have consolidated the foundation of India-Bangladesh relations. Despite few misunderstandings between the two neighbours, their bilateral relations have reached a new high through several agreements and mutual understandings by addressing areas of concerns as equal partners, and successfully resolving certain outstanding issues.

The future holds numerous potential for both countries to further advance their bilateral relations, provided that the two neighbours interact with each other with more understanding and openness, keeping the regional aspirations and nuances of each other in mind.[1] Moreover, India's endeavours of 'Act East Policy' can be more effectively realised with the assistance of the "Land of the Bengals". In March 2021, the Prime Minister of India visited Bangladesh to commemorate the centenary year of Bangabandhu Sheikh Mujibur Rahman, celebrated as the 'Mujib Borsho'. This was in fact the first foreign visit by the Indian Prime Minister since the outbreak of the COVID-19 pandemic. Given our historical, cultural, linguistic, ethnic associations, and interdependence on each other, it is clear India values its relationship with Bangladesh.

Growth of Bangladesh. Since its birth as an independent nation, Bangladesh has progressed in almost every parameter of economy, human development indices, empowerment of women, micro financing, garment manufacturing and exports, and extensive participation and largest contribution in the UN peacekeeping missions. Bangladesh's growth rests on three prominent pillars: exports, social progress and fiscal prudence.[2] It is well poised to be one of the Asian Tigers due to its socio-economic progress. Bangladesh has already over taken Pakistan in 2019 to become the second largest economy in the subcontinent. Despite the ongoing pandemic, COVID-19, Bangladesh has recorded a relatively high GDP growth rate.

Challenges and Way Forward in Bilateral Relations

Improved Connectivity. Over the years, connectivity between the two countries has continued to improve progressively. The direct bus route between Kolkata and Agartala is only 500 kilometres long, as opposed to 1,650 kilometres if it travels through the Siliguri corridor and Assam. Bangladesh has also allowed the shipment of goods from its Mongla and Chattogram (Chittagong) seaports to be carried by road, rail and waterways to Agartala. Now, all the physical connectivity's will need to be translated into business ventures, development tools[3] and encourage people-to-people contact. Accordingly, the Indian Prime Minister Narendra Modi has reiterated the vision and progress in ensuring "HIRA" connectivity – a mesh of Highways, Information ways, Railways, Waterways and Airways between the neighbours. New routes and "innocent passage" routes for barges have been identified. Riverine traffic would cross the international boundary, while moving from one river port to another in either country, thus reducing time and costs.[4]

Land Boundary and Cross Boarder Movement. One of the most important bilateral agreements is the historic Land Boundary Agreement (LBA). It facilitated the transfer of 111 enclaves (17,160.63 acres) from India to Bangladesh, and India received 51 enclaves (7,110.02 acres) from Bangladesh. As can be seen, India offered more as a show of goodwill toward its neighbours. It also saw the demarcation of 4,096 kilometres long land border, to minimise the conflicts on the border. Now, the issues relating to identity crisis and governance of the enclaves would require attention of both the countries on priority.

Water Sharing. The Joint River Commission (JRC) that came into force in 1972, works for the common interests and sharing of water resources, irrigation, floods and cyclones control. However, the dispute over Ganga water has been an important component ever since the Farakka Barrage was constructed. An agreement on the sharing of Ganga Water between India and Bangladesh was signed on December 12, 1996: it essentially addresses the sharing of lean-season flow of water into Bangladesh. However, the unsolved Teesta water sharing issue deserves to be resolved through bilateral consultations at the earliest, in order to fulfil the objectives of a lower riparian and a friend of India.

Continental Shelf Issues in the Bay of Bengal. India has accepted an UN international tribunal verdict in favour of Bangladesh that resolved a four-decade old maritime boundary dispute to build confidence between the two countries.

Energy Cooperation. Undoubtedly, cooperation in the power sector has become one of the hallmarks of bilateral relations.[5] India has recently introduced the concept of the Regional Power Trading System, which will help various regions of the country in reducing the power deficit by transferring surplus power from another region. Bangladesh now hopes to have access to Nepal and Bhutan's power through India. Construction of the 130 kilometres long Bangladesh-India Friendship pipeline to supply 4 lakh metric tonnes of diesel to Bangladesh is also in progress. Moreover, India is in the process to set up nuclear reactors in Bangladesh, including technical cooperation and sharing of information in the fields of nuclear safety and radiation protection.

Trade Relation. As of now, benefits of trade and economic collaboration remain far below their potential. The cost of trading remains quite high, owing mostly to a lack of sufficient trade facilitation as well as logistical challenges and the resulting long lead time, which discourages traders. In the FY 2019-20, the bilateral trade went up to US$ 9.46 billion, representing more than double the value five years ago. Bangladesh is now also the biggest development partner of India. In addition to numerous Lines of Credits (including that for Defence related purchases), India has also been providing grant assistance to Bangladesh for various infrastructure projects. In addition, High Impact Community Development Projects (HICDPs) constitute an active pillar of India's development assistance. India has funded 68 HICDPs and another 16 HICDPs are being implemented.[6] Moreover, both countries are committed to address trade imbalance issues.

Both nations have also agreed to a review the trade deal, which would allow them to use each other's land and water routes to transfer goods to a third nation, removing the age-old barrier in regional trade. It has incorporated a provision that the deal would be renewed automatically after five years, if neither countries object. Modalities of public-private partnerships and cross-country joint private sector initiatives also need to be identified and realised. Therefore, there is a need to expedite the proposed Comprehensive Economic Partnership Agreement (CEPA), an advanced form of a free trade agreement that will ensure preferential and even tariff-free access to goods, services and investments in both countries. Recently, India and the G-7 member countries have agreed on an infrastructural proposal of Build Back Better World (B3W), which will also benefit both countries in the coming days.

Security Coordination. After Smt Sheikh Hasina returned to power in 2009, the Bangladesh government had acted swiftly to rip up anti-India insurgency and terrorist elements who were operating from its borders. It has assured that no anti-state elements are given sanctuary or help, and terror-financing bank accounts were frozen.[7] Bangladesh has also handed over many of India's most wanted anti-national elements and criminals. India has, in particular, praised the Government of Bangladesh's zero-tolerance policy and its unwavering commitment to safeguarding regional peace, security and stability in the entire region. The two countries are now close strategic partners in counter-terrorism and have closer cooperation to fight against extremist radical groups, terrorist organisations, smuggling of arms, drugs and also organised crime as a shared priority. Such efforts have impacted positively on peacebuilding and reduction of armed forces in the Northeast Indian states. However, both countries must exercise caution to ensure that religious fanatics do not derail the relationship's economic trajectory and goodwill.

Defence Relations. Both countries have also institutionalised joint border patrols, joint training exercises, visits and exchanges to further enhance Confidence Building Measures (CBM). In 2017, Bangladesh and India signed two defence agreements, the first such agreements between India and any of its neighbours, as well as series of Memorandum of Understandings in areas of Defence cooperation. These are mostly focused on the following:

- The militaries of the two countries will conduct joint exercises and training to deal with counter-terrorism issues, natural disasters, ensure Humanitarian Assistance and Disaster Reliefs (HADR). Some of the major ones are: the Army Exercise Sampriti (Harmony), and 'Shantir Ogroshena' (Front Runner of Peace); Naval Exercise Milan and CORPAT

'Bongosagar', and the Air Force Exercise 'Samvedna', (Empathy). These reflect the priority as part of Prime Minister Narendra Modi's vision of SAGAR (Security and Growth for All in the Region).

- India will help Bangladesh in establishing production and service centres for defence platforms, with the aim of achieving self-sufficiency in defence manufacture in Bangladesh, providing expert training, as well as technical and logistical support.
- Enhance cooperation for comparative and joint initiatives of education in the area of Field Strategy and Study of Military Operations, between the Defence Services Staff College and National Defence College of both countries.
- Increasing cooperation between the Coast Guards and boosting of Intelligence sharing.

It was good to see a 122-member contingent from tri-services of Bangladesh Armed Forces participating during the India's 72nd Republic Day celebrations at Delhi in 2021 for the first time.

Citizenship Amendment Act (CAA) and National Register of Citizens (NRC). The Indian CAA and the proposal to implement the NRC, brings in certain apprehensions among the population at large. Though, Bangladeshi Prime Minister Sheikh Hasina was critical of the CAA, describing it as "not necessary", but nevertheless affirmed CAA and the NRC were "internal matters" of India.[8]

Media Reporting. The media reportings, both National and International, maybe distorted by bad faith.[9] There has been an increase in the regularity with which context has gone lacking in reporting on other countries, which breads mistrust. Audiences therefore, need to read between the lines to make an informed judgement. What is acceptable for one may not be acceptable to the other. Hence, there is a requirement for more area study programmes, journalists posted abroad and humility in public discourse. This would help stem misperception, particularly on neighbours, and larger powers.

Bonding of Hearts and Minds. The ground-level stakeholders also need to be encouraged and facilitated based on ground up ideas to reap the benefits of connectivity. Regular exchanges between younger entrepreneurs and civil society should be pursued in areas such as culture, music, sports, films, and sharing of best practices in sustainable development, human capital development, gender equitable growth, amongst others. The rich cultural and natural heritage of this region holds enormous tourism potential. Offering combination of circuits can be a game changer in attracting mainstream tourists and complementing the mutual interests.

Constant Resolution of Challenges. Past memories will fade as new aspiring generations, nurtured in a digital era, inevitably rise in both countries. New political leaderships will also emerge in the future. Hence, both countries have to adjust to these new realties and plan for the future. Prime Minister Narendra Modi has said, "India would not like to impose anything which Bangladesh may find not suitable to its requirement. The bilateral document under consideration is aimed at institutionalizing the existing mechanism and streamlining the ongoing cooperation between both the countries."[10] All these have expanded multi-sectoral cooperation, which was almost unthinkable in the past. However, all ties need constant nurturing. Both countries should also ensure that all mutually agreed upon assurances and deals are honoured and implemented without any last minute changes, unless absolutely necessary.

Over the years, the two countries have established a well-structured network of more than 50 joint institutional mechanisms in a wide range of areas, which ensures sustained dialogue across the year to regularly monitor developments and work on resolving issues.[11] These joint commissions should work to find solutions which address the aspirations and are mutually beneficial to both countries to maintain peace, better relations and development in the region. For all this to happen, there is a need to jointly work towards a new paradigm that enables borders to act as "connector zones" for inclusive growth and prosperity.[12]

One also hopes that deeper ties between the two countries will help each realise its aspiration of becoming an economically developed, socially inclusive and environmentally sustainable country. All signs point to the conclusion that the bilateral relationship between the two South Asian countries – India and Bangladesh – will continue to gain momentum in the years to come for mutual benefit and the overall betterment of the region.

Notes

1. Sabyasachi Basu Ray Chaudhury, '50 years of India-Bangladesh relations: Marking maturity,' March 25, 2021, Observer Research Foundation. Available at https://www.orfonline.org/expert-speak/50-years-of-india-bangladesh-relations-marking-maturity/.
2. Mihir S Sharma, 'Bangladesh rises to be South Asia's standout star as India, Pak fall behind,' Bloomberg Opinion, June 1, 2021.
3. Mustafizur Rahman, 'Bangladesh-India ties: Time to seize the opportunities,' March 25, 2021, Observer Research Foundation. Available at https://cpd.org.bd/bangladesh-india-ties-time-to-seize-the-opportunities-mustafizur-rahman/.
4. Pinak Ranjan Chakravarty, 'Bangladesh-India ties: Crossing a threshold,' March 25, 2021, Observer Research Foundation. Available at https://www.orfonline.org/expert-speak/bangladesh-india-ties-crossing-threshold/.
5. Haroon Habib, 'Golden jubilee and beyond: India–Bangladesh relations,' March 25, 2021, Observer Research Foundation. Available at https://www.orfonline.org/expert-speak/silver-jubilee-beyond-india-bangladesh-relations/.
6. https://mea.gov.in/Portal/ForeignRelation/India_Bangladesh_MAR2021.pdf.
7. Saleem Samad, 'Are India-Bangladesh relations at a crossroad?', Observer Research Foundation, Raisina Debates, 25 Mar 2021. Available at https://www.orfonline.org/expert-speak/india-bangladesh-relations-crossroad/.
8. Seema Guha, 'CAA, NRC move triggers disquiet in Dhaka', *The Tribune*, February 5, 2020. Available at https://www.tribuneindia.com/news/comment/caa-nrc-move-triggers-disquiet-in-dhaka-35884.
9. Adam Pitman, 'How Indian media reporting on Bangladesh is Distorted by bad faith, June 28, 2021, Scroll. Available at https://scroll.in/article/997714/how-indian-media-reporting-on-bangladesh-is-distorted-by-bad-faith.
10. Wikipedia, 'Bangladesh-India Relations.' Available at https://en.wikipedia.org/wiki/Bangladesh%E2%80%93India_relations#:~:text=Prime%20Minister%20Narendra%20Modi%20said,not%20suitable%20to%20its%20requirement.
11. Joyeeta Bhattacharjee, 'Prime Minister Narendra Modi's Bangladesh visit boost ties,' Raisina Debates, April 5, 2021. Available at https://www.orfonline.org/expert-speak/prime-minister-narendra-modi-bangladesh-visit-boost-ties/.
12. Sabyasachi Dutta, 'Bangladesh-India relations: Empowering the third space for a way forward,' March 25, 2021, Observer Research Foundation. Available at https://www.orfonline.org/expert-speak/bangladesh-india-relations-empowering-third-space-way-forward/.

Notes on Editors

Lieutenant General (Dr.) **VK Ahluwalia**, PVSM, AVSM**, YSM, VSM (Retd), is the Director of Centre for Land Warfare Studies (CLAWS). The General Officer was commissioned in 1971. He commanded an infantry brigade, mountain division and corps in Uri-Baramulla, Kargil and Leh-Ladakh sectors respectively. He has also served in the North East and in the states critically affected by the Maoist insurgency in India. Lt Gen Ahluwalia superannuated as Army Commander, Central Command in March 2012. He holds a Ph.D in Internal Security and Conflict Resolution and has authored a book titled *Red Revolution 2020 and beyond* (Bloomsbury India). His recent co-edited books includes *Surprise, Strategy and Vijay: 20 years of Kargil and Beyond* and *Covid-19 and Its Challenges: Implications for India.*

Brigadier **AN Jha** (Retd), is Senior Instructor (SI), Promotion Exam Cell (PROMEX) at CLAWS. The Brigadier was commissioned into the JAT Regiment in Dec 1986. He later commanded an Infantry Battalion and Rashtriya Rifles Sector HQ in J&K and the Jat Regimental Centre. The Officer has held important appointments at Unit, Brigade, Sub Area, Division, Corps, Command and Army HQs. He has been an instructor in The Infantry School and Army War College, Mhow (MP). The officer is a recipient of two COAS Commendation Cards and three Army Commanders Commendation Cards. He is a M. Phil in Defence Studies and takes a keen interest in writing articles.

Notes on Contributors

Colonel **Narjit Singh** (Retd), was commissioned into 2 LANCERS (1978). The Colonel was entrusted with the project of making a documentary on Kargil War. The documentary named "The Kargil War" was widely released and was well appreciated for giving the factual accounts of the Kargil War. He has won the Services Squash title four times and represented India in six International Tournaments. The officer is also a keen reader and a passionate writer.

Lieutenant General (Dr.) **JS Cheema**, PVSM, AVSM, VSM (Retd), is presently the Vice-Chancellor of Maharaja Bhupinder Singh Punjab Sports University. The General superannuated from the Indian Army as Deputy Chief of the Army Staff. He has done his Doctorate from Panjab University in Defence and National Security Studies.

Ms. **Shreya Das Barman** is currently working as Publications Manager at CLAWS. Ms. Barman holds a Post Graduate Degree in East Asian Studies with area of interest in China and a Graduate Degree in Sociology. She also has a basic knowledge of Chinese (Mandarin) language. She was awarded by the VCOAS for her contribution in publication of various articles at CLAWS.

Brigadier **Behram Panthaki** (Retd), was the ADC to General (later Field Marshal) Sam Manekshaw. The Brigadier was commissioned into 8 Gorkha Rifles in February 1964. He has co-authored with his wife, Zenobia, a coffee table book titled *Field Marshal Sam Manekshaw: The Man and His Times*. The entire royalty from it is donated to the War Wounded Foundation and War

Widows Association of India. He has also been the director of the Kingsbury Center Human Institute.

Brigadier **Ajit Apte** (Retd), was commissioned into the Regiment of Artillery and is an alumnus of the National Defence Academy Khadakwasla. The Brigadier fought the India- Pakistan War of 1971 on the Eastern Front in the Jessore-Khulna Sector. He also commanded an Artillery Brigade of a Strike Corps on the Western Front during the Kargil Conflict in 1999.

Major General **Ian Cardozo**, AVSM, SM (Retd), was commissioned into the 5th Gorkha Rifles (FF) in June 1958 and has fought in the wars of 1962, 1965 and 1971. The General was wounded in the battle of Sylhet (1971) wherein he lost a leg and was the first war-disabled officer to be approved for command of an infantry battalion and brigade. Post retirement he has served as the Chairman, Rehabilitation Council of India , GoI.

Colonel **Ashok Kumar Tara**, VrC (Retd), was commissioned into Brigade of the Guards. Colonel Tara fought in the Battle of Gadra-Rajasthan (1965) and the Battle of Gangasagar (1971) and was awarded Vir Chakra. Also, unarmed and single handedly he rescued the Sheikh Mujibur Rahman Family from the captivity of the Pakistan troops. He has been conferred an award "The Friends of Liberation War Honour" by Bangladesh.

Colonel **Vijay Yeshwant Gidh**, VSM (Retd), was commissioned in 13 Punjab (Jind). The Colonel served as an Instructor in NSG Training Centre; UN Peacekeeping Mission in Angola; Battalion Commander, NDA and Centre Commandant, The Punjab Regimental Centre. He commanded 14 Punjab (Nabha Akal) in J&K, Manipur and Nagaland. His son, Col Varun Vijay Gidh, SM is presently commanding the battalion.

Lieutenant General **JBS Yadava**, PVSM, AVSM, VrC, VSM (Retd), was commissioned in 5/11 GR in 1964. The General retired as DCOAS. He fought in 1965 war in Sialkot Sector and 1971 war in NW Sector East Pakistan. He also commanded 8 Mountain Division in Srinagar Valley and 16 Corps in Jammu.

Lieutenant Genenral **ARK Reddy**, PVSM, AVSM, (Retd), raised and Commanded 14 Bihar in 1977. The General held the appointment of GOC, Delhi Area. He held the appointment of COS in Northern Command before retirement.

Brigadier **BM Daniels** (Retd), was commissioned into 10 Mahar on 20 December 1970. The Brigadier is an alumni of NDA, IMA and DSSC, Wellington and was an instructor at NDA and JC Wing, College of Combat, Mhow. He is a war veteran of the 1971 War. He was involved in Counter Insurgency operations in Nagaland, Arunachal and J&K.

Major **Biren Borgohain** (Retd), from Assam Regiment joined the Civil Services and was the CVO, Executive Director, NEEPCO, a PSU under GoI. The Major holds BA, LLB degree, and has a diploma in Management. He also holds a diploma in 'Guide for Graduate' Sr Perspective Management from Oxford Centre for Management Studies, Oxford, UK.

Lieutenant General **Ghanshyam Singh Katoch**, PVSM, AVSM, VSM (Retd), presently is the Deputy Director and Editor at USI, India. The General was commissioned into 2 JAK Rif in 1977 and commanded 9 JAK Rif. He superannuated in 2016 as the Director General Strategic Planning (DGSP) after having commanded 12 Corps. He holds a MS Degree in Defence Analysis from the Naval Postgraduate School, Monterey, California.

Brigadier **Onkar Singh Goraya** (Retd), was commissioned in Artillery in December 1960. The Brigadier, in 1971, as Brigade Major at Agartala was responsible for providing artillery support during the battle of Akhaura and subsequent advance of the Indian Forces to Dhaka. He published his experiences in a book titled *Leap Across Meghna-Blitzkreig of 4 Corps*. He has also authored two other books titled *Operation Blue Star-1984* and *Voice of Reason : A call to Atheism*.

Major **Probal Das Gupta** (Retd), is currently the managing director (South Asia) for a global consulting firm. The former infantry officer was commissioned into 5/11 Gorkha Rifles. He has been a Braun-Myers Fellow and Tata Scholar at Columbia University, New York (USA). A historian and international affairs strategist, he authored the book titled *Watershed 1967: India's Forgotten Victory Over China.*

Lieutenant General **M Harun-Ar-Rashid,** Bir Protik (Retd), is currently the Managing Director of Rashid Krishi Khamar Limited and Vice President of the Sector Commanders Forum: Liberation War 1971. The General was commissioned in the Pakistan Army on September 06, 1970 and posted into the 4th Battalion of the East Bengal Regiment. He superannuated as the Chief of Army Staff (Bangladesh Army) and have participated in the India-Pakistan War of 1965 as a member of Pakistan Air Force. During the Bangladesh War of Liberation in 1971, he fought in greater Komilla area and conducted offensive operations against Pakistani Defences at Padua BOP, Kala Chara Tea Estate and Chandrapur-Lathumura.

Ambassador **Shamsher Mubin Chowdhury,** Bir Bikram (Retd), graduated as a Regular Commissioned Army Officer in 1969. Ambassador Chowdhury took active part in the Liberation War of Bangladesh in 1971. For his bravery in the battlefield, the Government of Bangladesh conferred upon him the gallantry award Bir Bikram. As a diplomat, he served as the High Commissioner of Bangladesh to Sri Lanka, Ambassador to the Federal Republic of Germany, Vietnam and the United States of America. He was also Foreign Secretary of Bangladesh from 2001 to 2005.

Group Captain **Shamshul Alam,** Bir Uttam, Swadhinota Padak, psc (Retd) was part of the East Bengal Air Force during the 1971 Bangladesh Liberation War. The Group Captain lead the Operation Kilo Flight Mission, which was one of the crucial turning point of the war.

Ambassador **Selina Mohsin** (Retd), is former Bangladesh High Commissioner to the Republic of Maldives and a Secretary of the Foreign Ministry. She joined the Ministry of Education in 1971 and was a Fulbright Scholar in USA and UNESCO Scholar in France. She was also an International Diplomat at the Commonwealth Secretariat, London, UK.

Air Commodore **Ishfaq Ilahi Choudhury**, retired from the Bangladesh Air Force in 2003. The Air Commodore holds a Master's in Defence Studies (MDS) from Defence Services Command & Staff College (DSCSC) and an M.Phil from the National Defence College (NDC), Dhaka. He was also a directing staff in the DSCSC and the NDC.

Lieutenant General **Zameer Uddin Shah**, PVSM, SM, VSM (Retd), superannuated as the Deputy Chief of Army Staff (Planning & Systems). The General is an alumnus of St Joseph's College, Nainital. Thereafter, he served in the Armed Forces Tribunal, Principal Bench, New Delhi and also held the appointment of Vice-Chancellor, AMU. The officer was conferred the 'Honoris Causa', The Doctor of Letters by Integral University, Lucknow (India).

Major General **PJS Sandhu** (Retd), superannuated as the Chief of Staff of 1 Corps. The General was commissioned into 8th Light Cavalry and later commanded 47 Armoured Regiment. During the 1971 War, he was posted on the staff of HQ 16 Independent Armoured Brigade. Post retirement, he was the Deputy Director & Editor at USI of India.

Major General **AJS Sandhu**, VSM (Retd), was commissioned in June 1967. The General served in the Punjab Sector during the 1971 India-Pakistan War, and in operationally vital regions of J&K and Ladakh, during the critical periods of the Siachen Conflict and Operation Vijay (1999). His authored books are titled *Battleground Chhamb: The Indo-Pakistan War Of 1971* and *With Honour and Glory: Five Great Artillery Battles*.

Lieutenant General **Raj Sujlana** (Veteran), was commissioned in 9th Battalion the Sikh Regiment and baptised in battle during the India-Pakistan War (1971). In later years, he had three tenures in active CI/CT J&K (Op Rakshak) and Assam (Op Rhino) and tenanted the appointment of the Colonel of the Sikh Regiment. As official spokesperson of the Army, he handled the media, psychological warfare and pioneered the Right to Information in the Army. Post retirement he served as Chairman, Punjab Public Service Commission.

Colonel **JKV Singh** (Retd), was commissioned in the 1st Battalion 9th Gorkhas on June 15, 1969. He fought the 1971 War as the Intelligence Officer of the Battalion.

Captain **D C Berry** (Retd), was commissioned into the 2nd Battalion of the Mahar Regiment. The Captain was Support Company Commander during 1971 War, and was actively involved in the assault and capture of Parbat Ali. The Battalion was bestowed with Battle Honour for Parbat Ali and Theatre Honour for Sind.

Captain **David Muthumani**, SM (Retd), was the RMO with 10 Sikh LI during Battle of Naya Chor in the Pakistan-Sindh Desert. The Captain served in the ADS during the War. Thereafter, he was posted to 2 Grenadiers at Srinagar. He was also an outstanding basketball player.

Dr. **Jyoti M. Pathania**, is Senior Fellow and Chairperson, Outreach at the Centre for land Warfare Studies. Dr. Pathania is the founding editor of *Online Indian Journal of Peace and Conflict Resolution*. She has 23 years of teaching and research experience in various universities and research institutes in India and abroad. For excellence in research, she was awarded by Chief of the Army Staff (General Rawat). She is also the recipient of Prof Randhir Singh Award and an honoured member of the NTS Consortium/RSIS/NTU Singapore.

Vice Admiral **Suresh Bangara**, PVSM, AVSM (Retd), is former Commandant National Defence Academy (NDA) and Flag Officer Commanding-in-Chief, Southern Naval Command. The Vice Admiral is a graduate from St Josephs College Bangalore, the Royal Naval Staff College, Greenwich-London, National Defence College and is an alumnus of the John F Kennedy School of Government (Harvard University). As a young Lt he was the Commissioning EXO of INS Veer – one of three Missile boats that sank ships off Karachi on 04 Dec 1971.

Commodore (Dr.) **Mani Singh Mamik** IN (Retd), is an all-round naval aviator having flown jets, large Maritime Anti-Submarine patrol aircraft as well as helicopters besides serving on ships ranging from patrol boat, patrol ships, frigates, tanker and an aircraft carrier. He is former Deputy Director, Naval Aviation Plans and Staff Requirements as well as Deputy Director General, Defence Planning Staff. He was also Strategic Adviser to CNS as head of Strategic and Doctrine Division and was DS in Staff College as well as Commodore Joint Ops with ARTRAC.

Ms. **Soumya Nair**, has earlier worked as a Research Assistant at the Centre for Land Warfare Studies. She is an independent researcher and journalist who writes on maritime affairs, geopolitics and emerging technology.

Air Vice Marshal (Dr.) **Arjun Subramaniam**, AVSM (Retd), currently occupies the President's Chair of Excellence in National Security at the National Defence College. The Air Vice Marshal has authored many books including *India's Wars: A Military History: 1947-1971* and its newly-released sequel in two versions titled *Full Spectrum: India's Wars 1972-2020* and *A Military History of India since 1972*.

Group Captain **AG Bewoor**, was commissioned in the IAF in 1965 and retired in 1993. Thereafter, the Group Captain worked with an Indian multinational. He led the airborne assault into Maldives in November 1988 by landing the first IL-76 with 200 paratroopers. He writes frequently on military issues.

Air Marshal **Harish Masand**, VrC, VM (Retd), is a fighter pilot of repute who retired in 2006 and spends his time in writing and speaking on defence and security issues.

Air Commodore (Dr.) **Ashminder Singh Bahal**, VM (Retd), is a Visiting Fellow at the Centre for Land Warfare Studies. The Air Commodore is currently Consultant Dean at ICAI – a regulatory body of the GoI. He was a diplomat at High Commission of India, Bangladesh. His authored book is titled *Emerging Politico-Security Scenario 2025: Vision for an Emerging Air Force*.

Mrs. **Sita Bhalla**, is the wife of late Squadron Leader Anil Bhalla. Mrs. Bhalla is an alumnus the Baldwins Girls High School, Bangalore. She did her higher studies in Germany and is a keen traveler and is an avid reader.

Colonel **AD Patole** (Retd), was commissioned in 1971 into the 19th Batallion of the Maratha Light Infantry. The Colonel Officer later was transferred to AOC in 1976. He served as an as Instructor at CMM Jabalpur. The author specialises in Receipt Inspection of all type of A vehicles imported from foreign countries. He superannuated as DDOS HQ Bengal Area.

Colonel **Lali Gill** (Retd), served as Instructor IMA, GSO1 MO Directorate. The Colonel Commanded 2 Para and was Instructor, DSSC. He was former Managing Director ESPARM, Germany.

Brigadier **Rajeev Williams,** YSM, SM (Retd), was commissioned into 10 GUARDS and went straight into war in the Shakargarh Sector. The Brigadier was later posted to 8 JAK LI (SIACHEN), which captured Bana Top at 21,143 feet. During Kargil operations (1999), he was responsible for the media war and thereafter commanded the Drass Brigade.

Brigadier **Balraj Kapur** (Retd), was fortunate to have gained battle experience immediately after commission. The Brigadier, in later years, participated in Counter Insurgency operations in Mizoram, Sri Lanka and Rajouri Sector in J&K. He commanded a Mechanised Infantry Battalion and an Armoured Brigade.

Major General (Dr.) **GG Dwivedi,** SM, VSM* (Retd), is currently Professor Strategic & International Relations. The General was commissioned into 14 JAT in November 1971 and took part in the Bangladesh War as 2 Lt, later commanded 16 JAT in Siachen, Brigade and Division in intense counter Insurgency environment; superannuated as Assistant Chief. He served as Defence Attaché in China, North Korea and Mongolia.

Colonel **Ajinkya Jadhav** is a Senior Fellow at CLAWS. Colonel Jadhav was commissioned into and commanded 7 PARA. He has rich experience of combat in Op Vijay & Op Rakshak. He has been an instructor in the NCO Academy and the Army War College. He has contributed immensely in modernising the Parachute Regiment with latest military technologies.

Major General **ANM Muniruzzaman** NDC, psc (Retd), is currently, the President, Bangladesh Institute of Peace and Security Studies(BIPSS) and Chairman, Global Military Advisory Council on Climate Change (GMACCC). The General served in the Bangladesh Army in different command and staff appointments. He was a member of the faculty at Defence Services Command and Staff College. An experienced UN peacekeeper, he has the distinction of heading the post-election UN Mission in Cambodia.

Other Contributors

A large number of headquarters, units and formations have contributed towards the successful compilation of the book.

Index